OPENING THE TREASURE OF THE PROFOUND

Opening the Treasure of the Profound

Teachings on the Songs of Jigten Sumgön and Milarepa

Khenchen Konchog Gyaltshen

EDITED BY

Khenmo Trinlay Chödron

SNOW LION
BOSTON & LONDON
2013

Snow Lion
An imprint of Shambhala Publications, Inc.
Horticultural Hall
300 Massachusetts Avenue
Boston, Massachusetts 02115
www.shambhala.com

9 8 7 6 5 4 3 2 1

First Edition
Printed in the United States of America

⊚ This edition is printed on acid-free paper that meets the
American National Standards Institute Z39.48 Standard.
♻ This book is printed on 30% postconsumer recycled paper.
For more information please visit www.shambhala.com.

Distributed in the United States by Random House, Inc.,
and in Canada by Random House of Canada Ltd

Designed by Gopa & Ted2, Inc.

Library of Congress Cataloging-in-Publication Data

Konchog Gyaltsen, Khenchen.
Opening the treasure of the profound: teachings on the songs of
Jigten Sumgön and Milarepa / Khenchen Konchog Gyaltshen;
edited by Khenmo Trinlay Chödron.—First edition.
pages cm
ISBN 978-1-61180-070-8 (pbk.: alk. paper)
1. Mi-la-ras-pa, 1040–1123. 2. 'Bri-guṅ Chos-rje 'Jig-rten-mgon-po,
1143–1217. 3. Spiritual life—Bka'-rgyud-pa (Sect). 4. Tantric Buddhism.
I. Trinlay Chödron, Khenmo, 1953– II. Title.
BQ7950.M557K68 2013
294.3'4432—dc23
2012049323

Contents

Preface   vii

Introduction   ix

  1. Supplication to the Kagyu Gurus for the Mist
     of Great Blessings   3

Part One: Vajra Songs of Jetsün Milarepa

  2. Distinguishing Happiness from Suffering   39

  3. The Eight Bardos   57

Part Two: Vajra Songs of Lord Jigten Sumgön

  4. Vajra Song on Attaining Enlightenment   73

  5. Song of the Fivefold Profound Path of Mahamudra   79

  6. The Song That Clarifies Recollection   111

  7. Vajra Song at Tsa-uk called "Tsa-uk Dzong Drom"   131

  8. Song of the Six Confidences   149

  9. Supplication to the Seven Taras   171

Part Three: The Life and Liberation of Lord Jigten Sumgön

  10. The Life of Jigten Sumgön,
      by Drigung Kyabgön Padmai Gyältsen   185

  11. The Precious Jewel Ornament, by Ngorje Repa   197

  12. Jigten Sumgön: The Second Nagarjuna,
      by H. H. the Drigung Kyabgön Chetsang Rinpoche   215

Glossary of Enumerations   251

Glossary of Names and Terms   261

Selected Bibliography   267

Index   271

PREFACE

THIS BOOK PRESENTS commentary on nine vajra songs from the Tibetan masters Jetsün Milarepa and Lord Jigten Sumgön. Vajra songs first became popular with the eighty mahasiddhas of ancient India. The songs of Saraha, Tilopa, and Naropa are particularly well known. A vajra song, also called a "doha," is a lyrical Dharma teaching that is imparted spontaneously from the wisdom mind of a great master. They arise whenever needed to confer concise and precise teachings to a disciple. The term "vajra" has great significance in this context. A vajra is unchangeable, unpierceable, impenetrable, incombustible, and indestructible. Vajra songs have the same profound characteristics because they were taught from the point of view of the dharmakaya, or enlightenment. Thus, it can be difficult for the ordinary, unenlightened mind to penetrate their meaning. Whether short or long, each vajra song encompasses a complete form of the Buddha's teachings. We need strong devotion as well as mental clarity to comprehend their full depth.

In Tibet, vajra songs became popular when Milarepa achieved enlightenment and started giving teachings in that style to his disciples when they requested teachings. This tradition has influenced all Buddhist schools, particularly the Kagyu lineages. Monks, nuns, and ordinary people commonly memorized such songs and sang them with beautiful melodies to remind themselves of their Dharma practice and cultivate devotion for the lineage masters so that they could follow the path to freedom from suffering and confusion.

My retreat master and other great teachers introduced me to these profound teachings and passed their transmission on to me. I began memorizing some of them and was inspired to receive their benefits. When I came to the United States, I wanted to share them with others, so I translated a few songs from Kagyu masters with the support of Dharma practitioners. I was very happy that we were able to publish them in a small book called

Prayer Flags. I started giving explanations of these vajra songs at various Dharma centers, and many people were inspired by the profound nature of those teachings.

Also included in this book are my translations of three accounts of Lord Jigten Sumgön's life—one short, one middle length, and one longer version. The first was written by Drigung Kyabgön Padmai Gyältsen, the fourth Chetsang Rinpoche and twenty-seventh successor of Jigten Sumgön, in the eighteenth century. The middle-length account was composed by Ngorje Repa, one of Jigten Sumgön's highly realized direct disciples. The longest account is a contemporary work written by the current (thirty-seventh) Drigung throneholder, H. H. the Drigung Kyabgön Chetsang Rinpoche. I am deeply appreciative that he allowed it to be included here.

As a special project, Khenmo Trinlay Chödron took responsibility to transcribe my talks, edit them, and put them together into a book. I am grateful for the many hours she spent doing that. My longtime friends and cotranslators Rick Finney and Victoria Huckenpahler, as well as Kay Candler, read the manuscript thoroughly and provided many good suggestions. Without the support of these individuals, this book would not have been completed. This book is also a result of support from the many Dharma practitioners who have dedicated their lives to Dharma study and practice. On behalf of all the readers, I would like to express my deep gratitude to the publisher for making this book widely available.

May this kindle the light of wisdom, dissolve all confusion into wisdom, free all beings from samsara, and lead them to enlightenment!

Introduction

As long as sentient beings—those who have consciousness—exist, the desire for happiness and freedom from suffering will naturally be in their minds. These desires fall into two basic categories: psychological and physical. To satisfy mental desires, many different methods have been invented to respond to the needs of various cultures and ideologies. For example, many people receive comfort and benefit from the myriad religions and philosophies that have been founded on concepts that depend on the mental capacity of their founder. In recent times, fulfilling desires for physical comfort and pleasure through science and technology has been more in the forefront.

We have five sense organs and there are five objects to complement them: form for the eye, sound for the ear, odor for the nose, taste for the tongue, and tactile forms for the body. Attachment to these sensations leads to involvement in the eight worldly concerns: gain and loss, praise and blame, pain and comfort, and fame and disgrace. These are universal distractions, regardless of culture, belief system, language, or lifestyle. Beings oriented toward worldly concerns believe that experiencing the four positive concerns (gain, praise, comfort, and fame) will bring peace and happiness for themselves and others. So much is sacrificed for worldly concerns that some even go to war for gain or fame. The four negative concerns (loss, blame, discomfort, and disgrace) are widely believed to cause suffering, and we expend considerable energy to avoid them. But if we investigate carefully, all eight concerns are nothing more than elaborate expressions of attachment and aversion.

Everything in samsara exists on the basis of this duality. We project the thought that something external to ourselves will fulfill all our wishes and desires. But all of these conceptions, whether spiritual or material, are the products of mental invention or discovery. So many things have been discovered in the past to ease our suffering—many different technologies such as engineering, construction, and manufacture of planes, railways, and other vehicles. Many types of medicine are made from chemicals and herbs, and various healing technologies have been invented. Then there is singing and dancing, books, movies, sports and games, delectable food, and lovely textiles. We rely on systems of mathematics and economics. Many different languages are used for communication, as are the Internet, mobile communication devices, computers, and logical debate. We have even invented weapons in our attempts to secure peace. Societies have developed governments to create safety and well-being. Science has given us physics and countless other disciplines. Every one of these is a method that attempted to create peace and happiness.

We go through considerable hardships and sacrifices to become expert in these subjects so that our lives will be comfortable. Throughout history, countless brilliant people in both the secular and religious realms discovered these wisdoms, methods, and approaches to a better life for themselves and others. Sometimes we introduce our way of doing things to others and try to convince them that our social and political structures are better. If they don't agree, we reinforce our persuasions and sometimes use force to try to make them understand.

Basically there are two kinds of happiness: the relative and the absolute. The relative happiness that we try to achieve through material objects and physical comfort is limited. When the mind is disturbed by afflictions and counterproductive emotions, a comfortable bed or a delicious meal won't solve the problem. Having millions in the bank won't calm the mind when the disturbing emotions manifest. Not only that, but these materials and power can give rise to negativity such as greed, jealousy, anger, resentment, and so forth. When we are unaware of these side effects, we continue to feed the causes of suffering. Therefore, it becomes important to learn about the mind and its capacity.

The mind is immaterial consciousness, so it is difficult to penetrate the world of the mind through material technology. Only when the mind is calm and relaxed, and imbued with love and compassion, is there real peace and harmony. That is the nature of genuine happiness. Because of this, scientists nowadays are starting to pay attention to the importance of the mind. They observe the negative health effects of a mind filled with hatred, greed, anxiety, or depression, and conversely see the benefits of a mind filled with love, compassion, and peace. They are coming to understand what the Buddha taught—that mind is limitless.

The historical Buddha went through mind training for many years. In the end, he captured the nature of infinite mind with limitless wisdom and compassion. His enlightenment has benefited people regardless of their status by allowing them to recognize suffering, its causes, and the means to become free of it. The Buddha's realization has generated great spiritual masters for more than two millennia and has now been passed down to us. This book, *Opening the Treasure of the Profound,* contains some of these profound and deep teachings. In particular, these vajra songs contain teachings related to mahamudra, which is concerned with directly revealing the nature of mind, the dharmakaya. There, confusion has no place; it cannot function or even exist.

The Four Dharmas of Gampopa, a very famous formulation of the path, says:

> Grant your blessings so that my mind may follow the Dharma.
> Grant your blessings so that Dharma may become the path
>   to enlightenment.
> Grant your blessings so that errors may be dispelled from the path.
> Grant your blessings so that confusion may dawn into wisdom.

The meaning of "confusion dawning as wisdom" is not easy to understand and is especially difficult to realize. To approach that meaning, beginning practitioners reflect on the impermanence of all composite phenomena, see the nature of suffering in samsara, and turn their minds toward Dharma by studying and practicing how to free themselves from these sufferings. They can come to understand the cause of suffering and renounce it, and embrace virtue, the cause of peace and happiness. In that way, they can clearly see the total nature of samsara and the advantages of enlightenment, and are inspired to channel their minds toward enlightenment.

As they progress on the path, they may encounter obstacles that could derail them from the Dharma. Strength of mind is needed to contend with such problems, so they build it by cultivating and enhancing the practices of love, compassion, and both relative and absolute bodhicitta. With the support of compassion and the wisdom of emptiness, we use systematic methods to gradually develop courage and strength of mind. Practitioners with high capacity can directly see the mode of abiding of obstacles and experience how none of them exists inherently. When one has this eye of wisdom, the confusion that causes samsara for ordinary sentient beings vanishes into emptiness. To achieve that state, to dissolve the notion of duality and free the mind from elaborations, an individual must have strong motivation and exert rigorous effort. The result is called "confusion dawning into wisdom," because all confusion is nothing other than primordial wisdom. This result is a place of everlasting peace and joy infinite as space, which cannot be expressed in words but can only be experienced. This is what was experienced by the Buddha and many highly advanced masters in India and Tibet, and it is the subject that these vajra songs address. In addition, I offer some simple meditation practices related to various subjects, especially in the commentary to the "Song of the Fivefold Profound Path of Mahamudra." Those who are interested can adopt and practice them, and they may be useful.

These vajra songs reflect the enlightened mind of their authors, Jetsün Milarepa and Jigten Sumgön. Milarepa was one of the iconic figures of the Buddhist world. By merely hearing his name or reading his life story and vajra songs, many throughout the world have been moved and inspired. His life story has already been translated into many different languages, so I haven't repeated it in this book except for a short section in the commentary to "Supplication to the Kagyu Gurus for the Mist of Great Blessings." It also appears in *The Great Kagyu Masters* along with the life story of Jigten Sumgön. Three accounts of Jigten Sumgön's life and liberation are contained in this book. These masters' experience of Dharma was not merely intellectual; they personally experienced enlightenment and revealed the meaning of nonduality. With impartial compassion based on that wisdom, they taught the Dharma sincerely to help others. These teachings comprise a method to explore our inner mental qualities by avoiding the delusions and afflictions that are the direct cause of suffering. When, with the eye of wisdom, you see the mind that cannot be seen, ultimate peace and happiness will be achieved. It is not easy to experience this meaning by relying on the intellect.

We who are in samsara should be tired of this never-ending cycle of suffering, but somehow we aren't. Time and again, we choose the illusion of happiness over genuine peace. Shouldn't we try to use profound wisdom instead, and follow the path to absolute peace and happiness? If we do this, we will fulfill the purpose of life and be able to rejoice in our accomplishment. We'll be able to say, "I am glad I chose this."

Opening the Treasure of the Profound

1. SUPPLICATION TO THE KAGYU GURUS FOR THE MIST OF GREAT BLESSINGS

Nagarjuna realized the profound emptiness free from extremes. His coming was foretold by the Tathagata in many sutras; he was reborn as the meditating bhikshu Rinchen Päl, the Protector of the Three Worlds, the Great Drigungpa. Once when Jigten Sumgön was staying at Jangchub Ling, there was a great drought in the region of Drisewa. The patrons and monks supplicated and requested him [to end the drought]. In response to their requests, Jigten Sumgön composed this song and said to Düdsi Shikpo, "Chant this song of mine near the spring behind our monastery, and rain will fall."

Namo Guru!

In the vast sky of the glorious dharmadhatu,
you pervade all dharmas without limitation of boundary or center.
Remembering again and again great Vajradhara, the dharmakaya,
I supplicate you with one-pointed mind filled with yearning.
Guru! Grant your blessings that I may be realized like you.

Clouds gather in the east over the land of Sahor.
Billowing mists of blessings arise.
Remembering again and again Tilo Prajñabhadra,
I supplicate you with one-pointed mind filled with yearning.
Guru! Grant your blessings that I may be realized like you.

Red lightning flashes over Pushpahari in the north.
You underwent twelve trials for the sake of the Dharma.
Remembering again and again the learned mahapandita Naropa,

I supplicate you with one-pointed mind filled with yearning.
Guru! Grant your blessings that I may be realized like you.

The turquoise dragon thunders over the valley of Drowo Lung
in the south.
You translated the teachings of the Hearing Lineage into Tibetan.
Remembering again and again the great translator Marpa Lotsawa,
I supplicate you with one-pointed mind filled with yearning.
Guru! Grant your blessings that I may be realized like you.

A gentle rain is falling in the highlands of the Lapchi snow range.
The instructions of the Hearing Lineage flow together into a lake.
Remembering again and again glorious Shepa Dorje,
I supplicate you with one-pointed mind filled with yearning.
Guru! Grant your blessings that I may be realized like you.

The earth is soaked in the Daklha Gampo hills in the east
by the continuous stream of the waters of clear light.
Remembering again and again the Lord, the King of Physicians,
I supplicate you with one-pointed mind filled with yearning.
Guru! Grant your blessings that I may be realized like you.

Shoots sprout in the land of Phagmo Dru.
You opened the treasure of the profound secret tantra.
Remembering again and again the Lord, the Self-born Buddha,
I supplicate you with one-pointed mind filled with yearning.
Guru! Grant your blessings that I may be realized like you.

The six grains ripen in the region of Drigung in the north.
These six grains pervade all the six realms.
Remembering again and again the kind Lords of Dharma,
the uncles and nephews,
I supplicate you with one-pointed mind filled with yearning.
Guru! Grant your blessings that I may be realized like you.

Upon the crown of my head, on a sun and moon disk seat,
sits my kind root lama, inseparable from the glorious Vajradhara.
Remembering you again and again,

I supplicate you with one-pointed mind filled with yearning.
Guru! Grant your blessings that I may be realized like you.

INTRODUCTION

THIS SUPPLICATION was composed to invoke the blessings of the great masters of the Kagyu lineage. We study and practice the precious Dharma teachings in order to free ourselves from samsara, which is, after all, merely a creation of our negative thoughts and delusions. To achieve this goal, we must purify our negative thoughts, and to accomplish that, our practice must be as fruitful as possible.

In order to practice effectively, we repeatedly remind ourselves of our precious human life. A *precious* human life is a rare opportunity that not every human being has. It comprises eighteen favorable conditions. Those who don't have all eighteen conditions are considered ordinary human beings without a "precious" existence. Like all other sentient beings, they desire happiness and wish to be free from suffering, but they lack the supporting conditions required to accomplish this. If we analyze this carefully, we can see how very rare a precious human life, with all its favorable conditions, is. The Buddha used the well-known example of a blind turtle to illustrate this point:

> Suppose the entire world were covered by an ocean. Swimming in that ocean is a blind turtle that only rises to the surface once every hundred years. A wooden yoke with a single hole in the center floats on the ocean surface, constantly moved about by the currents and winds. Now, it is possible that, as the turtle rises to the surface for a breath, his head could come up inside the hole in that yoke, but that would be very rare. It is rarer still for one to obtain a precious human life.

When we understand how many causes and conditions it takes to make up a precious human life, we will come to appreciate it when we have one. But if we don't investigate this carefully, we're more likely to take it for granted, and it won't mean so much to us.

Not only is this human life rare, but it also affords us an astounding opportunity to resolve all conflict and confusion into complete enlightenment. It holds every possibility, every opportunity, to achieve the freedom of enlightenment, the liberation from all suffering through which we can benefit countless sentient beings. Thus, it is important for Dharma practitioners to acknowledge this opportunity and use it without wasting even one precious moment.

We are able to read the stories of great teachers, so we must have created positive karma during previous lifetimes. Divination isn't needed to see that this is true and we don't need to ask fortune-tellers or astrologers. We know the nature of our past karma because of the results we are presently experiencing. Now it's up to us to take advantage of this opportunity, to exert ourselves to reinforce positive habits. Our positive past won't do us any good if we don't take advantage of this precious human life. The responsibility to practice bodhicitta, meditation, and purification is ours alone.

Whether we notice it or not, every sentient being wants to achieve happiness and be free of suffering. For that reason, we exert ourselves in many different fields such as politics, business, science, and so forth. We think that by achieving a goal we will gain some level of happiness. We work very hard to achieve something that will make our lives seem useful and, perhaps, will give us some measure of happiness or a sense of satisfaction. Humans have been doing this for countless numbers of years. Has it ever made anyone unconditionally happy?

Upon careful investigation, you can see that Dharma is the direct source of joy and that it possesses every cause and condition needed to purify our inner obscurations. No matter how advanced and powerful computers are, they have not yet been able to show the nature of mind itself. Modern technology cannot measure the wholesome and unwholesome deeds that cause happiness and suffering. On the other hand, Dharma can precisely show us the way causality functions to create the world of samsara and nirvana. Only Dharma shows us the nature of our mind; so we must make every effort not to waste this opportunity. This means we should learn how to reflect on the mind and develop our mental qualities. Appreciation of our precious human life inspires us and becomes the key to our steadily, joyfully, and happily engaging in Dharma practice.

This precious human life doesn't stand alone, even for a second. It is impermanent and transitory in nature—a mere moment in time. Sometimes when we think of impermanence, we conceive of it as a long process: we get old, we get sick, and we slowly die. But it does not necessarily happen that way. Life can unexpectedly last just one second more, be only one moment long. See whether this is true in your own experience. Your own experience is very important in Buddhism. Although the Buddha explained the details of many subjects, we must study and contemplate what he said in order to understand them deeply and personally. In this way, we will gain confidence and comfort in the refuge of the Buddha, Dharma, and Sangha. We'll know from the depths of our heart that life is precious—rare and beneficial.

The great masters mentioned in this song practiced Dharma joyfully and happily. No matter what obstacles or difficulties they encountered, they were completely victorious. When we study their life stories, we can realize that we have the same opportunity they had. They didn't have more opportunities and we don't have fewer. It's just a matter of our dedication and reverence, of whether we respect and take advantage of this opportunity to study the precious Dharma teachings.

Ask yourself what brings real happiness. Samsara provides nearly infinite guidelines on how to create suffering and even more opportunities to delude our minds with obscurations. Do they really work to bring lasting, unchanging happiness? Observe and follow the examples of the great masters, and see for yourself whether they bring peace and happiness into your life.

This is something that we have to practice every moment. Every single moment is the only life we have; the past is gone and the future has not arrived. Whether we are happy or suffering in this present moment, this very second is all we have. It is like the shimmering of water—flickering for an instant, then fading away. We cannot deny this or escape it; we have to go through each moment, and each one holds vast potential. By realizing this, the great masters understood that they could not waste a single instant.

Dharma teachings give us the wisdom to see this nature. The enlightenment state is contained in this present moment. Suffering and delusion are also here in this moment. When we investigate the nature of samsara carefully, we see it's like coals that appear cool on the surface but which are still burning hot underneath. Unaware of the danger, we get burned and suffer. In other words, despite samsara's seductive appearance, it is not possible to achieve total happiness within it. It is, by definition, a state of suffering. We are not making samsara into something bad or unnecessarily negative; this is how it is constituted by its own nature. Reflect on this and try to see samsara plainly for what it is. The great masters attained enlightenment using this wisdom.

Our human mind holds more potential than anything else in the world. There is no greater power than the mind. When we make friends with our mind, when we know our own mind, when we know how to relate to our mind, then all happiness, peace, and joy come to us. Conversely, when we don't know how to make friends with our mind, when we make our mind an enemy and set it on delusions, then every type of suffering arises. Sometimes people even commit suicide because of their suffering. Why? Because they don't know how to handle suffering or see the mind. They become an enemy of their own mind. When the pure nature of mind is insidiously polluted by defilements and then deeply rooted in delusion, we don't have a chance to enjoy this life but instead are made miserable.

Mind is the most important subject on which the Buddha taught. The mind can support us, bring us every good quality, and give us the opportunity to become the happiest person in the world. The best means to accomplish this is the cultivation of bodhicitta, the mind of enlightenment. Cultivating bodhicitta is the impeccable way to reveal the absolute nature of the mind. When we cultivate bodhicitta nothing is hidden; that is the universal mind. With the power of bodhicitta, everything that exists in samsara can be seen as an illusion and nothing can agitate us. We have to meditate on these Dharma teachings not just once but repeatedly. We should reinforce them every day until they are completely realized.

The Buddha said that when a person first becomes a monk or a nun he or she should practice the same teachings as the monastic who has been practicing for many years. And those monastics who have been practicing for a hundred years should practice the same Dharma teachings as the person who became ordained today. What is important is not how many new things we learn, but how much of the Dharma we actually experience in practice. If we practice, everything becomes fresh and every time we hear a teaching it's like new. If we don't practice, then the teachings become an old, boring story we've heard many times.

The account that accompanies this vajra song starts by explaining that Jigten Sumgön was a reincarnation of the exalted master of the second century, Nagarjuna:

Nagarjuna realized the profound emptiness free from extremes. His coming was foretold by the Tathagata in many sutras; he was reborn as the meditating bhikshu Rinchen Päl, the Protector of the Three Worlds, the Great Drigungpa.

In an earlier lifetime, Jigten Sumgön was born as the layperson Vimalakirti, who was a disciple of Buddha Shakyamuni and was renowned as a great master. His scholarship and mind were so advanced that even Shariputra, the monk with the sharpest intellect, and Manjushri, the embodiment of wisdom, could not surpass them. A famous sutra called the *Vimalakirti Nirdesha* contains a discourse between Vimalakirti and Manjushri that took place by the blessings of the Buddha.

The Buddha foretold that Vimalakirti would be reborn under the name of Nagarjuna four hundred years after the Buddha's passing. Nagarjuna's coming was also mentioned in many sutras, such as the *Mahamegha Sutra,* the *Lankavatara Sutra,* the *Manjushrigarbha,* and many others. Fully actualized in the realization of buddha mind, Nagarjuna is regarded as one of the greatest Buddhist teachers. In fact, many consider him a second Buddha. He came at a time when Buddhism in general, and the Mahayana in particular, were experiencing a decline and facing possible extinction. The Buddha said in the *Lankavatara Sutra* that Nagarjuna would transcend the two extremes of nihilism and eternalism, and that he would reintroduce understanding of the nature of emptiness, free from boundaries and elaborations. Because Nagarjuna manifested in the world, he was able to revitalize Buddhism, particularly the Mahayana and Vajrayana. Nowadays, his philosophy is well-known in the Buddhist world as the Middle Way School.

The *meditating bhikshu* mentioned here is Jigten Sumgön, the reincarnation of Nagarjuna and founder of the Drigung Kagyu. *Bhikshu* means a fully ordained monk. While he is best known as Jigten Sumgön, *Rinchen Päl* is one of his epithets in Tibetan. It is Ratna Shri in Sanskrit, and it is with this name that many sutras and tantras predicted his coming. *Protector of the Three Worlds* is the translation of "Jigten Sumgön"—*jigten* means world, *sum* means three, and *gön* means protector.

> Once when Jigten Sumgön was staying at Jangchub Ling, there was a great drought in the region of Drisewa. The patrons and monks supplicated and requested him [to end the drought]. In response to their requests, Jigten Sumgön composed this song and said to Düdsi Shikpo, "Chant this song of mine near the spring behind our monastery, and rain will fall."

Jangchub Ling (Center of Enlightenment) is the monastery Jigten Sumgön established in the Drigung area. On one occasion, that region experienced a severe and extended drought. As a result, many monks and laypeople gathered and requested Jigten Sumgön to create a rainfall.

Droughts, as well as earthquakes, epidemics, and other natural disasters, are dependent on causes and conditions. When our minds are deluded by fundamental ignorance and give rise to negative thoughts, we manifest negative activities that harm our environment, community, and ourselves. These are the causes that bring about unfavorable conditions. Wisdom and compassion are the root causes that bring about good weather and other beneficial conditions. Therefore, we should encourage the good mental conditions that create corresponding good external conditions. Generate positive thoughts of loving-kindness and compassion, and keep the mind peaceful and harmonious. Each individual has a responsibility to do this.

Because of the sincere requests of his disciples, Jigten Sumgön composed this song to inspire their devotion. The interdependence of the blessings of the great Kagyu masters and the devotion and confidence of their disciples created actual changes in the environment, and the drought ended.

This beautiful composition is an extended metaphor that starts with the beginning verse and continues all the way to the end, like a chain or a mala. The sequence of the metaphors depicts a step-by-step process: from the vast sky to the formation of clouds, from the clouds to the appearance of lightning, from the lightning to resounding thunder, from the thunder to falling rain, and from the rain to moisture in the ground that makes the crops grow. Everyone then enjoys the abundant harvest. The Dharma teachings (represented by the rain) help mature the minds of sentient beings, just as rain helps crops grow and mature. Each of these steps is a verse supplicating one of the great Kagyu masters: Tilopa, Naropa, Marpa, Milarepa, Gampopa, Phagmo Drupa, and Jigten Sumgön. You can read a more detailed account of their life stories in *The Great Kagyu Masters*.

COMMENTARY

Namo Guru!

Namo Guru is a Sanskrit phrase of homage to the guru or lama. *Namo* means to pay homage, and *guru* is Sanskrit for lama or teacher.

**In the vast sky of the glorious dharmadhatu,
you pervade all dharmas without limitation of boundary or center.**

Remembering again and again great Vajradhara, the dharmakaya,
I supplicate you with one-pointed mind filled with yearning.
Guru! Grant your blessings that I may be realized like you.

In this case, *dharma* refers to phenomena and *dhatu* means element, which is the absolute reality of phenomena. *Dharmadhatu,* then, refers to all phenomena that are sealed by emptiness. That sphere of reality is unlimited, without *boundary or center,* free from elaboration. It is all-pervading and all-encompassing like the sky, so it is called *vast.*

At our beginning level, buddhahood is understood as being of four types or forms: the dharmakaya, sambhogakaya, nirmanakaya, and svabhavika-kaya. From the point of view of an enlightened being, there are no such separations or differentiations, just as there is no difference between the nature of samsara and that of nirvana. Yet these classifications are useful so that we ordinary people can begin to comprehend the fullness of buddhahood. This is an example of the Buddha's skillfulness and how sentient beings benefit from that skill.

The great *dharmakaya* is the wisdom of a limitless mind free of delusion. It is the complete perfection of the Buddha's qualities, such as the ten powers, four fearlessnesses, and eighteen unmixed qualities. These perfect, exceptional, pure qualities, when considered together, are called dharmakaya. We cannot see them with our ordinary, physical eyes for they can only be seen with the perfect wisdom eye. Even great bodhisattvas cannot measure a buddha's qualities; only a buddha can comprehend their fullness. If the Buddha spoke about the qualities of a buddha for hundreds of kalpas, there would still not be enough time for him to complete his discourse. The Buddha could explain a single word such as "karma" for many years and not reach an end to the explanation, because there is no limit to a buddha's wisdom.

The sambhogakaya and nirmanakaya forms manifest from the dharmakaya, but their nature is not separate from it. Buddhas manifest in these emanation bodies to benefit sentient beings according to their capacity or disposition. In the sambhogakaya form, buddhas display their infinite qualities to inspire bodhisattvas to attain buddhahood. This can only be perceived by great bodhisattvas, especially those who are at the eighth bhumi and above.

There are three types of nirmanakaya:

- ▸ a supreme emanation body, such as the historical buddha, Shakya-muni, who exhibited the twelve deeds and taught all the various

levels of Dharma depending on the needs, capacities, and dispositions of individuals;

▸ a craft emanation, who displays skills in various engineering arts,
music, and so forth; and

▸ an inferior emanation, who takes the form of a rabbit or other
animals, or manifests in inanimate forms such as a bridge or tree—
whatever will benefit and help a sentient being. For example,
statues and paintings create inspiration and help beings make a
connection with the Buddha.

Svabhavikakaya (nature body) is the form of the other three in combination. We repeatedly bring this to mind, recalling the qualities of buddhahood
again and again, in the figure of Vajradhara, the dharmakaya personified.

When Jigten Sumgön says, "*I supplicate you with one-pointed mind filled
with yearning,*" he is expressing a strong desire to receive blessings and actualize the Dharma. Supplication is a special method that arises out of devotion and confidence. It connects our mind with the mind of enlightenment
that we yearn to achieve, and helps us progress on the path step by step.

A *one-pointed mind* is a very powerful mind, indivisible, without doubt
or hesitation. A mind that has no doubt or hesitation can penetrate the
mind of enlightenment. A divided mind, one with doubt, has little power
to experience the enlightened qualities. These can only be experienced by a
mind with confidence.

Guru is a Sanskrit word; in Tibetan, the word is *lama.* Translations of
guru describe the qualities of a guru as "heavy with wisdom and compassion" or "the well-established mind of a person of vast knowledge and great
compassion."

In the past, some Western historians called Tibetan Buddhism "lamaism"
and the monasteries were known as "lamaseries," with the implication that it
was a degenerate form of Buddhism. This misinterpretation was perpetu-
ated by those who did not understand how the monks studied and practiced
within the monasteries. In reality, Tibetan Buddhism maintains a pure and
complete form of Buddhism. The Buddha originally taught in many different languages, but nowadays only two of these remain, Pali and Sanskrit.
The Tibetan Buddhist canon was primarily translated from Sanskrit. All
three of the collections of teachings that form the foundation of Buddhist
study and meditation practices were included. Commentaries written by
the great Tibetan masters contain many quotations from the sutras. The
masters often did this to demonstrate that they weren't making up their own

ideas; rather, they were basing their teachings on the validity of the Buddha's teachings. They were convinced that we must depend on the Buddha's words to have a correct understanding of the Dharma.

We supplicate the guru to look upon us and grant his blessings. Blessings, like everything else, are interdependent phenomena. When the guru's compassion meets the disciple's confidence and devotion, the disciple receives blessings. The guru's compassion is like a ring and the disciple's devotion and confidence are like a hook. When all three come together they interdependently result in blessing. It is like a rock climber stuck on a high, rocky precipice who throws a hook attached to a rope and catches a ring set at the top of the mountain. Once the hook and ring meet, he can pull himself to safety.

For example, a lama who gives an empowerment should have the ability, quality, wisdom, and compassion to perform the ceremony and explain all the related instructions. A disciple who is a proper vessel has a keen interest in the Dharma teachings along with confidence and devotion. Such a disciple can receive blessings through the powerful experience of the ritual. However, if the disciple has devotion, but the lama does not have the ability to explain the instructions, the disciple may not experience as much. Likewise, if the lama has the wisdom and qualities, but the disciple does not have the right mindset, then what the lama says will not make an impression. This is why blessings are said to be an important, interdependent experience.

The supplicant prays to become *like you,* like the ultimate guru Vajradhara who embodies the complete state of buddhahood. We have buddha nature. We have a precious human life. We have the complete teachings to study and practice. So, the only thing obscuring buddhahood from our experience is our own mind and its habitual delusion. We can and must transcend these delusions and become buddhas ourselves.

> Clouds gather in the east over the land of Sahor.
> Billowing mists of blessings arise.
> Remembering again and again Tilo Prajñabhadra,
> I supplicate you with one-pointed mind filled with yearning.
> Guru! Grant your blessings that I may be realized like you.

To benefit sentient beings, the dharmakaya manifests in varied forms, just as clouds spontaneously manifest in the sky in limitless shapes. In this verse, the dharmakaya appears in the form of Tilopa, one highly accomplished in scholarship and realization. This happened in *Sahor,* a place in eastern

India or Bangladesh, perhaps in the area around present-day Chittagong. Tilopa is believed to have been born there in 988 C.E. and he spent many years in that area. The image of *billowing mists of blessings* arising brings to mind his vast qualities and blessings. *Prajñabhadra* (Good Wisdom) was his personal name.

At his birth, Tilopa was recognized as an exceptional being. When he was a young buffalo herder, an old woman with thirty-two ugly signs appeared and instructed him. Her thirty-two ugly signs correspond to the thirty-two major marks of a buddha and symbolize the nature of samsara, that there is no essence, nothing to grasp. She told him first to herd buffalo, which was a sign to cultivate compassion and bodhicitta. Later he was to give that up, meaning to renounce attachment, and go to Oddiyana to receive all the teachings. Tilopa traveled westward to Oddiyana where he encountered Vajrayogini in person and received the entirety of the Vajrayana teachings.

At times Tilopa would say, "I have no human teachers; my only teacher is Vajradhara." This caused him to be disputed by scholars who said that pure teachings could only come from the Buddha's lineage and, therefore, he clearly did not have them. To refute that argument and restore the confidence of those who had lost faith in him, Tilopa also received the complete Vajrayana teachings from four great lineages: those of Charyapa, Nagarjuna, Lawapa, and Dakini Kälwazangmo. That is how he established himself with magnificent miraculous powers and was able to subdue unruly human and nonhuman beings.

The name *Tilopa* comes from the Sanskrit word for sesame, *til*. It means "one who produces sesame oil." This moniker was given to him because he pounded sesame seeds and because he attained enlightenment while doing so. By recognizing that the interdependence of the mortar, pestle, seeds, and his own effort was needed to produce sesame oil, Tilopa saw the complete nature of the dependent origination of all phenomena. He then composed a beautiful mahamudra song:

> Even though sesame seeds have oil,
> in the beginning you have to know that oil is there in the seed.
> To produce oil from the seed,
> you need a mortar, pestle, and roasted seed.
> Then you must pound and press.
> Through the interdependent combination of all this,
>   you produce the oil.

Likewise, each sentient being has the oil of buddha nature.
But if you don't know that, you are fully deluded in samsara
with no way to be freed from it and no way to reveal the excellent
    qualities.
To receive all the instructions,
you need an authentic spiritual master and must be a sincere
    disciple.
Then practice according to that instruction, purify the obscurations,
    and accomplish the meditation practice.
Through these interdependent conditions, you reveal the oil of
    buddhahood.

Tilopa is fully established in the state of buddhahood and benefits count-less sentient beings through his impartial wisdom and compassion. Thus, the verse ends with Jigten Sumgön's supplication and request for blessings. He is expressing his total confidence in Tilopa's realization of buddhahood. When we recite this we are also supplicating Tilopa to bestow his blessings on us so we can become free of samsara and reach his level of realization.

Red lightning flashes over Pushpahari in the north.
You underwent twelve trials for the sake of the Dharma.
Remembering again and again the learned mahapandita Naropa,
I supplicate you with one-pointed mind filled with yearning.
Guru! Grant your blessings that I may be realized like you.

This beautiful poem continues its progress from the sky to clouds, and now there is *lightning* dramatically flashing from the clouds. *Pushpahari* is in northern India, about an hour north of the site of Nalanda University. Later in his life, the great Naropa didn't stay in any particular place. On Marpa's third trip to India, he had to search for many months for Naropa, and finally found him in Pushpahari. Naropa asked Marpa, "What causes you to come here?" Marpa replied, "I have a disciple named Milarepa who received advice from a dakini to get special instructions on how to achieve enlightenment in one lifetime. Since I don't have this teaching, I came here to ask it of you." Naropa was very moved by the mere mention of Milarepa's name, "In that dark land of Tibet to the north, there is a great being who is like the sunshine that dispels all the darkness on the mountains." Naropa then joined his hands at his heart and made three prostrations toward Tibet.

At that moment the trees and mountains bent toward Tibet. Later, a substantial temple was built at that spot, the ruins of which remain today.

Naropa was an exceptionally great master. As a young man, he was a gifted student who quickly mastered the various aspects of knowledge, such as astrology, meditation, medicine, language, and logic, in addition to Buddhist philosophy. He became the chancellor of Nalanda University and protector of the northern gate, largely because he was so expert in debate. When masters debated in those days, the loser and his disciples had to start following the winner's beliefs and path. Because Naropa always won, the other scholars could depend on him and Nalanda was at ease. It grew very famous and gained a large number of students during this period—ten thousand, according to one account from the sixth century.

Although he was a distinguished scholar well versed in all classes of Buddhist study, when Naropa looked at his mind, he noticed that it did not remain still for even a short moment. He realized that his vast scholarship didn't protect his mind and that he needed a teacher to help him calm and purify his mind. He decided to recite the short mantra of Chakrasamvara approximately seven million times, after which he heard a disembodied voice telling him to go to the east to meet Tilopa.

Under Tilopa's guidance, Naropa underwent *twelve* major and twelve minor *trials,* twenty-four in all, to purify his remaining obscurations and to build the courage needed to realize enlightenment. All this was done to cut Naropa's attachment to himself, his ego, and his body. For example, in one of the trials Tilopa directed Naropa to jump off a cliff. Without any hesitation or fear, he jumped from the cliff and his whole body was crushed. But due to his devotion and confidence in his lama and because of Tilopa's blessings, Naropa revived. On another occasion, he again had to release his attachment to his body when leeches attached themselves to him. It's not that Tilopa enjoyed torturing Naropa; he put him through those challenges only to help him purify his mind. After each of these trials and hardships Naropa purified an obscuration related to one of the channels. One by one, he purified the twelve obscurations related to the twelve links of interdependent origination, and his realization grew profound.

Similarly, we are trying to accomplish purification with the ngöndro (preliminary) practices of prostrating, reciting Vajrasattva's mantra, making mandala offerings, and supplicating. When we do prostrations, our body becomes very uncomfortable because we are so attached to it. When we are able to give up this attachment, we become peaceful and calm, and can come to enjoy doing prostrations. Even in the midst of chaos no one will be able to bother us. Otherwise, no matter how we are protected, as long as attachment is present something will always bother us. When we release these nets of attachment, which are nothing more than confusion and delusion, we will feel joy—but the process can be long and difficult. Nonetheless, we must abandon our excuses and use all means at our disposal to accomplish this. This is very important because, without purification, our bodhicitta will remain artificial.

Naropa's twelve trials represent the pain and suffering we endure while purifying our negative habits. We were raised in such a way that what we want most is to satisfy our ego and attachment. Sacrificing ourselves is very difficult and painful. For example, suppose I don't like someone who gives me a hard time. In order to get rid of my resentment, I have to go through hardship because deep down I don't really want to give it up. Purifying that resentment is like a trial, a hardship, but without purifying the resentment I cannot develop sincere and genuine bodhicitta and enjoy true peace in my mind.

Without the purification of obscurations, there is no way to realize the Buddha's mind.

After Naropa underwent all those hardships, Tilopa finally gave him the ultimate empowerment. Using the sky as an example he said, "This is self-awareness, the primordial wisdom beyond speech, beyond conceptual thought. I, Tilopa, cannot show it to you by any verbal or physical means whatsoever. But you should realize it by looking at your own mind." At that moment Naropa received the fourth empowerment and fully realized enlightenment. After this, Tilopa said, "If anyone wishes to receive teachings, let them go to Naropa." Tilopa also prophesied that Marpa, the future founder of the Kagyu lineage in Tibet, would come to Naropa and that Naropa would impart all the precious Dharma teachings to him. Naropa then made the Buddha's teachings flourish by giving teachings in many places.

We should keep in mind that, even though Naropa was well versed in the Buddha's teachings, that alone was not enough to free him from samsara. Just as Naropa went through hardships to disentangle himself from his samsaric habituation and directly realize mahamudra, we, too, must go through some hardship without becoming discouraged in order to attain complete enlightenment. This account should be a good example for us.

Naropa bore the title *mahapandita* because in Sanskrit, *maha* means great, and *pandita* is a scholar, one who knows the ten types of knowledge. Recalling his extraordinary life story and accomplishments, we supplicate Naropa to ask for his blessings so that we, too, may actualize the teachings as he did.

> The turquoise dragon thunders over the valley of Drowo Lung
>   in the south.
> You translated the teachings of the Hearing Lineage into Tibetan.
> Remembering again and again the great translator Marpa Lotsawa,
> I supplicate you with one-pointed mind filled with yearning.
> Guru! Grant your blessings that I may be realized like you.

In Tibetan legend, it is said that dragons stay under the ground to hibernate in the winter. Then in spring, the dragons fly into the sky to make thunder and cause rain. It is also said that if a dragon's tail touches the ground it will create a destructive tornado. Thunder is called the "sound of clouds" that can be heard for miles around. In this song, Marpa is the *turquoise dragon* who creates the resounding *thunder* of Dharma that wakes us up from the deep sleep of samsara.

The *valley of Drowo Lung* is the place in southern Tibet where Marpa was born, established his seat, and taught the Dharma. Marpa is, of course, best known as a great translator. *Lotsawa* is a Tibetan word that was derived from the Sanskrit *lokchakshu,* meaning eye of the world or the light that harmonizes the world. His family name was Marpa and his personal name was Chökyi Lodrö, which translates as "one who has the discriminating wisdom of the Dharma." He was exceptionally intelligent and courageous, making three trips to India and spending more than twenty-one years there.

As a young boy, Marpa was very tough and sometimes quarrelsome. In his teens, he was sent to study with Drokmi Lotsawa, who had traveled to India to study Sanskrit as well as Buddhism. Marpa studied with him for three years but was not satisfied, so he decided to go to India himself. He went home and asked his parents, "What portion of our homestead is mine? Please give it to me now because I need money to go to India and study the Dharma." His parents were reluctant because travel to India was quite treacherous. Nowadays, it is largely deforested, but at that time India was full of dense forests with wild animals and bandits. Having heard such stories, his parents were afraid to let him go, but Marpa was determined. He finally received his inheritance, which he converted into gold. He first traveled to Nepal with some friends and stayed there for a while to acclimate to the temperature because India would be even hotter than Nepal. While in Nepal, he befriended one of Naropa's disciples, studied some Sanskrit, and learned about that great teacher.

Marpa journeyed in the forest, carrying all his possessions on his back. Even though his mind was in a stable meditative state, his body would tremble when he heard tigers roar and snakes rustling in the bushes. This is the way that he and many other brave Tibetans fully sacrificed themselves to study and practice the Dharma. Eventually, Marpa made it to India and met Naropa, who accepted him as a disciple. By day, Marpa received the teachings and studied diligently to understand them. Then by night, he practiced in order to experience them deeply.

Naropa was not an easy master. He would send Marpa to different teachers to receive teachings. For example, he sent Marpa to Kukuripa for the Guhyasamaja teachings. Marpa had to travel for days and cross a poisonous lake to reach him. The poisonous waters caused his skin to shed like a snake's. On another occasion Naropa sent Marpa to Maitripa to receive mahamudra teachings and, upon his return, Naropa gave him the same teachings all over again but at an even more profound level. Marpa thought, "Why does he send me to those faraway places when he knows all the teachings himself?" Of course Naropa knew them, but he wanted to give Marpa more opportunities for training and purification.

During his visits to India, Marpa received teachings from 108 teachers in all. Thus, he thoroughly established himself as a great scholar in general Buddhist subjects and particularly in the Vajrayana teachings. He came to embody the ocean of teachings and to perfectly realize enlightenment. After translating everything he had into Tibetan, Marpa transmitted those teachings to many disciples, including Milarepa. Tibetan historians consider Marpa one of the key figures who brought the light of the Dharma to Tibet.

For a long and harsh time, but with great skill, Marpa trained Milarepa to achieve buddhahood. For example, Marpa required him to construct buildings of stone, tear them down, and build them up again. The training was so difficult that at one point Milarepa became suicidal and was ready to jump into a river. Another of Marpa's disciples, Ngok Ton Chödor, found him in time, grabbed him, and said, "Please don't do this." When Marpa heard this news, tears welled up in his eyes and he said, "This is what it means to be a vajra disciple. Today is the day that Milarepa will be my chief guest." Marpa then gathered all his disciples together and explained his actions. "Everyone has a reason for what they do. Milarepa is desperate to receive teachings and he has tried everything to get them. My wife, Dagmema, tried every way she could to give comfort to Milarepa." Marpa went on, "I also have a reason for what I've done to Milarepa. If it had been for my own benefit, I would have nicely asked Milarepa to construct a building. However, the building was not for me; it was completely for Milarepa's sake, to purify his negative karma and build his courage. From now on, no one should be mistaken about any of this because Milarepa is now the principal guest in my house." At that moment Milarepa saw Marpa as the Buddha himself and had no words to express his feelings. This shows Marpa's great wisdom and compassion, and that he had no attachment to self-interest. He had the power and skill with which to test his disciples. This is the way we should remember him.

There were other great translators at that time, but few are remembered as widely as Marpa. He gave such fresh, vivid teachings! He was wrathful, but compassionate and strong, with determination and courage. Without that kind of personality he could not have survived all those difficult journeys to India. No one with a fragile mind could have done what he did. Marpa had a wife and children but remained untouched by the mud of samsara. His life was like a lotus that blossoms fresh and pure above the water. Milarepa said, "My teacher, Marpa, is like a lion with all the capacity and wisdom to achieve the state of perfection. I am like a fox. And if a fox tries to jump like a lion, he will only break his back."

The essence of the Buddha's teachings, the pith instructions, are passed from teacher to disciple and then put into practice. The Kagyu, or *Hearing Lineage,* contains all the teachings and instructions that you must hear in order to practice. Remember *again and again* that Marpa brought buddha-hood into Tibet. We cannot repay his kindness and great courage, so we supplicate Marpa in order to become actualized like him, to be free from samsaric action and thought. May our mind fully blossom with the qualities of the Buddha!

A gentle rain is falling in the highlands of the Lapchi snow range.
The instructions of the Hearing Lineage flow together into a lake.
Remembering again and again glorious Shepa Dorje,
I supplicate you with one-pointed mind filled with yearning.
Guru! Grant your blessings that I may be realized like you.

After the thunderclaps, a *gentle rain* falls over the *Lapchi snow range*. A hard rain would just run off the surface, but a gentle rain will really soak in. Milarepa visited many holy places, Mount Kailash, and so forth, but as Marpa had prophesied, Lapchi was the place where he attained enlightenment.

Milarepa is one of the most inspirational masters who ever figured in Buddhist history. Anyone who reads his life story or hears his songs can be moved by his teachings and his example. Milarepa was born into a relatively wealthy family. His father was a successful businessman who unfortunately died early. Afterward, the family's wealth was stolen by Milarepa's aunt and uncle. As a result, he, his mother, and his sister were reduced to poverty and endured many hardships. Milarepa's mother encouraged him to avenge them by learning black magic. Milarepa was very successful at this but later came to regret his actions. By understanding karma and fully acknowledging his unwholesome deeds, Milarepa's mind was turned toward Dharma.

"Karma" simply means action, which can be either mental or physical. All thoughts based on ignorance, whether wholesome or unwholesome, cause a future result. All physical and verbal expressions will have a result similar to the initiating action. Karma is such a tyrant! Once the cause is created, there is no choice about the result. So, to avoid unfortunate results we must be aware of our thoughts and actions, and not create the karma that will lead us into unhappy circumstances. Karma is not just a belief system or a cultural tradition; it is a universal law. Milarepa understood that if he died with the terribly negative karma he had created with his black magic, there was only one way he could go—to the lower realms.

Thus aware of his condition, Milarepa was desperate to meet a teacher and receive Dharma teachings. He first went to a dzogchen master, who gave him profound teachings and said, "The instructions that I am giving you will allow you to reach enlightenment immediately or at least within a week. Those who are fortunate enough don't even need to meditate. They can achieve enlightenment just by hearing these teachings." Milarepa thought, "I must be a fortunate one because I was so successful with black magic and now I am lucky enough to receive these precious Dharma teachings. Maybe I don't need to meditate."

Milarepa listened to the teachings and then just relaxed. After a week, the master asked Milarepa, "What kind of experiences have you had?" Milarepa answered, "Nothing special." So the teacher said, "Maybe you do have to meditate." So Milarepa meditated for one week, but still had no experience. The master was shocked and said, "Everyone is supposed to be able to attain enlightenment within one week with these teachings. Maybe you need a special teacher." The dzogchen master had heard of a Marpa Lotsawa who had been to India and suggested that Milarepa see him. Just hearing Marpa's name, Milarepa was inexpressibly moved with peace and joy. He set off and journeyed day and night hoping to meet Marpa as soon as possible.

At that same time Marpa had a dream that Naropa was giving him a stained vajra. In the dream Naropa said to Marpa, "Polish this and put it on the top of the victory banner." In the dream, Marpa did what Naropa asked and the polished vajra's light shone all over the world. Marpa knew the dream was significant, and so the next day he masqueraded as a farmer plowing his fields and waited to receive his new student.

When Milarepa, who was carrying all his possessions on his back, saw Marpa, his mind was overwhelmed, but he did not recognize the farmer. He asked, "Do you know where I can find the great master Marpa Lotsawa?" The farmer replied, "I will show you Marpa later, but first drink this beer and then finish the plowing." Milarepa was grateful for the offer because he was very thirsty after the long journey. Marpa left and Milarepa finished plowing the field. Those two events hold symbolic significance: drinking the beer signified that he would receive all the teachings that Marpa had; plowing the field completely meant that he would have success with the teachings that he received and would benefit sentient beings infinitely.

After a while, a young boy appeared and led Milarepa to Marpa. Milarepa recognized that the farmer was Marpa and felt intimidated. He said to Marpa, "I am a very sinful person from the upper part of Tibet. I come to you to receive instructions and attain enlightenment in one lifetime. I offer you all of my body, speech, and mind. Please give me teachings, food, and clothes." Marpa answered, "Your being a sinful person has nothing to do with me. Attaining enlightenment in one lifetime is up to you; it depends on your own effort. If you want food, I will give you food and you can get Dharma teachings from others. If you want Dharma teachings, I will give you Dharma teachings and you should get food from others. I cannot give you both." Milarepa answered, "Please give me Dharma teachings and I will find food elsewhere."

Milarepa went around collecting alms and received a good amount of barley and other supplies. He exchanged some of the barley for a copper pot. When he returned, Marpa was giving teachings to a large group of disciples. Milarepa was very tired and threw his bundle on the ground; in doing so, he jarred the house. Marpa said, "Hey, do you want to destroy my house?" Milarepa thought, "I must be more careful," and then offered the cauldron and half of the barley to the master. Marpa meditated for a few moments. With tears in his eyes, he beat the cauldron very hard which made a loud sound in all directions. He took the cauldron into the shrine and filled it with butter to make it into a butter lamp for use day and night.

The next day, Marpa asked Milarepa to build a house in each of the four directions. When they were nearly finished, Marpa asked him to dismantle them and build different ones. Finally, Marpa asked Milarepa to build a nine-story tower in the center of the Drowo Lung valley, which Milarepa did all by himself. Because of all this hard work, Milarepa developed terrible wounds on his back. When Marpa's wife saw them she was filled with compassion and tears. She had never seen such wounds on a man before, only on donkeys and horses. She thought that it was a disgrace for a great lama to treat his disciple in such a harsh manner and said as much to Marpa, who answered, "Let him come here." He looked at Milarepa's wounds, covered them with a piece of cloth, and told him to continue working. Milarepa attended Marpa this way for a total of six years and eight months.

This hard method was a way of purifying and building unwavering strength in Milarepa's mind. With a fragile mind and fragile body, one cannot practice Vajrayana. A strong mind is required, one that can endure any challenge with courage as stable as Mount Meru. That is why Marpa trained Milarepa in this manner.

During a Chakrasamvara initiation that Marpa Lotsawa performed, he asked the disciples to visualize Chakrasamvara in the space in front of and above them. Milarepa actually saw Chakrasamvara vividly and clearly, and received the name *Shepa Dorje* (Laughing Vajra) from him. He thought, "Is this real or a dream? If it is a dream, may I not wake up. Let me hold on to this dream a little longer."

After imparting the complete teachings and instructions, Marpa told Milarepa to go into retreat:

> Now go and practice.
> If you practice sincerely, you will be happy.
> That happiness comes from nowhere.
> I will be joyful.
> That joy comes from nowhere.

Later, Marpa reluctantly advised Milarepa to return to his homeland without any intention of coming back to the Drowo Lung valley. So Milarepa left the valley as instructed. He returned to his home and found that his mother had died and his sister was wandering aimlessly. The beautiful house that his father had built was now only a roost for birds and pigeons. Even the roof had collapsed. When Milarepa went into the house he had a true experience of the nature of samsara and impermanence, and composed this song:

> When my father was here, his son was not.
> When the son comes here, the father has left without a trace.
> Even if son and father meet together, there is no essence.
> When my mother was here, her son was not.
> When the son comes here, the mother is a corpse.
> Even if son and mother meet together, there is no essence.
> When my sister was here, her brother was not.
> When the brother comes here, the sister is wandering.
> Even if brother and sister meet together, there is no essence.
> When the house was here, there was no owner.
> When the owner comes here, the house is broken.
> Even if the house and owner meet together, there is no essence.
> Samsara has no essence so I will dedicate my whole life to studying
>   and practicing Dharma in retreat.

Milarepa clearly saw that samsara consists of chasing rainbows and mirages. Things seem beautiful and tempting, but in the end we get nothing and are exhausted. Milarepa fully realized this. As a result of this experience, strong renunciation arose and Milarepa repeatedly dedicated his life to the Dharma. This motivated him to do retreat in the mountains. Sometimes he didn't have any food or clothes, but still he utilized every moment for enlightenment.

Sometimes, a person can feel revulsion even when given good food as, for example, when he is suffering from motion sickness. That is how Milarepa felt about samsara. Once, his sister found him and was so disgusted by his situation that she said, "We are the most unfortunate people in the world. There should be a better life for us. Maybe you should serve another lama, at least we could get enough food that way." Milarepa answered her, "That is not the issue. I see that remaining in samsara is like staying within a burning fire." It's not that he hated this world, but he realized that samsara offers no real happiness or peace.

People who chase samsara with determination are deluded victims of confusion. With great determination, compassion, bodhicitta, and devotion, Milarepa dedicated his life completely, one hundred percent, to the practice of Dharma. As a result, he attained enlightenment. His example still gives us comfort because it contains great bodhicitta. It gives us wisdom because of his great accomplishment of wisdom. It gives us courage and inspiration because Milarepa himself embodied indomitable courage.

Regardless of lineage, Milarepa inspires all of Tibet, and now the whole world. This is very rare because he was an ordinary person. He was not born in a miraculous way. He had no need to be approved as a reincarnated teacher, nor was he prophesied by the Buddha. Milarepa started his life with hardships and difficulties much like our own. He met teachers, received teachings, studied and practiced sincerely, and finally attained complete enlightenment. Afterward, Milarepa gathered disciples, such as Gampopa and Rechungpa, and the lineage was well established.

Out of his great compassion Milarepa said, "In the future, whoever hears my name with devotion will not be reborn in the lower realms for seven lifetimes." Not everyone can hear his name and not all who hear his name will have devotion. To develop devotion, we must have faith that Milarepa was someone special. That is what will make the connection between him and future generations. Since Milarepa was such an instrumental teacher in the lineage, we supplicate him and say prayers with a *one-pointed mind full of yearning* to be free from samsara. Every practitioner can take Milarepa as an example. We can all do just as he did.

> **The earth is soaked in the Daklha Gampo hills in the east**
> **by the continuous stream of the waters of clear light.**
> **Remembering again and again the Lord, the King of Physicians,**
> **I supplicate you with one-pointed mind filled with yearning.**
> **Guru! Grant your blessings that I may be realized like you.**

The *Daklha Gampo hills* are east of the Lapchi snow mountains. The Buddha prophesied that Gampopa would go to that place, as had his master Milarepa.

When the mind is in total equipoise, absorbed in meditation supported by special insight, all the defilements and obscurations are uprooted. The mind becomes gentle, flexible, workable, clear, and peaceful. That is the state of *clear light*. In the absence of obscurations, one can sustain precise awareness without a gap, like a *continuous stream of water*. In the clear light state, the deep sleep of ignorance can be realized as the nature of primordial wisdom. When that state becomes *continuous,* one has realized the nature of mind and attained complete enlightenment.

Gampopa was born at the beginning of the eleventh century as the son of a famous medical doctor. He himself studied medicine when he was young, and he became an expert healer, which is why he is called *King of Physicians*. He also studied Buddhist philosophy and the Vajrayana teachings early on. After his family passed away in an epidemic, he became a monk in the Kadampa tradition where he studied all the Kadampa teachings, the sutra system, and some Vajrayana. His primary studies were Mind Training, *Mahayanasutralankara, Uttaratantra, Madhyamakavatara,* Vinaya, *Abhisamayalankara,* and Stages of the Path. He was exceptionally accomplished in scholarship, and his conduct was very pure and compassionate, gently precise. In short, he had all the necessary good qualities. Those around him had great expectations and hopes that he would become the next great teacher of the Kadampa.

But somehow, Milarepa's fame reached Gampopa's ears. As soon as he heard Milarepa's name, his mind quivered like a leaf blown in the wind. He could no longer meditate well and thought, "What is wrong with me?" His mind was completely pulled by the name "Milarepa." So he set off on a journey to find him.

It is a long journey to Lapchi from Central Tibet. Gampopa walked alone carrying all his possessions. He traveled day and night and continuously supplicated Milarepa as he went along. Once, he became sick and fell to the ground unconscious beside the road. A monk happened by and tended to him. Gampopa regained consciousness after a while, asked for a cup of water, and then felt better. At that same moment Milarepa was giving teachings to a group of his students. While giving these teachings, Milarepa stopped to meditate quietly, and he smiled. His disciples wondered what was happening and inquired. Milarepa answered, "Nothing special. A monk is coming here from Central Tibet. He fell sick and fainted, but someone helped revive him and he will arrive soon."

Soon after this, Gampopa did arrive to finally meet Milarepa. Gampopa offered him gold coins and a brick of tea, but Milarepa said, "This old man doesn't agree with gold and I have no pot in which to boil the tea. If you want to follow the practice lineage, take my life as an example and do as I did. Do not place so much emphasis in beautiful words, but instead look at the meaning of the Dharma and put it into practice. Later we will discuss this further." He gave back the gold and said, "Use this for your provisions during your Dharma practice." Gampopa attended Milarepa for about three years, receiving teachings during the day and meditating at night. During these periods he received all the Vajrayana instructions, including the Six Dharmas of Naropa and mahamudra.

Milarepa advised Gampopa to travel toward the east, to Daklha Gampo, to continue his meditation in retreat. "There, you will achieve certainty in the absolute nature of mind, complete enlightenment. At that time, you will see me as the Buddha. Afterward, you will establish a monastery and gather disciples." Even though he had never been there, Milarepa gave precise directions. Gampopa went there and meditated for a long time. He was not interested in giving teachings and preferred to stay in retreat. One day he made a special commitment to meditate for twelve years, but a dakini appeared to him and said, "Instead of meditating for twelve years, it would be better for you to give teachings. You are ready to do that." Thousands of disciples gathered as soon as Gampopa started to give teachings. Thus began Gampopa's lineage, called the Dakpo Kagyu. It grew very powerful all over Tibet. Later it spread throughout India, Nepal, and China, and now it can be found throughout the world.

Several accounts of Gampopa's life are available. He intentionally took birth in Tibet at the right time and in the right place. At the time of Buddha Shakyamuni, he was called Bodhisattva Youthful Moonlight, which is Dawai Shünu in Tibetan or Chandra Prabhava Kumara in Sanskrit. It was the bodhisattva Chandra Prabhava Kumara who requested the Buddha to give the teachings recorded in the *Samadhiraja Sutra* (*King of Meditative Absorption*). In that sutra, the Buddha praised Gampopa's previous lifetimes.

For example, countless eons ago Gampopa was born as the bodhisattva Mentok Dazey (Flower of the Beautiful Moon). It was a time of degeneration of the teachings of the buddha of that era, so the bodhisattva Mentok Dazey stayed in the All-Good Forest with seven hundred other bodhisattvas without attachment or aversion. To connect sentient beings to enlightenment, he once went to a nearby kingdom to teach. He gathered thousands of people, including many of the ministers and queens. He planted the seed for their enlightenment by teaching day and night without stopping. The king, named Pawai Jin, felt threatened and jealous because so many people in his kingdom were being influenced by this monk. He asked a ruthless butcher to kill the monk, and the butcher did so.

For seven days Mentok Dazey's body did not change. Instead of decaying, the body radiated light and manifested auspicious signs. Upon seeing this, King Pawai Jin deeply regretted having ordered the death of this innocent monk and said, "This was not an ordinary person. I have committed a heinous crime against a saint. I will surely be reborn in a hell realm as a result." A disembodied voice from the sky confirmed, "Yes, you did an evil deed." The king felt intense remorse. To make amends, he built a stupa to enshrine the monk's remains and relics. Every day King Pawai Jin purified his negative karma by cultivating bodhicitta, making offerings, and circumambulating the stupa, but after death he still was born in the hell realm for a long time. Buddha Shakyamuni said, "The bodhisattva Mentok Dazey who was killed is now the bodhisattva Chandra Prabhava Kumara. I was the king at that time. Because I cultivated bodhicitta and purified the rest of my karma, I have become a buddha."

After the Buddha gave the *Samadhiraja Sutra* teachings, he asked the bodhisattvas present, "In the future, who will accept responsibility to benefit sentient beings through these teachings?" No one volunteered except Chandra Prabhava Kumara, who stood up and said that he would do it. Other bodhisattvas then also stood up and said to Chandra Prabhava Kumara, "When you give these teachings to other sentient beings, we will help you." The Buddha then said, "I will also come at that time and help you promote these teachings and help sentient beings become free from samsara." Thus the Buddha clearly prophesied Gampopa's coming in the future.

These are only a few details from Gampopa's life. If you read the histories carefully, you will see that Gampopa was a prominent teacher who was responsible for establishing a complete form of Buddhism in Tibet. He practiced the sutra, vinaya, and Vajrayana systems without any contradiction and attained full enlightenment. The example of Gampopa's life has inspired many great practitioners regardless of lineage. This was foreseen by Milarepa in a dream that he had the day after Gampopa left him. Overjoyed, he recounted, "A giant vulture flew from me and landed on a mountain. Many yellow geese gathered near that vulture, each goose was surrounded by no fewer than five hundred geese. After some time, the whole sky filled with geese. This means that many monks will follow Gampopa. I, a yogin, have served the Buddha's teachings." Thus, the Buddha's teachings flourished and served many sentient beings. So we, too, should supplicate

Dharma Lord Gampopa from the bottom of our hearts to receive his blessings and become like him.

> Shoots sprout in the land of Phagmo Dru.
> You opened the treasure of the profound secret tantra.
> Remembering again and again the Lord, the Self-born Buddha,
> I supplicate you with one-pointed mind filled with yearning.
> Guru! Grant your blessings that I may be realized like you.

After the ground of meditation was softened in Daklha Gampo, the *shoots* of tantra *sprout in the land of Phagmo Dru*. This verse is a supplication to another great teacher, named Phagmo Drupa. Phagmo Dru, or Phagdru, is the name of a place, and Phagmo Drupa is the person who stayed there. He was the rebirth of the first buddha of this kalpa, Buddha Khorwa Jik (Tathagata Krakucchanda).

Phagmo Drupa was born to a poor family in the Kham region of Tibet. Because of his inclination toward the Dharma, he was able to study with many of the best teachers and masters of his time. He studied almost every Buddhist philosophy and became known as a great scholar and meditator. In particular, he became one of the closest disciples of a master named Kunga Nyingpo. After Phagmo Drupa achieved the great qualities of bliss and a clear state of samadhi, Kunga Nyingpo declared that he had achieved the first bhumi.

One day, Phagmo Drupa met a monk from his birthplace who was a disciple of Gampopa and they decided to visit their homeland together. Gampopa's disciple said, "Before we leave for our homeland, I want to visit my master." Phagmo Drupa agreed to go with him, so they stopped there and stayed with the master for a few days. Phagmo Drupa obtained an interview with Gampopa, who asked him what he had studied and what experiences he had had. Phagmo Drupa described all the study he had done and said, "My teacher confirmed that I have attained the first bhumi and special insight." Gampopa was eating tsampa at the time and said, "Perhaps this handful of tsampa is more useful than your special insight." Phagmo Drupa was confused by this reply. They talked some more, and over time Phagmo Drupa grew more serious and thought, "Maybe there's something here that I am missing." The next day Gampopa taught him how to really achieve special insight, and told him to go to a rock to meditate. Phagmo Drupa meditated on that rock, and genuinely realized special insight. After that Phagmo Drupa became one of Gampopa's most important disciples, to the point that one day Gampopa announced, "Phagmo Drupa is no different from me." Thus, he became one of the Kagyu lineage holders. Phagmo Drupa is also considered a manifestation of Vajrayogini.

Phagmo Drupa went to Phagdru to establish his monastery, and thousands of disciples gathered there. It became well known that Phagdru was a buddhafield, that the lama there was a sambhogakaya, and that the disciples were great bodhisattvas. Phagmo Drupa is considered a sambhogakaya because *he opened the treasure of the profound secret tantra,* meaning that he taught the profound Vajrayana teachings. He had such skill articulating the teachings from Milarepa and Gampopa to his disciples that he produced many highly accomplished students.

Five Kagyu lineages sprouted from Gampopa: the throneholder of his main seat at Daklha Gampo, and the Kamtsang, Barom, Tsalpa, and Phagdru. Phagmo Drupa's followers created eight additional Kagyupa lineages: the Drigung, Taklung, Drukpa, Trophu, Yabsang, Shuksep, Yelpa, and Martsang. In addition to being great intellectuals, these disciples were also accomplished meditators who received all the instructions from great masters and dedicated their lives to meditating in mountain caves. There were thousands of disciples of whom we have very little record; they just went into the mountains and practiced, became enlightened, and passed away there.

Since Phagmo Drupa was an enlightened master, his wisdom and compassion pervade the whole of samsara and nirvana. His activities will continue until the end of samsara. So we supplicate him with a one-pointed mind to receive his blessings and to free every sentient being from samsara.

> The six grains ripen in the region of Drigung in the north.
> These six grains pervade all the six realms.
> Remembering again and again the kind Lords of Dharma, the uncles
>   and nephews,
> I supplicate you with one-pointed mind filled with yearning.
> Guru! Grant your blessings so that I may be realized like you.

The shoots that sprouted in Phagdru are now ripening as grain in *Drigung,* north of Phagdru. The *six grains* are barley, corn, rice, wheat, pea, and mustard, and they represent all the foods of Dharma that support our life and mind. When they ripen, they pervade the six realms of samsara and nurture them. Likewise, the fully ripened realization of Dharma also pervades everywhere and provides sustenance for complete peace and happiness in samsara and in the enlightened state.

Jigten Sumgön was the Dharma heir of Phagmo Drupa. He was born into a prominent family, the Kyura. At a young age he could read and memorize quite easily. When he was in his seventies, he recalled that he had begun meditating when he was nine years old. A natural inclination for compassion manifested throughout his life. Jigten Sumgön received teachings on sutras and tantras from several masters. However, when he was twenty-five, he heard of Phagmo Drupa and all his attention was drawn in that direction.

Jigten Sumgön made the long journey from Kham to Phagdru in Central Tibet, and attended Phagmo Drupa for about thirty-two months. As soon as he arrived, Phagmo Drupa said "Now all my disciples are present." Then Phagmo Drupa told him, "You will be the greatest meditator of all, and for that I rejoice." While Jigten Sumgön was studying with Phagmo Drupa, he was very simple and modest. In the assembly of monks, he would sit in the back as if he knew nothing, but he was actually in a constant meditative state. Phagmo Drupa then entrusted him with the lineage and declared, "You will hold my throne of Dharma."

After Phagmo Drupa passed away, Jigten Sumgön went into retreat in the Echung cave for five years, took a short break, and then returned for two more years of retreat. After he attained enlightenment at age thirty-five, he said, "For the first five years of retreat I did not know how to meditate well. During the last two years, I came to understand how to meditate and, because of that, I achieved a vast result." Upon his enlightenment, he had visions of all the deities. He even received a vision of Ananda, who was the Buddha's attendant and who had memorized all of his teachings. In this vision he received everything the Buddha taught. Thus, he was able to establish himself as a master who could teach every level of Dharma from that of the rank beginner to the tenth-level bodhisattva.

For the next two years Jigten Sumgön visited many places, including Phagdru. While there, Phagmo Drupa came to him in a clear vision and said, "Now leave this old seat, go to the north, and build a new seat. You will benefit many sentient beings in that area." That is why Jigten Sumgön went to Drigung when he was thirty-seven and established his seat there. As a result, thousands of disciples gathered until he passed away at the age of seventy-five. Because he performed his enlightened activities in Drigung, whoever goes to that monastery makes a connection that will prevent rebirth in the lower realms.

Many of the disciples who gathered around Jigten Sumgön also attained enlightenment in one lifetime and, in this way, a great lineage was established. On three occasions, he sent disciples to the three most holy places: Tsari Mountain, Lapchi Mountain, and Mount Kailash. The first time he sent around eighty disciples to each mountain; the second time, nine hundred to each; and the third time, fifty-five thousand disciples went to each mountain. Each time, a still greater number of disciples gathered in the Drigung area.

Jigten Sumgön's enlightened mind permeates all sentient beings, and his blessings are there for anyone who meditates in the mahamudra state. He said that if one meditates on mahamudra, he himself will be present because his dharmakaya and the luminosity of the meditator's mind are no different. If one remembers Jigten Sumgön at the time of death, it will surely bring about rebirth in Sukhavati, Buddha Amitabha's pure land, or Abhirati, the eastern buddhafield where Buddha Akshobhya dwells.

There are many accounts of Jigten Sumgön being an incarnation of Nagarjuna. The deity Tara told this to Shakya Shri Bhadra directly. Other great masters also said this to Jigten Sumgön, so he himself accepted that he was Nagarjuna's reincarnation. This is mentioned in "Meaningful to Behold," a poem published in *Calling to the Lama from Afar:* "Even though this body is not Nagarjuna's body, all his teachings are in my mind." For example, Nagarjuna explained all the Buddha's teachings, absolute and relative, within the context of interdependent origination. Jigten Sumgön taught the same philosophy based on the mode of abiding of all phenomena, which has the same meaning, just using different words.

Che-nga Sherab Jungne, one of Jigten Sumgön's closest disciples, once visited the Mount Kailash area with five hundred disciples. The king of the nagas living in nearby Lake Manasarovar offered Che-nga Sherab Jungne a special statue of the Buddha. Many years before, the Buddha had given teachings at Bodh Gaya to human beings, gods, and nagas about the great benefits that come from building a statue of a buddha as an object of veneration and offering. Deeply inspired by this, the naga, human, and god kings each commissioned statues for their own realms that were blessed by the Buddha himself. Mahakala had gone to Bodh Gaya and brought the statue belonging to King Bimbisara, the human king, back with him. The Buddha instructed Mahakala and the naga king to keep the statue jointly. The Buddha said, "In the future a great teacher called Ratna Shri will appear in the eastern direction. At that time, one of his principal disciples will come to this area with five hundred other disciples. Give this statue to him, and many sentient beings will benefit." When Sherab Jungne arrived in the area with five hundred disciples, the naga king remembered what the Buddha had said. He offered the statue to Sherab Jungne, saying, "The Buddha instructed us to give this statue to you." Sherab Jungne wondered, "What should I do with this statue full of blessings like the Buddha himself? Should I leave it here or take it to Drigung?" The statue itself spoke, "I will stay here." As Jigten Sumgön had prophesied, they built the famous monastery called Gyangdrak on that spot, and he sent fifty-five thousand retreatants to stay there. The statue has remained as the main installation of the shrine ever since.

In one way samsara is very forceful; its suffering is dreadful and endless. On the other hand, when we have the opportunity to connect with an authentic lineage and receive the precious teachings, enlightenment is not so far from us. Because samsara is not ultimately real, we simply need mindfulness, strength, and devotion to cut through it. Sacrificing negative habits is very painful because we are so habituated to them. But if we learn how to practice diligently, they become nothing. In order to accomplish this, we need to trust the qualities of the enlightened beings. Without that, our practice will be very fragile and we may be derailed from the precious path to enlightenment. So we should *remember again and again* the kind lords of the Dharma who embody the teachings. They did not merely learn intellectual expression; they entered retreat in solitary places and fully experienced the ultimate meaning through realization. Jigten Sumgön said, "Whatever Dharma I teach, I have experienced through practice." So we *supplicate* him with a *one-pointed mind* in order to dissolve all our delusions into emptiness, and from there manifest all the enlightened qualities.

> Upon the crown of my head, on a sun and moon disk seat,
> sits my kind root lama, inseparable from the glorious Vajradhara.
> Remembering you again and again,
> I supplicate you with one-pointed mind filled with yearning.
> Guru! Grant your blessings that I may be realized like you.

Above the crown of your head, your root lama in the form of Vajradhara gently rests on moon and sun disks upon a lotus flower. Vajradhara, embodiment of all the buddhas and bodhisattvas in the ten directions and three times, inseparable appearance and emptiness, is surrounded by all the lineage masters, buddhas, and bodhisattvas. Before them all, we pray, "May I become like you, free from gross and subtle delusions. May I breathe compassion and wisdom. May you completely pervade my mind from all directions. I have been born in samsara from beginningless time and have experienced endless suffering. Today, I take refuge in you. Please protect me!"

First, we take an outer lama as root teacher, receive the teachings, supplicate to receive blessings, and experience those teachings in our heart. Then we take the Dharma texts as a teacher, read them again and again, and enrich our experience by persistently reminding ourselves of the practice. Once we have experienced these teachings in the depths of our heart, we take our own mind as the root teacher. Maintain that state without wavering, without being driven by the waves of delusional negative thoughts.

In these degenerate times our minds are capricious, unstable, fickle, changeable, and momentary. We may take someone as our root lama out of brief emotional inspiration but quickly abandon them when our emotional wishes are not fulfilled. If we develop negative thoughts about this experience, then we can destroy all the virtue of the Dharma practices we have done. This unfortunate circumstance comes from a lack of understanding of, and experience with, the purpose of Dharma practice. To prevent this from happening, we should take great masters like Milarepa, Gampopa, or Jigten Sumgön as our root lama. It doesn't matter whether they are alive because their wisdom and compassion extend to all sentient beings. Of course, it would be very good if living teachers all had direct experience of these precious Dharma teachings and if disciples had invincible courage and devotion.

In the space in front of you, visualize Vajradhara surrounded by the lineage teachers. Recite the mantra OM AH MULA GURU VAJRA DHRIK MAHA MUDRA SIDDHI PHALA HUNG many times and say prayers. When we recite prayers and meditate, we glimpse the blessings of the great masters. At the end of practice, we meditate that these great masters dissolve into one another from Vajradhara to Tilopa, to Naropa, to Marpa, to Milarepa, to Gampopa, to Phagmo Drupa, and to Jigten Sumgön, and they all dissolve into Vajradhara, the root lama at our crown. With devotion and confidence, we meditate that they dissolve into us at the crown of our head and permeate our whole being and body. Alternately, we can meditate that we receive the four empowerments in sequence and then meditate in the uncontrived state. We meditate that all our obscurations of body, speech, and mind are fully purified and that we are established in the nature of Vajradhara. The mind, now free of artificial elaboration, thus establishes itself in the unfabricated state. Meditate in this state of mahamudra for a few moments at the end of the session, and say dedication prayers.

CONCLUSION

All these great teachers—Tilopa, Naropa, Marpa, Milarepa, Gampopa, Phagmo Drupa, and Jigten Sumgön—are human manifestations of the Buddha himself. This should encourage all Dharma practitioners. If we supplicate them and take any one of them as our root lama, their blessings will always be with us, just as they were for the disciples who were present when these great teachers were alive. Jigten Sumgön clearly stated that, if in the future someone should need a root lama, they should take one of the great masters of the past. They actualized the mind of equanimity; therefore, they don't discriminate among sentient beings. Their wisdom and compassion permeate every sentient being until the end of samsara. They each cultivated bodhicitta and practiced it to perfection. They pledged to benefit sentient beings until the end of samsara and, since samsara has not yet ended, their blessings are as powerful now as they ever were.

When we study the gurus' teachings from books, we should also supplicate them and ask for their help in understanding the teachings. We supplicate them as root lamas, so we gain the same benefits from them that their direct disciples received. Jigten Sumgön said, "The Buddha's blessings are not greater for me or less for you." This is true because our own buddha nature and the buddha nature that has been actualized by the great masters are not different. So, let us build confidence, develop devotion, and practice tirelessly to realize that our negative thoughts and obscurations are only temporary. Purify them without exception and realize buddhahood.

Part One

Vajra Songs of Jetsün Milarepa

2. Distinguishing Happiness from Suffering

Recognizing the essence of his own mind, the yogin who realizes the true nature is always happy.
Pursuing delusion, the practitioner who increases his misery always suffers.

Resting within the uncontrived state, the yogin who realizes the unchanging nature, pure within its own place, is always happy.
Pursuing feelings and thoughts, the practitioner who freely accumulates attachments and aversions always suffers.

Realizing all appearances to be the dharmakaya, the yogin who cuts through hopes, fears, and doubts is always happy.
Engaging in pretense and careless actions, the practitioner who doesn't quell the eight worldly concerns always suffers.

Recognizing everything to be mind, the yogin who takes all appearances as an aid is always happy.
Having spent his life in distraction, the practitioner who feels remorse at the time of death always suffers.

Having liberated thought processes in their own place, the yogin who has continuous meditation experience is always happy.
Pursuing words and terms, the practitioner who does not determine the nature of his mind always suffers.

Having given up worldly activities, the yogin who is without selfishness and personal objectives is always happy.
Struggling to gather provisions, the practitioner who is preoccupied with family and relatives always suffers.

Having inwardly turned away from attachments, the yogin who realizes
everything to be an illusion is always happy.
Remaining on the path of distraction, the practitioner who employs his
body and speech as servants always suffers.

Riding the horse of diligence, the yogin who progresses through the paths
and bhumis to liberation is always happy.
In the shackles of laziness, the practitioner who is anchored to the depths
of samsara always suffers.

Having cut through false assertions by listening and reflecting, the yogin
who looks at his own mind as entertainment is always happy.
Merely professing to practice the Dharma, the practitioner who engages in
negative actions always suffers.

Having cut through hopes, fears, and doubts, the yogin who remains
continuously within the intrinsic state is always happy.
Having handed over his independence to others, the practitioner who
ingratiates and flatters always suffers.

Having cast all wants behind him, the yogin who continuously practices
the divine Dharma is always happy.

INTRODUCTION

THIS VAJRA SONG was taught by Milarepa, one of the most popular
and iconic figures in the Buddhist world. He was instrumental in planting Dharma practice in Tibet. For centuries, great teachers have admired his
accomplishments. During his lifetime, thousands of people had an opportunity to meet him, receive his blessings and teachings, and eventually become
free from samsara. Among them were many great masters like Dharma Lord
Gampopa and Rechungpa. Lengom Repa was the disciple to whom Milarepa gave these particular teachings. Lengom Repa received all the proper
instructions from Milarepa, practiced what he had learned, and experienced
great results. Then he said to Jetsün Milarepa, "Thank you so much. Because
of your kindness and all the teachings you gave me, I now understand what
should be given up and what should be accepted. Without effort, good
qualities now arise by themselves."

"That's right," Milarepa replied. "My son, one who practices the Dharma according to the Buddha's instructions on what should be abandoned and what should be accepted—such a Dharma practitioner will always be happy. When these conditions are reversed, the practitioner will always suffer." This shows that even Dharma practitioners should not miss the point by not knowing how to practice and making mistakes in the name of Dharma.

Even though the actions to accept and reject are listed in many places, it is always helpful to refresh one's mind and reinforce our focus on the purpose of our study and practice. The ten nonvirtues are the causes of suffering and predicaments in both secular society and in the spiritual realm:

- Taking the life of other living beings; directly or indirectly taking things that do not belong to oneself; and sexual misconduct— these are called the three physical nonvirtues.
- Telling lies, particularly about spiritual achievements that one does not have; dividing a group, couple, or society out of jealousy, attachment, or hatred; using harsh words out of anger or resentment; and senseless idle talk without any benefit—these four comprise nonvirtuous speech.
- Covetousness and greed; aversion and resentment; and wrong views related to causality or the absolute nature of reality—these three are related to a nonvirtuous mental state.

All the conflicts between people and countries, all undesirable conditions and predicaments are caused by these actions.

The ten virtues are these:

- Respecting and protecting others' lives, especially human life; practicing generosity and sharing; and keeping moral conduct— these three are the virtuous physical actions. To these, we can add abstaining from intoxicating drugs and alcohol.
- Speaking the truth; harmonizing divided societies or individuals; using an elegant voice and gentle words; and conducting meaningful conversations—these are the four virtues of speech.
- Contentment and appreciation; contemplation of loving-kindness, patience, and tolerance; and right view concerning infallible cause and result, and accepting the view of interdependent origination—these are the three virtuous mental states.

No matter who practices them and leads a life accordingly, these ten virtues create an environment of peace and tranquility. This is living a life of nonviolence, peace, and joy. Regardless of culture, religion, or ideology, everyone can accept and practice them as a foundation for true peace. They are the foundation for spiritual growth, an indispensable aspect of the path that frees us from samsara. Without them, we are building our mansion on a sandbar or on ice. With the ten virtues as a base, we can go on to tame the unruly mind, to study and practice loving-kindness, compassion, and bodhicitta. This is the consummate method, so it is important to remind yourself of these things repeatedly. Especially after you read the full commentary on Milarepa's song, you will be in less danger of wasting this precious human life.

COMMENTARY

> Recognizing the essence of his own mind, the yogin who realizes the
> true nature is always happy.
> Pursuing delusion, the practitioner who increases his misery always
> suffers.

First, although the song says "his" own mind, it is important to understand that mind has no gender. Gender operates merely at the outer level of physical phenomena. Nor do buddha nature, bodhicitta, and so forth contain any concept of male or female; neither does emptiness. The opportunity that we each have to study and practice transcends such duality. This is why it is said that the Buddha's mind is no different from the mind of sentient beings. The Buddha's bodhicitta and a sentient being's bodhicitta do not have the slightest difference. However, we must individually take responsibility to follow the path. Milarepa used a male pronoun because he was addressing Lengom Repa, but this teaching is intended for all sentient beings impartially.

The positive example here is a practitioner who recognizes *the essence of his own mind.* Our mind belongs to us alone, so we alone have the responsibility to know ourselves. It is important to encourage ourselves to make the realization of mind's true nature a priority in our life. Once we realize it, the universe is in our hand. We are fully satisfied; and when we are fully satisfied, we are happy. Otherwise, we have to keep searching, searching for happiness from outside.

Although we may have received many teachings, full comprehension often remains beyond our grasp. If we don't put the teachings into practice, we are still lost, no matter how much information we've collected. This point is crucial. Milarepa studied under Marpa, who taught him completely. Milarepa could stay alone in the mountains full of joy and contentment because he put those teachings into practice and fully experienced them. He didn't have to go anywhere, see anything, or do anything more. So his advice for us is to meditate, practice, get used to the teachings and practices, master them, build confidence, and become enlightened. Happiness will then be inevitable.

The opposite example given here is of a practitioner who chases after delusions, one after another. We may study Dharma, but in practical terms we are more involved with the eight worldly concerns. Many practitioners go here and there in the name of Dharma but never find their own minds, because they think they can achieve happiness from outside themselves. This can never happen. Happiness is within. Pursuing delusion only brings more misery. The more we follow the eight worldly concerns and other distractions, the more our suffering will increase. As Dharma practitioners, we should really understand this.

> **Resting within the uncontrived state, the yogin who realizes the unchanging nature, pure within its own place, is always happy. Pursuing feelings and thoughts, the practitioner who freely accumulates attachments and aversions always suffers.**

Here again, we have a contrasting pair of examples. The happy yogin has realized the true nature of his own mind and simply rests in that nature, *the uncontrived state.* "Uncontrived" means that there is no need to make things better or change them in any way. You just realize mind directly, as it is. When clouds disappear from the sky, it doesn't make the sky better; space just is as it is. It is the same with mind. When delusions and afflictions disappear, the mind is free from elaboration—unfabricated, unchanging peace.

Contrivances are artificial constructions and, therefore, changing. Our conventional mind is like the ball in a soccer game, being kicked back and forth between good and bad, wrong and right, like and dislike. From beginningless time, we have been chasing delusion without finding any place of rest. We search and search for happiness, but it continually slips away from us. The way to rest is to become free from elaboration, to experience the uncontrived nature of mind, which is pure just as it is. Take water as another example. When we purify dirty water, all we can do is remove the pollutants.

The water itself remains unchanged; it was always pure. In the same way, we cannot alter the pure nature of mind. Recognizing that and resting there is happiness and joy.

On the other hand, a Dharma practitioner who is continually *pursuing feelings and thoughts* has a problem. He runs back and forth after his feelings of hope and fear, and therefore suffers by continually bouncing between likes and dislikes, attachments and aversions. When one has a strong attachment to one's own happiness, achievements, joy, and so forth, this will lead to suffering as a side effect. Likewise, when one has a strong reaction to hatred, that anger will bring suffering into our being. We should learn how to relax. Otherwise, the suffering will be constant.

Basically, this verse describes the difference between samsara and nirvana. Samsara is a constant condition of suffering, while resting in nirvana is continual happiness. The distinction is easy to see, but we have to learn how to go from one to the other. First, there is bodhicitta. It is very important to have this principal method as a foundation. Then we can practice mahamudra, and when we practice well, we will experience great joy and peace. This kind of happiness is called "fearless" because there is no fear of losing it.

Realizing all appearances to be the dharmakaya, the yogin who cuts through hopes, fears, and doubts is always happy.
Engaging in pretense and careless actions, the practitioner who doesn't quell the eight worldly concerns always suffers.

All appearances are illusion, like a mirage. Their nature is emptiness. Seeing this *cuts through hopes, fears, and doubts*. There's nothing to expect, nothing to hold, nothing to fear. Hesitation and doubt are cut off. Thus abiding within the dharmakaya, one *is always happy* and experiences great peace.

The study of impermanence, suffering, and causality are indispensable as preparation for these kinds of realization. When we study impermanence, we see that all composite phenomena are of a transitory, momentary nature. They come and go. Impermanence can be summarized by these four things that we know to be true:

> ▸ Everyone will die. There is no record anywhere in the world of someone having been born who did not die. If they had not died, we could see them now.
> ▸ The end of all accumulation is dispersion.
> ▸ The end of all meeting is separation. We may meet many people, but we will always part, either by leaving them or through death.

▶ The end of all construction is destruction. Everything that has been built—buildings, roads, airplanes—will one day fall apart. It's just a matter of time.

Contemplate this in order to release attachment and anger, and free the mind.

We can see how the study of impermanence is very helpful to an understanding of the illusory nature of phenomena. As a result of engaging in this kind of contemplation, a more precise way of thinking will arise, and that will lead to incisive awareness. Life is like ripples in the water, moving every moment. Without such awareness, we unsuccessfully try to make things concrete, and then we suffer. On the other hand, if we realize that the nature of phenomena is emptiness, that realization will cut our fears and doubts. Without fear and doubt, we will always be happy.

Suffering is based on confusion; the root cause of suffering is our great ignorance. Ignorance is a mental factor that has the nature of contrivance and fabrication. It prevents us from perceiving the pure nature of mind as it is. As long as confusion remains, physical and mental suffering must also persist. Therefore, everyone in the world will live under the condition of suffering until confusion is dispelled. There are two types of causality: causes conditioned by confusion and causes based in wisdom and compassion. The result of causes conditioned by confusion is suffering. The results of causes based in wisdom and compassion are peace and happiness. All the peace and happiness in this world and beyond are the result of an unafflicted mind.

The practitioner who engages in *pretense and careless actions* pretends to be good but is actually careless when it comes to discipline. That is like being trapped in a prison. If you have taken precepts or vows but are not keeping them well, you have to pretend in front of people that you are a genuine practitioner or scholar. Sometimes you pretend that you are accomplished. But if the reality is that you are careless regarding your precepts, this pretending will be like a prison, and you will suffer because you cannot act freely. Precepts are not something meant to strengthen your ego. Precepts are just a part of Dharma practice, a part of life, not a cause for pretense.

When our actions are uncontrived, they are more natural and flow freely, like a stream flowing from a mountain into the ocean. If our life flows like that, there is such great peace and joy. If we always have to pretend, then we'll always be tight. That approach does not *quell the eight worldly concerns* but rather makes them worse. The eight worldly concerns are listed in many different places, but are repeated here as a reminder. Gain, praise, comfort, and fame—these are the positive states we seek to achieve. Everyone in the world, from a street cleaner to a country's leader, will sacrifice their life to obtain these four and thereby will create many undesirable causes. Loss, discomfort, blame, and disgrace—these are the four objects of aversion. It's hard for us to accept responsibility for these four; people repeatedly create masses of confusion to cover them up or deny their existence. If we genuinely desire peace and happiness, we have no choice but to avoid these eight worldly concerns.

Everyone should watch their mind, but especially those who are practicing bodhicitta and mahamudra. When any of these eight concerns arise in the mind, purify them. We should see them as bubbles, mirages, or magical displays. We should relax the mind naturally within the sphere of wisdom.

To achieve a free-flowing, relaxed life, we have to practice Dharma well. We must transcend our negative thoughts and bad habits. We should practice to purify the causes of our suffering. We should practice to purify delusions, not to make ourselves into something special or to obtain a high title. We should investigate for ourselves whether this is true.

> **Recognizing everything to be mind, the yogin who takes all appearances as an aid is always happy.**
> **Having spent his life in distraction, the practitioner who feels remorse at the time of death always suffers.**

How are we to understand that everything is mind? For example, is this table your mind? No, we are not saying that. Fabrications about the table, such as good, bad, big, or real, clearly exist only in the mind. They are not inherent to the table. But the table didn't appear by itself. It was constructed from parts into a form that we call "table." The concept of a table was a creation of the mind; a mind designed it, planned it, and figured out how to put it together. Therefore, we say the mind created it. Similarly, we can say that our perception of all of samsara and nirvana is just mind, because directly or indirectly they are both created by the mind. We label each phenomenon and impute a fabricated meaning on this basis.

When Jigten Sumgön was studying, he heard the teaching that says everything is just mind. He questioned his lama, saying, "If everything is just mind, then when the Buddha attained enlightenment, everything else should have become enlightened, too. The bodhi tree at Bodh Gaya should have been enlightened. But the bodhi tree is still there unchanged. Why?" The lama replied, "When the Buddha attained enlightenment his perception of the bodhi tree was enlightened. Since we are not enlightened, our perception of the tree is not enlightened. When we are unenlightened, our mind is obscured by defilements, so we perceive everything as impure. When one is enlightened, all obscurations and defilements dissolve into emptiness, so one perceives everything as pure."

It is important to understand the connection between phenomena—that is, objects of the mind—and how mind perceives phenomena. Shantideva taught this in the *Guide to the Bodhisattva's Conduct*. In that text, he posed the question, "Who could have created the intense heat of hell, the guardians, and the excruciating pain of the beings living there? The Buddha said that it is all a result of negative thought." Negative thought creates samsara and suffering; a positive mind creates the enlightened nature and the buddhafields.

When we are aware that everything is just our mind, then we know to relax our mind. We can always reshape our mind. We can exercise the mind on this basis, and then *appearances* become *an aid* to help the mind. When something goes wrong, instead of sinking in helpless agony, look at the situation in a different way. For example, suppose you lose a possession. You lost it because you owned it; if you hadn't had one, there would have been nothing to lose. This is an example of an appearance aiding our understanding of Dharma. We get sick because we have a body. If we didn't have this body, there would be no reason to age, get sick, or die. There's nothing to blame. It's just a question of how we perceive the situation. Changing our perception protects our mind from suffering. There are many stages to this kind of practice. When you know how to accept adversity, how to relate to events in your life and in your Dharma practice, you will always be happy.

A practitioner who wanders from place to place with a mind scattered in distraction will feel *remorse at the time of death*. He will recognize that he didn't practice well and couldn't experience the Dharma, even though he met with such a precious teaching. When there is deep regret like this, there is intense suffering. But no matter how much you suffer, you still follow the same pattern. You chase after suffering, just using a slightly different method each time. We end up with our entire life span occupied by laziness—what a waste! So, practice Dharma as much as possible. Turn away from the wrong direction toward the right, and always investigate the mind.

Reflecting on impermanence, especially as exemplified by death, is crucial to Dharma practice. If we didn't have Dharma teachings, it would be useless to reflect on death, because we couldn't do anything about it. It would be better to put that thought aside. But since we have these precious teachings and skillful methods, we can transform suffering and the causes of suffering into an aid to enhance bodhicitta. We are going to die anyway; that much is certain. So we should develop the confidence to face it with a positive attitude. This is the way to be true to oneself, to take care of one's own best interest.

> Having liberated thought processes in their own place, the yogin
>   who has continuous meditation experience is always happy.
> Pursuing words and terms, the practitioner who does not determine
>   the nature of his mind always suffers.

For practitioners and nonpractitioners alike, the *thought process* arises continuously, and we cannot stop it. There are many different types of thoughts, some positive and some negative. Nonpractitioners have few methods to handle these thoughts, let alone to consider liberation. But a Dharma practitioner has a good opportunity to relate to his thoughts and become liberated through the wisdom of the Dharma.

Liberated thought processes are unfabricated and uncontrived. When a thought arises in the mind, do not chase after it or make anything of it; just knowing its nature while remaining in the unfabricated equipoise state is itself liberation. Then, there is no grasping or no fixation. When you draw a figure on the surface of water, it disappears immediately without a trace. We should liberate our mind in the same way. Treat the thoughts that come like that drawing, and let them disappear in their own unfabricated place. As the drawing is liberated within the water, let thoughts disappear back to their source. If we hold the mind, grasp at thoughts, are attached to our thoughts, or hate them, then we just suffer. In contrast, through meditation practice our mind can become stable and clear. When this stability and clarity are *continuous,* one is *always happy.* This happiness is not like samsaric pleasure, which is temporary. This happiness arises from the enlightened nature and is total freedom.

A so-called practitioner who is only involved with philosophical analysis, who is intellectually sophisticated but lacking in experience of the teachings, is not really paying attention to the mind and therefore *always suffers* in hope and fear. Of course, we have to study some philosophy to know what we're doing. But the reason for becoming a scholar, for understanding the Buddha's teachings, is to apply them by focusing on the mind.

If we don't pay attention to the nature of mind but only focus on the *words and terms* and analysis without experience, then in the end suffering will continue without end.

> **Having given up worldly activities, the yogin who is without**
> **selfishness and personal objectives is always happy.**
> **Struggling to gather provisions, the practitioner who is preoccupied**
> **with family and relatives always suffers.**

True Dharma practitioners are convinced of the impermanence of all phenomena, know that everything is illusory and transitory, and understand that materials have no essence. They understand that no matter how rich or famous one may be, everyone in samsara remains in the condition of suffering. Pursuing the eight *worldly activities* may keep one very active, but it is still spiritual laziness, even if done in the name of the Dharma. This verse is not suggesting that we should do nothing at all. The activities to abandon are those that involve samsaric concerns, goals that are pursued for selfish reasons and personal gain. Without such things, the yogin *is always happy.*

Instead of being lazy, yogins study the profound teachings of the Buddha and practice them, particularly bodhicitta and mahamudra. In this way, they purify the unruly mind that is at the center of all the afflictions. They develop the mind of enlightenment by dispelling *selfishness* or attachment to oneself. This allows them to build the indomitable courage to free themselves from all limits. Discarding *personal objectives* and embracing the pristine mind of luminosity, they rest in the uncontrived state and are always happy.

One who is involved in the Dharma but doesn't take Dharma to heart is the opposite. Such a person is actually involved in samsaric activities such as *gathering provisions,* and struggling for wealth, fame, and authority. On the basis of attachment, these so-called practitioners are *preoccupied with family and relatives;* they are enslaved by the need to support their family and relatives. Instead of purifying their delusions and mental afflictions, they promote their ego and attachment by pretending they are highly accomplished meditators. Aversion arises when someone opposes their wishes. The result of all this is only suffering. Therefore, it is important to take full responsibility for exercising our good and wise judgment by choosing the path that ends suffering.

Having inwardly turned away from attachments, the yogin who
realizes everything to be an illusion is always happy.
Remaining on the path of distraction, the practitioner who employs
his body and speech as servants always suffers.

Sometimes the word "yogin" is misunderstood as meaning a married lama.
The Tibetan word here is *naljor*. *Nal* refers to the uncontrived nature, and
jor is the meditator who has unified his mind with that uncontrived state.
That could be anyone; whether they are a monk or married is irrelevant.
A true yogin looks within and rests within the uncontrived state. This means
that he has unified samadhi and special insight.

As was described before, all the different types of suffering are caused by
afflicting emotions. When afflictions and karma work together, confusion
and suffering continuously arise from without and within. A yogin who has
skillful means does not chase outside, objective phenomena. His project
is to calm the mind and relax, to pacify all the gross and subtle afflictions
with samadhi. With that support, he lights the fire of special insight that
consumes the darkness of confusion. The yogin then enjoys total peace and
satisfaction. Such a mind is free from attachment and, because of that, it
realizes *everything to be an illusion*.

One who spends his time being entertained by TV, the Internet, or movies is always distracted. All his life energy is expended to fulfill attachment
to this life. His *body and speech* become *servants* to attachment and ego.
All his resources are sacrificed to no purpose; in the end, nothing has been
accomplished to promote Dharma. This is like chasing rainbows or trying
to quench thirst with a mirage.

Riding the horse of diligence, the yogin who progresses through the
paths and bhumis to liberation is always happy.
In the shackles of laziness, the practitioner who is anchored to the
depths of samsara always suffers.

Practicing Dharma is more than chanting some mantras, doing a few prostrations, turning a prayer wheel, and going on pilgrimage to the holy sites.
Dharma means peace based on wisdom, free from delusion and confusion.
Practicing Dharma, then, means reducing the causes of suffering at every
level. Look at the ten virtues and nonvirtues, and then work to develop
a positive frame of mind. Through this, skillfully purify the cause of suf-

fering and simultaneously develop the cause of the uncontrived mode of abiding. One who progresses in meditation practice in this way is *always happy* because his or her mind is healthy and strong within the framework of bodhicitta. The *horse of diligence,* or joyous effort, will easily take you through the five *paths* and the ten *bhumis.* The paths and bhumis are precisely described in *The Jewel Ornament of Liberation.* Please refer to that book if you would like more detail on this subject.

Unfortunately, many are chained by *laziness.* One whose time is taken up in this manner *always suffers.* There are basically three types of laziness: the laziness of discouragement, attachment to the pleasures of this life, and busyness for this life's benefit.

The laziness of discouragement consists of thinking things such as, "I'm not smart enough. I can't do this. I'm not strong enough. The Dharma is so profound and I feel so small. How could I absorb this Dharma? It's not for me." This is actually just your making excuses by looking down on yourself. Look carefully at this approach. Will this kind of excuse exempt you from suffering? Because you have this flaw, will samsara have compassion for you and allow you alone not to suffer? The better approach is to recall buddha nature and the precious human life. Recall that you are not helpless, because you have the teachings on virtue and nonvirtue. You can understand samsara and nirvana. Somehow, even insects can eventually be freed from samsara, so why not you? Starting from that point, you will soon be free from the *shackles of laziness.* This doesn't mean to encourage arrogance and looking down on others. Here, we develop confidence that will enable us to study and practice Dharma, to progress on the path, and to cultivate bodhicitta with a courageous mind. With these methods, we can escape the laziness of discouragement.

Going on picnics, watching movies, wasting time on gossip and idle talk, and enjoying meaningless speech are examples of the laziness of attachment to the pleasures of this life. The antidote is to reflect on impermanence. Think, "Even if I passed my entire life this way, what would I have in the end?" Suppose you went to the mountains on vacation and had a wonderful time. What essential things would you achieve through this? Instead, climb the mountain of bodhicitta, watch the movie of mind, and unreservedly enjoy the uncontrived state. Reflect on Dharma teachings, practice them, and purify the mind. If you had taken the time you spent on entertainment and used it for meditation, think about the difference it would have made now! Which one do you choose for the future?

An example of the third kind of laziness, busyness for this life's benefit, can be seen in the way workers are sometimes so busy they don't even take time to eat lunch. So many deadlines! In the end, how much benefit will you get from this lifestyle? Try to be more balanced. It's all a matter of your point of view. You can still do things for this life, but do them with a focus on liberation. When you drive, take a shower, cook, or do any activity, you have a chance to practice Dharma by continually practicing mindfulness.

Some find themselves *anchored to the depths of samsara* by four perverted mindsets:

- ► holding the unclean to be clean;
- ► holding the impermanent to be permanent;
- ► holding suffering to be happiness; and
- ► holding the selfless to possess a self.

Our body, composed of five aggregates, is nothing more than a skeleton covered with unclean material, but we cherish it as if it were clean. This body is fragile and impermanent, a conglomeration of many causes and conditions, but we see it as a single, solid thing. This very body is the basis of all suffering, but we confusedly take it to be the basis of happiness. Being a composition of many factors, it has no self-entity, no inherent existence; but through our delusion we hold this "self" to be very important. This perverted mindset firmly anchors us to samsara, where we waste all our resources in cherishing and protecting our body.

> **Having cut through false assertions by listening and reflecting, the yogin who looks at his own mind as entertainment is always happy. Merely professing to practice the Dharma, the practitioner who engages in negative actions always suffers.**

By *listening and reflecting* we receive the Dharma teachings and gain the skills to *cut through false assertions,* which will free us from doubt and hesitation. There are many Dharma texts taught by the Buddha and written by great teachers. Aspiring Dharma practitioners should study these texts, memorize them, and receive word by word explanations of their meaning. After such study, it is beneficial to use contemplation and debate as means to delve deeper into their meaning and gain a clear understanding of their purpose. Then we should meditate more seriously and use our mind to witness the Buddha's wisdom and to gradually reduce the afflicting emotions that cause confusion. This way, positive qualities will naturally manifest.

The very first step of Dharma practice is to look at the mind. There are many different ways to do this. In the beginning, just witness what is present in the mind. So many thoughts arise, mostly anger, attachment, arrogance, and jealousy. Uncover these defilements and purify them by applying their antidotes. Make them less and less powerful and then rest in the uncontrived state.

We may be interested in practicing Dharma, but what of our conduct in daily life? When the Buddha saw some of his disciples acting negatively, he said, "I taught in order to free people from samsara, but they are creating samsara in the name of Dharma. Why should I create additional causes for suffering? Perhaps I should stay quiet and let people play in the samsara that is already manifest." Our Dharma centers are places where we need to pay attention to these things. The way we manifest our activities there is especially important. We are supposed to be creating an opportunity for people to study and practice, but if it becomes a place to exercise ego and power, then the center is merely another place of confused conflict. No matter how much we work, no one will appreciate it. All the effort will be wasted as it increases suffering and develops a negative environment. Knowing this, be mindful and appreciate the Dharma as a remedy to purify all shortcomings. Meditate on a daily basis. Such a practitioner will *always be happy* and will develop the resources to help others as well.

Of course, since we are not enlightened, these negative habitual tendencies will arise. When negative thoughts arise, pay attention and apply the Dharma as an antidote. Then as our Dharma centers progress, they will become useful. In the outside world, few people understand kindness and meditation. Some will even say we are crazy. So we create an environment where people can come to study and practice peace sincerely. We do this as a Dharma service; we don't expect appreciation. But if we do things the right way people will appreciate it anyway. Do just one little thing; do it sincerely, and it can benefit so much.

> Having cut through hopes, fears, and doubts, the yogin who remains continuously within the intrinsic state is always happy.
> Having handed over his independence to others, the practitioner who ingratiates and flatters always suffers.

Abandoning *hopes, fears, and doubts* is a skillful way to practice. Worldly activities are nothing but hope and fear. Our entire life is spent bouncing between these two. We hope that a project will go well, and at the same time we fear that it may fail. In between, there isn't much clarity of mind. There are many attractive and prestigious goals to achieve in samsara. We are considered successful when we gain wealth, fame, or power, so we invest a lot of hope in these things. At the same time, we fear that we will lose them. We waste our time in maintaining our position in life. Ordinary people and inexperienced practitioners will continue to suffer until they let go of hope and fear.

Dharma practice is the only solution. Through the wisdom of the Dharma, we have the opportunity to perceive things clearly, to see that everything is just a manifestation or reflection of the mind. Phenomena and events come and go. With this wisdom, rather than expecting our happiness to come from outside ourselves, we look into the mind. True happiness and joy are there. When we fully understand our mind through the wisdom of the Dharma, we can regard it as a wish-granting jewel. We must never lose our understanding but always safeguard it in the treasury of mindfulness. Maintaining that *intrinsic awareness* continuously brings happiness, so protect your own mind.

On the other hand, if we continually try to please others while our mind remains in a state of dense delusion, we will *always suffer*. This does not mean we should ignore harmony with others; that would be going too far. This verse concerns using flattery and ingratiation to promote our own self-interest. As long as we are in samsara, it is not possible to protect others' minds or to make others happy. So, we should first protect our own mind with the *intrinsic state* of awareness. Once we can sustain that state of mind, we can make other people happy, because we will have lost all selfish concerns.

Having cast all wants behind him, the yogin who continuously practices the divine Dharma is always happy.

Having cast all wants behind him means that the meditating yogin has no attachment to this life. Whatever he happens to get, good or bad, he is content. Without aversion or attachment, he is completely focused on enlightenment. One who always relies on the Dharma, *who continuously practices the divine Dharma, is always happy*. The pure Dharma purifies delusion and uproots the cause of samsara. Relying on that will always lead to happiness.

If practitioners make mistakes, that is their own problem, not a fault of the Dharma. Sometimes when a Buddhist makes a mistake, people say, "Look what kind of people those Buddhists are!" And if a lama causes a problem, even Buddhists will say, "You see that lama? He made a big mess. This is what Buddhism can do to you." This reflects our misunderstanding of the Dharma rather than something being wrong with Buddhism itself. Not every practitioner can practice perfectly according to the Dharma. So, instead of depending on an individual, always depend directly on the teachings. Look at the meaning of the Dharma, not at the behavior of individual practitioners.

Dharma is the true refuge. A doctor is important for diagnosing an illness and prescribing the right medicine. But the cure then depends on the medicine. If the medicine is phony it won't help no matter how good the doctor may be. But if the medicine has good healing qualities, the patient will get better no matter who gives it to him. In the same way, the Buddha carefully prescribed the cure for samsara: this is suffering, this is the origin of suffering, this is nirvana, and this is the path to nirvana. It is up to the practitioner to progress on the path step by step by purifying his obscurations and afflictions. Because of this, we say that Dharma is the real medicine. If we drink the undefiled ambrosia of Dharma, there is no doubt that all physical problems and mental delusions will be healed. Please keep in mind how precious the Dharma is.

In the *Garland of the Sublime Path,* Gampopa says:

> When even in the lower realms and in the unfree states there is some slight temporary happiness created through the merit of wholesome virtuous deeds—this is by virtue of the sacred Dharma.

Suppose someone is so confused that no one values him. Somehow, that person encounters Dharma teachings, studies, practices, and begins to develop good qualities. Little by little he becomes a better person and people treat him a little better. After some time, he becomes a wonderful person, all because of Dharma. An ordinary person may take refuge in the Buddha, Dharma, and Sangha, start following the Dharma teachings, take the bodhisattva vow, and gain the respect of everyone around him. All this happens because of the Dharma. When someone attains buddhahood, the perfect state free from all obscurations, it is because of the Dharma. A buddha manifests ceaselessly and benefits countless sentient beings because of the Dharma. So recognize that jewel in your own hand. Cherish it and polish it, and happiness will follow like a shadow.

3. The Eight Bardos

I prostrate to the saintly lamas.
In particular, I go for refuge to the one who was kind.
Son, in answer to your prayer
I sing this song about the bardos.

Sentient beings in the three realms of samsara
and buddhas who have passed beyond suffering
are one in their actual true nature.
This is the bardo of view.

The various white and red manifestations
and the inexpressible innate mind
are inseparable, being one in the intrinsic state.
This is the bardo of meditation.

Delusory appearances in their various manifestations
and one's own nonarising mind
are one as nondual coemergence.
This is the bardo of conduct.

Last night's dreams arise from habitual patterns.
We know them to be false when we awaken.
These states are one in being illusion-like.
This is the bardo of dreams.

The impure five skandhas
and the pure five families of the victorious ones
are one within the nonconceptual completion stage.
This is the bardo of the generation and completion stages of the path.

The father tantras arising from skillful methods
and the mother tantras arising from wisdom
are one as the coemergence of the third empowerment.
This is the bardo of the essential point.

The unchanging dharmakaya for one's own benefit
and the unceasing form kayas for the benefit of others
are inseparable, being one in the intrinsic state.
This is the bardo of the three kayas.

The impure illusory body born from a mother's womb
and the pure form of the deity
are one in the luminosity of the bardo.
This is the bardo of result.

INTRODUCTION

MILAREPA'S STYLE of teaching is called "direct pointing out." This refers to instructions that pinpoint what should be rejected and what should be accepted, the causes of suffering and the causes of happiness, without a lot of intellectual argumentation. For centuries, people have benefited from studying his vajra songs. Now we, too, have the good fortune to study the songs of Milarepa and be similarly inspired to practice Dharma sincerely. Even though we may not fully comprehend what Milarepa said, it is crucial to rejoice in the opportunity to read his words. If we can do that, we will make a connection with Milarepa and receive his blessings through his songs. This isn't due to some magical power but rather is the natural result of understanding and practicing his teachings. In this song of the eight bardos, the profundity and vastness of his teachings are made clear to scholars and practitioners alike. If we keep them in mind, we will eventually arrive at buddhahood.

COMMENTARY

I prostrate to the saintly lamas.
In particular, I go for refuge to the one who was kind.
Son, in answer to your prayer
I sing this song about the bardos.

Milarepa begins by singing the praises of the *saintly lamas,* who are the great enlightened masters. Among them, Marpa was the *one who was* most *kind* to Milarepa because he is the one who gave Milarepa all the lineage teachings, which caused him to achieve complete enlightenment in a single lifetime. Gampopa is Milarepa's spiritual *son,* and the one who requested these teachings.

Bardo is a Tibetan word. The first syllable, *bar,* means "in between"; the second syllable, *do,* means "two." So together, they mean "place in between two." While the bardo between lives is the most well known, the word can be used to indicate a state between any two things: hungry and full, happiness and suffering, delusion and enlightenment, laughing and crying, this life and the next, or between meditation sessions. Our life constantly plays out in between, in duality. This song is a teaching on how to transcend duality or, in other words, how to purify the concept of duality. Since Gampopa was highly accomplished in meditation and scholarship, Milarepa explained these bardo teachings from the point of view of mahamudra. All appearances related to every subject manifest in dependence on causality from the mahamudra state, and they dissolve back into mahamudra. A great amount of wisdom based on meditation experience with nonduality is needed to capture the meaning of inseparable appearance and emptiness. This song explains it in terms of eight specific bardos:

- ► bardo of view
- ► bardo of meditation
- ► bardo of conduct
- ► bardo of dreams
- ► bardo of generation and completion stages of the path (also called bardo of the path)
- ► bardo of the essential point
- ► bardo of the three kayas
- ► bardo of result

Sentient beings in the three realms of samsara
and buddhas who have passed beyond suffering
are one in their actual true nature.
This is the bardo of view.

The *three realms* that comprise samsara are the desire, form, and formless worlds. The desire world is the largest, extending from the hells up to the six lowest desire god realms. In that world, beings are ruled by their senses and their desires are fulfilled by outer objects. For example, our human desires are fulfilled when we look at beautiful forms, hear beautiful sounds, smell lovely fragrances, taste delicious foods, and touch smooth objects. Beings in the four stages of the form world have a more subtle existence, and their desires are completely satisfied through meditative absorption. They feel so joyful and peaceful that external phenomena are of no interest. Instead of looking for outside stimulation as we do, they are content to abide inside the mind. Beings in the formless world are even more subtle and have no physical form. They have only a mental form that is so fully absorbed in equipoise it can remain so for many thousands of eons. They are satisfied with a meditation state that is even more profound than that of the form world. All the countless sentient beings are contained within these three contaminated worlds.

Buddhas are those who have transcended these three realms to reach full enlightenment. Their obscurations, both gross and subtle, have been fully purified. The two wisdoms are fully awakened within them.

Although these two—sentient beings and buddhas—are on two different levels, they share the same essential *true nature*. The difference is that sentient beings are bewildered in a jungle of confusion. They have failed to recognize their buddha nature and wander in helpless suffering as a result, whereas buddhas have purified their ignorance and revealed their true nature. Out of great wisdom and compassion, buddhas teach the Dharma based on the certainty that buddha nature makes perfect enlightenment possible for everyone.

The Dharma is not some kind of instant magic. We gradually follow in the footsteps of great masters like Tilopa, Naropa, Marpa, Milarepa, Gampopa, Phagmo Drupa, and Jigten Sumgön. One after another, they practiced and forcefully destroyed their delusions. Therefore, there is no doubt that we, too, can experience this. We only need courage, dedication, and strength.

The buddhas and great masters did not create their own view of reality; rather, they realized it as it actually is. They recognize the very ignorance that causes the perpetual suffering of samsara as primordial wisdom. When one sees everything clearly and precisely, there is no samsara to give up and no nirvana to achieve. Duality and all bardos are transcended. This is the principal point of all our Dharma study and practice.

A simple analogy can help demonstrate this point. Let's say you are suspicious of someone and think, "Oh, this is a terrible person. She gives me such a hard time." But after some time, you get to know her better, discover her good qualities, and become close friends. The other person is the same; the duality of her being good or bad does not exist from her side. But as you gained understanding, your perceptions changed. Similarly, as we develop more loving-kindness, compassion, and bodhicitta, our perception of negative thought purifies. Mental clarity grows stronger as we perceive with a healthier mind. We can even get to the point where we feel grateful when someone presents us with an obstacle.

There is an account of a bodhisattva in ancient times whose hand was cut off by a king. The bodhisattva reacted by saying, "Thank you so much for this opportunity to enhance my practice." His heart had been so transformed that instead of seeing a negative action, he genuinely felt grateful. With practice and confidence we, too, can transcend the duality of good and bad, buddha and sentient being, as Jigten Sumgön did. He expressed this in the "Song of the Six Confidences":

> I, a yogin, realized the unity of the guru, my own mind, and the
> Buddha.
> I have no need of superficial devotion.
> In non-effort, I, the yogin, am happy.
> This happy yogin experiences joy.
> This experience of joy is the guru's kindness.

This is the ultimate view: that the Buddha and we ourselves share the same nature. There are many, many high and profound views, but this one is the pinnacle. There is nothing higher that we might achieve. Actualizing this view is our goal, and until we arrive at that destination by transcending duality, we must exert whatever effort we can.

> **The various white and red manifestations**
> **and the inexpressible innate mind**
> **are inseparable, being one in the intrinsic state.**
> **This is the bardo of meditation.**

An infinite variety of experience will arise when we meditate. Manifestations can come while dreaming, during the meditation session itself, or afterward. There's really no predicting what, if anything, will manifest. But no matter what appears, it is all a manifestation from the innate mind. The mind cannot be described or limited by any sort of boundary. We cannot say that it exists one way or the other. In fact, we cannot pin down whether it exists at all. Its nature is *inexpressible* by any conventional means, yet that same mind is the basis of all our experiences, the *various white and red manifestations*. These are the myriad experiences that occur during meditation practice and during our various thought processes.

The mind is like an ocean, and all mental activities are like ocean waves. Ocean waves arise from the water and dissolve back into it. When a wave manifests, we can point to it and say, "This is a wave." But the wave is of the same nature as the water, so we can't truly separate them. Big waves and small waves may come, but the water itself is unchanged. Water with waves and water without waves is still water. They may temporarily appear to be separate, but upon examination they are actually seen to be of a single nature. Similarly, when we are skilled at meditation, we can see that all phenomena are manifestations of the innate nature of mind. Different experiences come and go, but when it comes to the mind itself, nothing has happened. The innate mind is utterly unchanged.

All mundane technologies are manifestations of our human mind. Buses, cars, trains, airplanes, and so forth, deadly weapons, and all the communication devices (phone, cell phone, Twitter, e-mail, and so forth) were created by mind. Every year, hundreds of thousands of books are written by means of mental contemplation. Buildings are constructed, as are towers, mansions, roads, and houses—all created by mind. Each city, district, country, and state has its own rules and regulations, each one a little different from the others. All these different solutions to the same problem were put together by the mind. There are even different aspects of enlightenment: four types of shravaka (stream enterer, once-returner, nonreturner, and arhat), as well as pratyekabuddhas, and ten levels of bodhisattvas, and then buddhahood. But, within the framework of mahamudra, they are all of the same nature—there is not a single difference. That is the ultimate mode of abiding. It is as if five differently colored pieces of cloth were burned in a fire. They would all turn to the same color of ash, their original distinctions dissolved into emptiness.

These are very profound teachings that are not easy to comprehend. The mind is as limitless and inexpressible as space. If you try to describe space, what can you say? Can you determine that it has a particular color? A shape? A center? Like the wave example given above, clouds arise and dissolve within the sky, but the sky remains unchanged. Clouds and the sky similarly appear to be separate but are inseparable, being one in the *intrinsic state*.

We should focus on the mind in our meditation, rather than getting involved with the myriad manifestations that arise within it. Look at the ocean and the sky, and don't be distracted by the waves and clouds. Let phenomena such as feeling good or bad manifest from mind and let them dissolve back into mind. Simply sustain awareness of the innate mind. This is the bardo of meditation.

Delusory appearances in their various manifestations
and one's own nonarising mind
are one as nondual coemergence.
This is the bardo of conduct.

We, and all others in samsara, are deluded and confused, blinded by ignorance, and mistake outer *appearances in their various manifestations* for reality. Not recognizing that they are illusory, we fixate on them and are continually disappointed. When we do not recognize the actual nature of these outer projections, they delude our mind even more, and the darkness thickens.

The deluded samsaric mind and the innate nature of mind seem to be two different things. But they are one, nondually coemergent. That very deluded mind is coemergent with the unborn mind of wisdom. The confusion is that we do not recognize this. The unborn mind is like water and the deluded mind is like ice. No matter how long it has been frozen, ice retains the nature of water; they are one and the same. Likewise, when the solid mind of ignorance, confused by appearances, melts into the expanse of the *nonarising mind,* there is no separation to be found.

Suppose you and a friend have been separated for a long time. By chance, you meet on the street but don't recognize each other. A third person introduces you, and instantly you know that this is your old friend. One moment earlier you were confused and didn't know that person. Now the two of you are as familiar as if you had never been parted. It is like that when delusion is removed and the once-confused mind meets the innate mind. When you are introduced to the innate mind by a skillful lama, all the illusory distinctions disappear.

There are six realms in samsara: hells, hungry spirits, animals, humans, demigods, and gods. These six realms manifest in their distinctive forms due to the varied mental formations of the afflicting emotions of those who inhabit them. As we know, even within this realm there are many different types of human beings: different colors, sizes, shapes, languages, different mental states—these are all the direct result of mental formations that are based on the afflicting emotions. Each individual experiences a different mixture of peace, happiness, and suffering; some are gross and others more subtle. All these manifestations arise from the clear, effulgent luminosity of the mind. When we are too confused to see that, we have strayed from our true nature. Suppose everyone eliminated the confusion of samsara, made effort in meditation practice, and returned to their own nature. There would be no disagreements; everyone would be harmonious.

We can habituate ourselves to this understanding when we meditate, especially when we dissolve into the mahamudra state. Pay close attention to that and experience the unceasing, nonarising mind. The duality of external projections, such as nonvirtues and positive thoughts, will fade. When you have developed the skill to recognize them, there are no poisons to give up. There is no medicine to seek. Everything falls into one pile. That is the nonarising mind.

Why is this called the *bardo of conduct*? This verse is about internal conduct, the actions of the mind. The mind makes the decisions, and then the body and speech just follow. Milarepa exemplified perfect conduct after he purified his delusions. His mind flowed as freely as air, with no attachment to good and no aversion to negativity. He functioned in perfect nonduality.

Last night's dreams arise from habitual patterns.
We know them to be false when we awaken.
These states are one in being illusion-like.
This is the bardo of dreams.

Dreams arise when we sleep. Most dreams arise out of our habitual tendencies, whether based in this life or some other lifetime. While we are dreaming, the experience seems true. When we go places in the dream, we perceive that we are really going there, meeting people, eating food, seeing things, and so forth. We don't see the dream as a dream until later. When we awaken we say, "Oh, that was just a dream, not something real." But when we interact with people in the daytime, we see that experience as real, as being fundamentally different from our dreams. In actuality, our dream experiences and waking experiences are both illusory. They have the same nature. For example, when you have a strong headache it is so real and painful. As soon as it dissipates, no trace of the pain remains, so then it is *illusion*.

When you awaken from a dream, where does that dream-world abide? Where did all those people and places come from? In a moment, all we have left is a memory of a vanished experience. Examine your daytime experience in the same way. Do all those people and buildings exist or not? You have a perception of solidity, of reality, but is it valid? After a while, all we have is a memory again—the day-dream has vanished, too. When we engage in purification practices, we have a better chance to understand what this means because our mind becomes very sharp and more relaxed through meditation. When the mind calmly abides, there is less suffering and greater wisdom. This wisdom can directly perceive all phenomena as a momentary display—and that is the purpose of *dream bardo* practice.

There is a special practice called dream yoga that is used to enhance the mahamudra meditation practices. Practitioners who are interested in this must be very serious, attend an authentic teacher, receive the teachings, and go into retreat. As a foundation, it is of utmost importance to have achieved single-pointed absorption. Dream yoga provides an opportunity to be aware of the illusion of dream while we are dreaming. That experience is then applied during the daytime in order to see the illusory state of all phenomena and to experience manifestations as being inseparable from mahamudra itself.

> **The impure five skandhas**
> **and the pure five families of the victorious ones**
> **are one within the nonconceptual completion stage.**
> **This is the bardo of the generation and completion stages of the path.**

The meaning here is similar to that in another of Milarepa's songs, "Mahamudra: Distinguishing the Provisional from the Definitive," which says:

> This skandha of form, which is brought about compulsively,
> when there is no realization, is a body of the four elements;
> sickness and suffering arise from it.

> When there is realization, it is the form of the deity, which is union.
> This reverses ordinary clinging.

Ultimately, there is no body.
It is pure like the cloudless sky.

At the center of our delusion is our conception of our own "self." We hold tightly to this collection of afflicted skandhas as if it had some independent existence. We are thoroughly attached to this body, which is nothing more than the basis of suffering. If someone spreads negative words about us, it is painful. It hurts the heart because we are so attached to the "I" as something tangible or concrete. On the other hand, if someone praises us by saying, "How beautiful and skilled you are," we feel so happy and excited and attached to ourselves.

Let's investigate this. The five skandhas of form, feeling, perception, mental formation, and consciousness—where do they exist? Are they in your name? your body? some part of your body such as the hand or the chest? A name can be changed, so it is clear that your name doesn't contain the self. If your hand were cut off, would you become someone else? Some say the self is in the mind. You yourself cannot find your own mind, let alone others', so how could you know whether a self is there? No matter how we investigate and analyze, we cannot prove that a self exists. This is what is called "illusory nature." We are not denying or ignoring the label of "I," we are just questioning whether it exists independently.

The hair of a turtle is a good analogy for the self. Suppose someone says that a turtle's hair is very soft and warm and that the fine and smooth cloth made from it is very expensive. Something can have a name and we can describe all its good qualities, but does that make it exist? This is also true of the self. The Buddha himself used conventional language when he said things like, "When I was in such and such place I did these things" and "This is my Dharma teaching." So the label of "I" can be used conventionally, but the self to which it refers does not exist in the way we perceive it. That's why we are said to be confused. Hard as we try, we cannot stabilize or establish as true that which does not exist. No matter how long we meditate, we will never see a self. We cherish ourselves so much that surely we should have seen it by now. Someone who will sacrifice anything to protect the self would have found it if it existed. But no one has seen a self-existent self. Grasping and cherishing that which does not exist is at the center of our suffering.

On the other hand, the buddhas have purified their misconceptions and realized that the five skandhas are illusory. In actuality, the heads of the five Buddha families are themselves the perfection of the five impure skandhas. The five buddhas do not exist apart from the five skandhas. The form skandha corresponds to Buddha Vairochana, whose purified aspect is mirror-like wisdom. The feeling skandha corresponds to Buddha Ratnasambhava, whose purified aspect is equanimity. The skandha of perception corresponds to Buddha Amitabha, whose purified aspect is discriminating wisdom. Mental formation corresponds to Buddha Amoghasiddhi, whose purified aspect is all-accomplishing wisdom. Finally, consciousness corresponds to Buddha Akshobhya, whose purified aspect is the all-pervading wisdom of the Dharma-expanse. This is another way of saying that samsara and nirvana are of one nature. When you realize this, you are a buddha. When you do not realize this, you are confused in samsara. This is the teaching of the Vajrayana.

The Vajrayana methods are so skillful! Through the empowerment ceremony, for example, you are introduced to the ultimate state of reality, and you gain the opportunity to manifest as a buddha right where you are sitting. Through the deity yoga practices, you learn to sustain yourself in that state. You begin to understand the continuity of arising as the deity, dissolving into emptiness, and manifesting again from within emptiness—in short, *the bardo of the generation and completion stages of the path.* You go back and forth arising as the deity and dissolving into emptiness. As you practice and progress, all your delusions, negative karma, and negative thoughts become purified. Then one day, you can attain buddhahood, inseparable appearance and emptiness, where there is nothing to give up and nothing to accept. When you have perfected the inseparability of the five skandhas and the five buddhas or wisdoms, then within nonconceptual thought the generation and completion stages have been perfected. But while we are still on the path, we need to follow those practices, step by step.

> The father tantras arising from skillful methods
> and the mother tantras arising from wisdom
> are one as the coemergence of the third empowerment.
> This is the bardo of the essential point.

Father tantras arising from skillful methods encompass all the skillful means that are manifestations of appearances and compassion, such as the first five paramitas, the first two of the three trainings, and the generation of oneself as the yidam deity with all the subsequent practices. *Mother tantras arising from wisdom* refers to development of the wisdom of emptiness, practices such as the last of the six paramitas, the third of the three trainings, and the completion stage with signs. All the different methods of dissolution into all-pervading emptiness are related to wisdom. When skillful means and the wisdom of emptiness are understood to be inseparably coemergent, the *third empowerment* is realized. Luminosity or appearances and emptiness are experienced concurrently. That is the realization of mahamudra.

The essential point here is the coming together of the various elements of tantric meditation techniques. For example, we often visualize white light coming from the forehead of the deity and flowing into us, transforming our body into the enlightened state. Then red light manifests from the throat and purifies our speech obscurations. Finally, blue light arises from the deity's heart and purifies our mind. This is called the third empowerment. Based on this skillful method, we transform our ordinary form into the enlightened state. Without that, there is no basis from which to meditate on emptiness.

For example, if you want to have lunch, you first collect vegetables, wash them, and chop them. Based on these preparations, you can cook a delicious meal. Or if you are driving, you need the skillful method of the car in combination with the wisdom of the driver in order to reach a destination. Likewise, we need the foundations of practice and skill, as they are the basis from which to attain enlightenment. Coming to a realization of the nature of mind by manifesting in the enlightened state is the *essential point* of all the Vajrayana methods.

> The unchanging dharmakaya for one's own benefit
> and the unceasing form kayas for the benefit of others
> are inseparable, being one in the intrinsic state.
> This is the bardo of the three kayas.

A Dharma practitioner who is fully convinced of the real nature of samsara will be inspired to study and practice the Dharma. One starts through the stages of understanding and then practices step by step to purify the gross and subtle adventitious defilements. Finally, the practitioner actualizes emptiness and fully awakens the two wisdoms: knowing reality as it is and understanding each and every object of knowledge. These two wisdoms are a single point without separation. One eventually achieves the dharmakaya, the dimension of the Buddha's perfect, excellent qualities. Upon the attainment of buddhahood, the dharmakaya, one is completely free from suffering and its causes. That accomplishment is said to be *for one's own benefit* because all the perfect, infinite qualities are fully realized.

To attain buddhahood, you must initially cultivate bodhicitta, which is the desire to benefit all sentient beings. Then you train to perfect that mind for a long and difficult period of time. Once you become a buddha with these excellent qualities, you will have the skills and methods to benefit others through the two enlightened *form kayas:* the sambhogakaya (enjoyment form) and nirmanakaya (emanation form). Sentient beings have to interact with a perceptible form because they cannot perceive the dharmakaya. Therefore, *the unceasing form kayas* are necessary in order to accomplish *the benefit of others.* By manifesting these forms, a buddha's activities are effortless and limitless and can adapt to the various dispositions of sentient beings. The sambhogakaya relates to the great bodhisattvas, who are highly accomplished in their spiritual realization. The nirmanakaya is for all. For example, Buddha Shakyamuni manifested as the nirmanakaya from the dharmakaya to demonstrate the path to enlightenment.

While they appear separately according to the needs of sentient beings, in reality these three kayas cannot be separated, because buddhas have completely transcended all such duality. Their unproduced, empty nature is dharmakaya, their luminous nature is sambhogakaya, and their infinite manifestations, as limitless as the objects of knowledge, are the nirmanakaya.

> **The impure illusory body born from a mother's womb**
> **and the pure form of the deity**
> **are one in the luminosity of the bardo.**
> **This is the bardo of result.**

The meaning here is similar to that of the verse about the impure skandhas discussed earlier. When you are born in this world *from a mother's womb,* the body is usually perceived as impure. Later, we see that it is illusory. Look at a reflection in a mirror—it is an illusory form. Or look at a bubble, here one moment and gone the next. Clouds appear and disappear without effort. These analogies help us understand that our own body is illusory. We know that a rainbow is illusory, but we still enjoy looking at its beauty. However, we would never try to capture one and put it in the closet. When we recognize a mirage as an illusion, we never try to drink its water. Look at your own body and see that it has that same nature. There is no difference at all. Sentient beings in samsara have such dense delusions regarding duality!

On the other hand, the pure illusory body is the deity form that we see in our mind when we practice. There, you can clearly see that this illusory form, inseparable appearance and emptiness, does not exist. The pure form is luminosity. This is the bardo of result. When you actualize the inseparable nature of the impure and pure illusory bodies, this is the ultimate achievement, buddhahood.

There is a special practice called "luminosity" or "clear light yoga" that is similar to the dream yoga mentioned earlier. Here again, the practitioner must be able to devote his or her life to retreat without wavering toward the eight worldly concerns. One's mind must be fully established in meditative equipoise and the practice instructions must be personally received from a vajra master. The essence of the practice is that one maintains single-pointed concentration throughout sleep, particularly during the deepest portion, when there is an opportunity to experience the luminous nature of the mind. When fully accomplished and stabilized, this experience transcends and purifies all aspects of duality.

Part Two

VAJRA SONGS OF LORD JIGTEN SUMGÖN

4. Vajra Song on Attaining Enlightenment

In three nights and four days,
my karma and obscurations were purified.
I realized the cause and result of interdependent origination.
The treasure of the profound tantra revealed itself!
In the nonduality of the great luminosity,
the two fixations of meditation and post-meditation were purified.
I recognize that I am [now] a lord of yogins.

THOUGH SHORT, this vajra song contains vast and profound meaning. Jigten Sumgön was born in 1143 and his birth was accompanied by remarkable signs. Even as a young child, he meditated and gave meditation instructions to his friends. As he grew up he met various teachers and received their teachings until, at the age of twenty-five, he encountered his root guru, Phagmo Drupa. Jigten Sumgön attended that guru for about thirty-two months, during which time he received the complete teachings of the lineage. He did not waste a moment of his short time with Phagmo Drupa, studying and practicing very diligently. He kept to himself so much that he became known as the "silent Kyura," with Kyura being his clan name. His pure conduct and diligence earned the admiration of everyone in the community, and he was particularly respected for his devotion to the master. Not only was he a scholar, but he also experienced the teachings through practice.

After Phagmo Drupa passed away, Jigten Sumgön dedicated his time to retreat. He spent seven years meditating day and night in a cave at a place called Echung. Toward the end of this retreat, he became seriously ill. This was a sign that his remaining *karma and obscurations* were ripening. By the power of his devotion to his lama and by the force of his bodhicitta, he fully *purified* his negative karma and recovered. Like a sun freed from an eclipse, he completely revealed the buddha mind. This experience is called "confusion dawning as wisdom." It was at that moment that he sang this song.

Jigten Sumgön realized the full complexity of *interdependent origination* in its outer, inner, secret, and ultimate aspects.

Outer interdependence is concerned with the external environment: the "container" consisting of this world, planets, galaxies, and stars as well as the mountains, plains, and oceans. None of this exists independently, but rather is made up of a combination of the four elements. Due to a kaleidoscopic shifting among the elements, we experience weather, climate change, seasons, and so forth. All these changes take place in the state of impermanence according to the causes we have created, either individually or collectively.

Inner interdependence has to do with the "contained" living beings: humans, animals, fish, birds, and so forth—any being with consciousness or a mind. Their existence and functioning are also based on interdependence and causality. These sentient beings are interconnected with each other to such an extent that none can exist by itself; they all support one another. Incisive wisdom is needed to perceive this interdependence, the true mode of abiding.

Every one of these beings desires peace and happiness and not one desires suffering. The causes of peace and the causes of suffering function unerringly, so it is important for us to understand the distinctions between them. If we create a cause of suffering while believing that our action will cause happiness, the result is still suffering, no matter how strong our belief is. Conversely, if we create a cause of happiness, the result will be happiness despite any contrary conceptions we might have. This is the universal functioning of causality. For example, examine the mind. When the afflicting emotions—attachment, pride, jealousy, and so forth—are present, peace and happiness will remain mirages no matter how hard we search for them. When we keep the mind in a state of love, compassion, clarity, or altruism, the result will be peace and happiness even if we don't wish it. Thus, it is clear that everything functions within interdependent origination.

In addition, both animate and inanimate phenomena are in a constant state of impermanence that changes in every moment. From the day we are born, our condition is that of impermanence. There is no need to speculate about other factors; the body will age and decay by itself. It changes according to the causes and conditions we have created. This being so, a wise person will choose to avoid the ten nonvirtues, which cause suffering, and will adopt the ten virtues, which cause peace and happiness. Taking and keeping at least the five lay precepts can only enhance our happiness.

Secret interdependence concerns one's own body and the causes and conditions that ensure its functioning and maintenance. For example, whatever food we eat or beverages we drink have physical effects, so we need a clear understanding of which dietary practices are beneficial. Similarly, tantric meditation instructions teach us about the subtle functioning of the body: the chakras, channels, wind energy, and bindus. With proper instruction and understanding, practitioners can engage in meditation practices that reveal inner knowledge. In any case, we should be like skilled mechanics who can tune the components of an airplane or car into a smooth-running machine on the bases of bodhicitta and emptiness.

Ultimate interdependence has to do with the Buddhist teachings on emptiness. Everything manifests from emptiness, and all these manifested phenomena dissolve back into emptiness. Through realizing that our innate nature is emptiness, we will have an opportunity to dissolve all confusion and delusion. Still, the causality and interdependence discussed before function within that very emptiness without contradiction. One who realizes that perfectly is one who has attained buddhahood.

All these different states of interdependence can be perceived by the mind, making mind the most powerful and universal force. But mind is a veiled subject and difficult for many people to pinpoint. Mind cannot be shown by machines or seen through a microscope; it can only be revealed through meditation. No matter how much we intellectualize, the profundity and vastness of the mind will escape us until we experience it through absorption and equipoise—until we learn to see nothing and everything at the same time.

The Buddha taught the sutra and tantra systems as paths leading toward enlightenment. Studying and practicing the sutra system enables one to begin following the path. Then, one can pursue the four classes of practice within the tantra system: action (*kriya*), conduct (*charya*), yoga, and unexcelled tantra (*uttaratantra*). There are many different ways to explain these categories. For instance, the Buddha taught them as progressive stages on the path. They can also be mapped against the four initiations: the vase initiation correlates to action tantra, the secret initiation to conduct tantra, the wisdom initiation to yoga tantra, and the fourth initiation to unexcelled tantra.

Tantric practice, or Vajrayana, includes many skillful methods for transformation that enable us to recognize our innate nature. Hundreds of enlightened deities are involved in tantric practice, with distinct teachings and meditations related to each one. All these different paths can be condensed into two: ripening and liberating. Ripening refers to the profound initiation rituals. Each class of tantra has its own system of initiation, and each introduces its own mandala, or cosmology. Liberating also has two components: the generation and completion stages. There is a different method of generating oneself into the deity for each individual deity. Completion is a complex system of meditation practices, either with or without signs. Here, one has an opportunity to destroy all obscurations and defilements as fuel is consumed by fire. When united with the emptiness state, one can transcend all manifested phenomena as they dissolve into emptiness and can uproot all grasping of duality, including the self.

When Jigten Sumgön attained buddhahood, he completely realized the profound and vast *treasure* of the Vajrayana teachings. The door was open to him; the teachings were *revealed* clearly and without any concealment. Because of this, many yidams, such as Chakrasamvara, Tara, and Chenrezig, vividly appeared to him as he was achieving enlightenment.

The journey to enlightenment can also be divided into five paths: accumulation, application, special insight, meditation, and perfection. The first two occur within samsara. When we see that all phenomena are nothing but suffering and understand the benefit of enlightenment, we will be inspired to begin the journey to freedom. When we reflect on the suffering of sentient beings, we can see that there are three types. The suffering of suffering is the obvious pain that everyone, even animals and insects, feels. The suffering of change is seen by ordinary people as a pleasant feeling, as something to seek out. However, that pleasurable sensation won't last and the end result is more suffering. The third type, the all-pervasive condition of suffering, is present so long as we have the afflicted aggregates of the five skandhas. No matter how much we cherish and care for our lives, past karma and afflicting emotions characterize our existence and leave us in the pervasive condition of suffering. When we directly perceive the coming and going of phenomena, we will gain a profound awareness of impermanence. For these reasons, those who are far-sighted will be inspired to achieve enlightenment to free themselves from this kind of suffering. They will first follow the path of accumulation to develop mental stability and then progress to the path of application.

After that, they pursue the third path, special insight, on which they realize the unfabricated reality of the Dharma-expanse. At this stage, there is a large gap between the absorption state of meditation and the post-meditation period. As the practitioner continues to gain experience with equipoise meditation and progresses through the ten bhumis step by step, he gathers the great accumulations of merit and wisdom. He requires less and less effort to meditate, and the gap between meditation and post-meditation gradually closes. At that time, *the two fixations of meditation and post-meditation* can be said to be *purified*.

After the tenth bhumi, one becomes a buddha. All obscurations have been fully transcended by the meditation state of total equipoise, and the unmistakable all-pervading dharmakaya is experienced. There is no gap between meditation and post-meditation as one remains in the Dharma-expanse state. Jigten Sumgön attained that state, so he can say without fear of contradiction that he is *a lord of yogins*. He gathered hundreds and thousands of disciples, some of whom were on the eighth, ninth, or tenth bhumi. He could perfectly relate to them all, fulfill their wishes, and cause them to achieve buddhahood. Therefore, for those Dharma practitioners who follow his path, who meditate as he instructed, and who supplicate him, there can be no doubt that the benefits and blessings will avalanche upon us.

5. Song of the Fivefold Profound Path of Mahamudra

These teachings were given to Jigten Sumgön by Phagmo Drupa. On obtaining certainty in them, Jigten Sumgön sang this song:

I bow at the feet of glorious Phagmo Drupa!

If the steed of love and compassion
does not run for the benefit of others,
it will not be rewarded in the assembly of gods and men.
Attend, therefore, to the preliminaries.

If one's body, the king of deities,
is not stabilized on this unchanging ground,
the retinue of dakinis will not assemble.
Be sure, therefore, of your body as the yidam.

If on the guru, snow mountain of the four kayas,
the sun of devotion fails to shine,
the stream of blessings will not arise.
Attend, therefore, to this mind of devotion.

If from the sky-like expanse of mind's nature
the clouds of conceptual thought are not blown away,
the planets and stars of the two wisdoms will not shine.
Attend, therefore, to this mind without conception.

If the wish-fulfilling gem of the two accumulations
is not polished by aspiration,

the results we have hoped for will not arise.
Attend, therefore, to this final dedication.

INTRODUCTION

EACH OF THESE vajra songs holds profound and vast meaning. In fact, the complete teachings of the Buddha, including both the sutra and tantra systems, are contained within each one. Therefore, we should cherish and contemplate them. They are short and their meaning is explicit, precise, and clear, so it is easy for us to reflect on them. In modern times, we are not left with much time to read long books, so these short teachings are practical and easy for us to apply in our lives. In past times, people would memorize these vajra songs and chant them on a daily basis in order to recall their meaning and to remind themselves of their meditation practice. Nowadays, we, too, can memorize them and chant them regularly.

Sentient beings are the same in that they all desire happiness, peace, and calm in their lives. Every being wants to be free from suffering. Human beings have an especially profound potential to create the causes of happiness and achieve good qualities, but we also have an enormous potential to create the causes of suffering and destroy our good qualities. This means that we carry an important responsibility to develop moral ethics based on our intelligence and wisdom.

We all keep busy with our daily activities, yet we rarely experience peace or harmony. No matter how much we strive, we are never completely free from suffering. These Dharma teachings penetrate to the very source of suffering, the delusion at the root of the problem. When properly implemented, these teachings provide an empirical method to achieve the complete cessation of suffering. Even an attempt to practice just a small portion of the teachings is useful and worthwhile. There are no negative side effects, only benefits.

In the past, hundreds of thousands of Dharma masters achieved their goal through these teachings. We can learn much from them. If we reflect on history, this path we are following is not a matter of liking or disliking the teachings, or of being spiritual or not spiritual. This is a matter of coming to understand the true meaning and purpose of life, of learning how to become free from suffering and how to attain peace and happiness at the relative level as well as the definite goodness of the ultimate state.

We are not alone either in the samsaric world or in the spiritual realm.

In the samsaric state we are interconnected through business, politics, science, technology, and so forth. Without the support of others we could not sustain life. In the spiritual world, we could not generate or develop such thoughts as love and compassion without the existence of others. Therefore, it is very important in both circumstances to understand how much we are connected to one another. Because we are all interconnected and interrelated, the altruistic thought to benefit all sentient beings, which is the mind of enlightenment itself, is crucial. With this thought of altruism in our minds, we will now turn to the five verses of the "Song of the Fivefold Profound Path of Mahamudra."

The meaning of the Sanskrit term *mahamudra* can be understood as follows. *Maha* translates as "great" or "highest." This refers to the ultimate realization of the nature of all phenomena as they actually exist, free from contrivance or mental fabrication. *Mudra* translates as "seal," and refers to the seal that is stamped on the totality of nature, the entire universe with nothing whatsoever left out, existing as it does within perfect emptiness and luminosity. Thus, mahamudra, the great seal, is the ultimate view, the highest understanding of samsara and nirvana, which is experienced as the radiance of our intrinsic luminosity or the buddha-dharmakaya.

All of nirvana and samsara manifest from the mind, whether we are deluded or not. Once you realize the coemergent mind that grasps both appearance and emptiness, there is no difference between samsara and nirvana. Both manifest from the mind, and they do not exist separately from the primordial nature of mind. However, samsara is based on confusion rooted in great ignorance, and nirvana is based on an enlightened mind. One who has fully realized the unfabricated nature of samsara has achieved nirvana.

The *fivefold profound path* mentioned in the title is the method by which we can actualize the state of ultimate realization of the primordial nature of mind, enlightenment. The five verses of this song correspond to these five paths: bodhicitta, yidam deity practice, guru yoga, mahamudra, and dedication. Each path is a special technique that can bring us closer to realization, and each verse of the song conveys the entire meaning of mahamudra, which is why this song is considered so profound. Vajrayana practitioners emphasize the study and practice of these five as individual methods to achieve enlightenment. But here, Jigten Sumgön has put them together into one song based on the instructions that he received from his guru and that he vigorously practiced and experienced. The achievement of buddha-hood is interdependent, and these five methods comprise an impeccable complete path.

COMMENTARY

I bow at the feet of glorious Phagmo Drupa.

These teachings were given to Jigten Sumgön by his root guru, *Phagmo Drupa*. In the early part of his life, Phagmo Drupa studied the Buddha's teachings with many great teachers and seriously practiced. He became fully accomplished in scholarship and meditation. So, when he met Gam-popa, Phagmo Drupa was well prepared to receive the pith instructions. During their discussion of Buddhist philosophy and the innate nature of mahamudra, Phagmo Drupa fully revealed the absolute nature of his mind. Gampopa became his most important teacher at that point and Phagmo Drupa stayed with Gampopa until he passed away. As a result, Phagmo Drupa reached enlightenment and Gampopa said, "There is no difference between him and me." After Gampopa passed away, Phagmo Drupa was acknowledged as his Dharma heir.

Phagmo Drupa gathered thousands of disciples of his own at Phagdru Monastery, and established them in the various stages of enlightenment. Among them, Jigten Sumgön was Phagmo Drupa's Dharma heir. Jigten Sumgön also learned the sutra and tantra teachings from many great teach-ers and he continually remained in a state of meditation. Phagmo Drupa put a great deal of emphasis on teaching the fivefold path of mahamudra, espe-cially in his instructions to Jigten Sumgön. Because of that, Jigten Sumgön was able to practice diligently and experience certainty in their meaning. The complete nature of his mind melted into the dharmakaya state, and he achieved the state of enlightenment.

When it became obvious that he had fully actualized the highest state and that nothing was hidden from him, Jigten Sumgön sang this song as a teaching. All his disciples were taught from this song and established on the path toward enlightenment, so it became renowned as a profound root text. Through the power of his wisdom and skill, Jigten Sumgön benefited human and nonhuman beings throughout the universe and became famous without any need for advertisement.

Bodhicitta

> If the steed of love and compassion
> does not run for the benefit of others,
> it will not be rewarded in the assembly of gods and men.
> Attend, therefore, to the preliminaries.

In order to win a prize, we train a horse to run stronger and faster. Similarly, we must strengthen our *love and compassion* in order to gain the ultimate "reward" of enlightenment. Over time, our entire being can become suffused with love and compassion, leaving no room for negative thoughts. Negativity cannot survive the presence of love and compassion, just as darkness cannot exist in sunshine. The resulting state of mind is freedom from delusions, total peace and harmony. In that state, we no longer have to chase after peace and happiness, but rather we discover that they are already here within us. Love and compassion are the primary causes for the cultivation of bodhicitta.

Enlightenment is achieved by progressing from the ground of perfection through the perfecting path, to the result—perfected mind. The ground or basis of perfection is the buddha nature with which every sentient being is naturally endowed. This buddha mind is the unadulterated nature of mind, inherently present and complete. In order to reveal this ground of perfection we use the perfecting path of cultivating bodhicitta. Bodhicitta is the method that opens us to the pure nature of mind. That opened, pure nature of mind is itself the result, ultimate bodhicitta. Therefore, it is clear that the cultivation of bodhicitta is the indispensable means by which to attain complete enlightenment.

It is vital that we first establish ourselves firmly in love and compassion so that we can fully actualize the Buddha's teachings. Without *preliminary practices* such as these we would have no basis to become free from samsara and attain enlightenment. It is like driving from our garage onto the road—navigating the driveway in between is the preliminary practice. The driveway cannot be regarded as unimportant; it is the first stage of reaching our destination, and without it we would go nowhere. So it is just as important, if not more so, to pay attention to the preliminaries as it is to focus on the main journey.

To develop love and compassion, try to practice them in your daily life as much as possible. For instance, while going about your everyday life doing things like working, driving, or cooking, do everything with mindfulness. That is the key. Focus on the practice of compassion for those who are suffering, and particularly for those who are creating the causes of suffering because they are overcome by negative thoughts. See them as true victims of their own making.

Of course, suffering is very painful for those who are experiencing it, but it is also a type of purification. When experiencing suffering, a person's karma is actually getting lighter. But a person who is creating suffering for others has a serious problem. We need a deeper kind of compassion for, and awareness of, beings who ignorantly disturb the peace, happiness, and lives of others. They are creating heavy negative karma, and because of that, they will experience suffering. Supported by wisdom, we must develop a powerful sense of compassion for them. When we have awareness and see the need for compassion, it encourages us to build strength of mind and work harder to actualize these precious teachings within our very being, penetrating to the "marrow" of the mind.

There are many other preliminary teachings besides those on love and compassion. For instance, the ordinary preliminaries include contemplation on the four foundations, also called the "four thoughts that turn the mind": precious human life, impermanence, the suffering of samsara, and karma or causality.

Precious human life. A human life contains the potential and, if utilized in the best way, provides the possibility to become free of samsara and attain enlightenment. However, not every human life provides the practical opportunity for enlightenment. Only those that do are called "precious." A precious human life is free from the eight unfavorable conditions and possesses the ten endowments. If even one of these is missing, there is no opportunity to reach enlightenment in that lifetime.

Those who have a precious human life are not only interested in this path, they also have the opportunity to study and practice. Compared to the number of people who are interested in Dharma, there are vastly more who are not interested. We can only cultivate compassion for these beings. They do not have the light of the wisdom eye to see and bring these teachings into their hearts. There may be some people who are very smart, but when it comes to this kind of teaching, they do not appreciate it or understand how important it is. As a result, these individuals will continue to create suffering.

Impermanence. Being young and healthy is no guarantee that you will not die tonight, tomorrow, this week, or next month. Life is so fragile; it can vanish in an instant. This is not meant to frighten you or to make you depressed. Rather, this is the reality of all animate and inanimate phenomena that are composed of causes and conditions. In short, *everything* is of a momentary, impermanent nature. All who are born are subject to dissolution. All who meet are subject to dispersion. All that we accumulate is subject to dissipation. All that is built is subject to destruction. It is easy to see, therefore, how tenuous the opportunity to obtain a precious human life really is.

Suffering of samsara. Suffering is created through many different causes, including our negative thoughts, delusions, afflicting emotions, and the results of the unwholesome deeds we performed because of these negative thoughts. The negative karma we create manifests as various states of suffering, which are generally categorized as three: the suffering of suffering, the suffering of change, and the all-pervasive suffering. Throughout the six realms, the suffering of suffering has two components—physical and mental. Physical suffering involves sickness, aging, death, lack of food or clothes, and so forth. Mental suffering encompasses depression, greed, anger, jealousy, and so forth. With experience, practitioners come to recognize temporary happiness as the second type of suffering, the suffering of change. Time after time, people see pleasurable circumstances change into suffering, yet they continue to grasp desperately at them. The wise will cultivate renunciation of such deceptive pleasures and develop nonattachment. Recognition of all-pervasive suffering is the most subtle of the three. It is the understanding that all of samsara is conditioned by suffering; as long as we are under the influence of afflicting emotions and karma, there is not one completely unafflicted moment to be found anywhere. While we may understand this intellectually, this truth can be perceived only by one with critical insight. So, suffering is not a Buddhist philosophical belief; it is the reality of samsara. Every individual has the responsibility to be aware of this and to investigate seriously its root cause.

Karma. Karma is a very complex, profound, and vast subject, so we need to hold the understanding of causality in high regard with respect. In addition to positive and negative karma, there are also individual and collective karma to take into account. Karma can ripen quickly or slowly, with great or small results. Whether heavy or light, karma may be purified through different practices. Only an omniscient buddha can comprehend all the details of cause and result. In the human realm we do experience occasional moments of temporary peace and happiness, which are the manifest results of afflicted but positive karma. But, such limited happiness and peace are not enough. To be completely peaceful and to achieve permanent happiness, we have to go beyond the state of samsara itself.

When we become convinced of this, we will sincerely study and practice Dharma and, minute by minute, appreciate our opportunity to have a precious human life. These preliminaries are crucial practices at the beginning of the path, and they are also very important in the middle to enhance our practice. They are the most important support that encourages us to perfect enlightenment. When we yearn to be free of suffering but realize that we don't know how to accomplish this, the method of taking refuge in the Buddha, Dharma, and Sangha arises. Refuge is a special method that leads us to buddhahood, the complete absence of suffering. It is a means to dispel the veil of confusion and open the door to enlightenment.

The Buddha taught the Dharma out of great wisdom and compassion in order to benefit all sentient beings. When we know the Buddha and the Dharma teachings, then we also know the Sangha. The Sangha is the community of those who wish to be free of samsara and who sincerely practice these teachings with an earnest, pure, clear, and calm mind that wholeheartedly desires all sentient beings to have happiness. This is the basis of refuge in the Buddha, Dharma, and Sangha.

As a foundation for study, and especially for meditation practice, we need to take at least the five precepts: not taking life, especially that of a human being; not taking others' belongings through any means; not engaging in sexual misconduct; not telling lies, especially regarding spiritual achievement; and not becoming intoxicated by alcohol or drugs.

Taking another's life could be motivated by attachment, ignorance, or hatred. In all cases, taking a life, especially a human being's, is a very heavy nonvirtue that creates an environment in which there is little room for virtue to remain.

Stealing is done mainly out of pernicious desire without respect or regard for others. Indulging in theft harms oneself as well as the other, and is also a strong nonvirtue that leaves little space for virtue.

Sexual misconduct is not appreciated either secularly or spiritually. Such activities, which are performed under the power of delusion and with strong attachment, create heavy nonvirtue.

Proclaiming that some achievement has been accomplished when one actually has no experience is generally caused by ignorance and self-aggrandizement. This is true for general subjects, but making false spiritual claims evidences a particularly distorted mind.

Intoxication results from mental delusion and attachment. When intoxicated, the mind has no clarity and no ability to distinguish virtue from non-virtue. Intoxication opens a door to many other faults.

In general, the vinaya is the foundation of all forms of Buddhist practice, whether Theravada, Mahayana, or Vajrayana. From within his omniscient wisdom, the Buddha explained the details of causality, the causes of suffering and the means to free ourselves. So unless they follow the discipline contained in the vinaya, practitioners cannot succeed or experience the results of the path. Those who keep the five precepts that counter the five nonvirtues are called "those with pure moral conduct." In the human realm, such practitioners are a special source of peace, joy, and trust. Those who engage in all or any of the nonvirtues are a source of confusion and suffering. For Dharma practitioners, these five precepts are an indispensable discipline to keep as a foundation for meditation and special insight. Both lay and ordained practitioners must preserve their precepts as they do their eyes. Thus, Jigten Sumgön repeatedly emphasized the importance of the vinaya.

When people begin to follow the path, they sometimes have adverse reactions. For example, some people feel uncomfortably vulnerable when they practice love and compassion. When they initially encounter the concept of renunciation, some get the impression that they have to give everything away immediately. Such reactions mean that they don't really understand the meaning of the Dharma. In actuality, when we practice, we receive only benefit.

Our practice of love and compassion develops from sincere renunciation, meaning that we renounce the causes of suffering, all mental afflictions or neuroses, and the negative actions they encourage. We see that the nature of samsara is suffering, and that it is not advantageous to make effort toward samsaric goals. So, to be free from all that, we cultivate the thought of bodhicitta, embrace it, and then repeatedly put it into practice in order to solidly integrate it into our mind stream. With that firm motivation, all the other practices we do and every opportunity that comes our way support our practice of bodhicitta. So, while this first stage of the fivefold path encompasses all the preliminaries, the main practice is bodhicitta.

To develop bodhicitta, first relax and generate a state of mind free from all tension, hatred, and negative thoughts. This method alone will broaden the space in your mind. Sometimes it may be difficult to cultivate that state. If this happens, contemplate the person who is closest to you—your mother, relative, friend, or whomever. Practice generating love and compassion with that person in mind, and then expand that thought to all the sentient beings who inhabit the eastern direction. Then do the same for all sentient beings who inhabit the north, then the south, and then west. Embrace not only human beings in this thought, but all sentient beings, including even small insects. Wish them all to be free from suffering by thinking, "May they experience peace and happiness." With the support of this altruistic thought, cultivate the mind of enlightenment and pray that these sentient beings attain buddhahood.

While the actual nature of mind is ultimate bodhicitta, we need relative bodhicitta in order to reveal it. Relative bodhicitta is the method that allows us to achieve perfection of the nature of mind, and it comprises aspiration and action, or engaged, bodhicitta. Aspiration bodhicitta is the mind that sincerely wishes to achieve the mind of ultimate bodhicitta, so we practice it first. An analogy often given is that the mind of aspiration is like a person who dearly wishes to take a train trip. But in order to make that trip, they have to actually get on the train and go. This is action bodhicitta. So, we cultivate action bodhicitta on the basis of aspiration in order to bring life to our aspiration. The *Guide to the Bodhisattva's Conduct* (*Bodhicaryavatara*) will give you explicit advice about both relative and ultimate bodhicitta.

Once we have cultivated bodhicitta, all our practices will naturally follow that path to enlightenment. In that way, all our Dharma practices become action bodhicitta. Whatever practice we do—even if we just sit in meditation for ten minutes, read a few lines of Dharma, or chant a dozen mantras—can enhance our bodhicitta. However, action bodhicitta is best developed through the six paramitas, also called the six perfections. These six comprise a systematic method designed to be followed step by step: the practices of generosity, moral ethics, forbearance, perseverance, meditative concentration, and wisdom awareness. These are described in more detail in *The Jewel Ornament of Liberation* and *A Complete Guide to the Buddhist Path*. Please refer to these texts to enhance your study. Our mental defilements of delusion and our negative thoughts are gradually purified by following this path. As the darkness of our negative thoughts slowly disappears, clarity of mind is revealed. This is a precise method to transform all our delusions into the enlightened state. We don't have to create anything new to make this happen; we just have to follow what the Buddha already taught.

If anything becomes an obstacle to our practice, we can wish for it to substitute for the obstacles of all other sentient beings, and for them to become purified through our own suffering. When we experience happiness and success in life, we can wish for our happiness to substitute for the suffering experienced by all other sentient beings so that they, too, can experience happiness. This practice is known as exchanging self for others.

There are different levels to handling obstacles. As a novice practitioner at the very beginning of your journey, it will sometimes be difficult to dedicate your happiness as a substitute for the obstacles that other beings may experience. We often mistakenly make efforts to defeat obstacles, but instead are overpowered by them. As we grow in the Dharma, there comes a time when we have a conviction about our understanding, and we also have some success in the special practices of love, compassion, and bodhicitta. We can then use obstacles as a special path to enlightenment. With this practice obstacles are no longer a burden but become a part of practice. You no longer are hesitant or afraid to face them and, in fact, will welcome them because they allow you to practice. Without obstacles, there is little chance to progress. Later, when you become more advanced in mahamudra practices, you realize that obstacles do not exist independent of your mind. You will see that they are just manifestations and reflections, merely of the nature of illusion. At that point, you will have the substantial authority and ability to benefit sentient beings.

But we cannot truly help other sentient beings without first establishing ourselves in the state of bodhicitta through the preliminary practices. Without bodhicitta we will have no ability or means to help others. That's why great masters spend their lives in retreat in the mountains. They are not being selfish. Rather, they are spending their time in mountain caves in order to practice and thereby successfully benefit others. Otherwise, as long as we still have afflicting emotions and discursive thoughts, we will not be effective in helping others even though we may wish to be. Instead of being beneficial, we will simply become more entrenched in delusion and bring more suffering to ourselves and others.

By practicing the Dharma, you come to understand that, layer after layer, there is more to purify, more to know, more to understand, and more to experience on the path. The nature of the Dharma teachings is deep and vast. Our mind has many levels to penetrate and, because of this, realization takes time. Dharma provides the means to achieve complete comprehension by going through all these different layers. Look at Milarepa's life story.

He spent his life in retreat in order to penetrate all the different layers of mind, until the true nature of his mind was fully and totally revealed, and he attained the dharmakaya.

The true nature of mind is composed of two factors: great compassion and special insight; through them, one can realize emptiness. These are the critical factors needed to penetrate the nonexistent nature of delusion. Love and compassion have the power to utilize that wisdom in an optimum way to bring about peace and harmony, both within the mind and for other sentient beings. So these two go hand in hand; you cannot separate them. If you were to separate them, they would not be as useful or effective, nor would the outcome be so healthy. That is the meaning of the line in this verse that reads *it will not be rewarded in the assemblies of gods and men.*

Here, briefly contemplate a concise cultivation of bodhicitta. Visualize the historical Buddha along with the buddhas of the three times surrounded by Dharma texts and great bodhisattvas. In front of these objects, sincerely take refuge from the depths of your heart with a great yearning to achieve freedom from the suffering of samsara. Repeat three times:

> By the power of all merit and virtue, I will cultivate bodhicitta for
> the benefit of all sentient beings. I will practice the six paramitas
> step by step until they are fully perfected.

Then dissolve the visualization into light, and let that light dissolve into you, allowing your mind and the mind of all buddhas and bodhisattvas to become inseparable. Meditate that bodhicitta is born within your mind. Finally, meditate with a mind free from all fabrication. Say dedication prayers when you are finished.

Yidam Deity Practice

> **If one's body, the king of deities,**
> **is not stabilized on this unchanging ground,**
> **the retinue of dakinis will not assemble.**
> **Be sure, therefore, of your body as the yidam.**

Once the mind of bodhicitta has been cultivated, it needs to be perfected. So, here, the song introduces Vajrayana practice, also called tantra or deity yoga. The Buddha, out of his omniscient wisdom and uncontrived, pervasive compassion, taught the complete methods by which all sentient beings can purify their many levels of obscuration and achieve the absolute state of enlightenment step by step. When an individual practitioner has developed sufficient capacity and ability, the Vajrayana provides many methods that allow one to realize buddha nature. In order to comprehend tantra, one must have aspiration, interest, and full dedication. Only then does one have the practical possibility and capacity to digest its profound and vast meaning.

There are two methods within the Vajrayana: initiation or empowerment (*abhisheka*) and liberation. Before one practices tantric meditation, one should receive all the components of an empowerment (the vase, secret, wisdom, and precious word) from an appropriate vajra master. Along with the ceremony, it is also important to receive the practice instructions and to understand them precisely. After receiving an initiation, there are two deity yoga meditation practices that allow one to perfectly actualize the teachings: arising and completion.

In the arising or generation stage, our buddha nature manifests in the form of a deity. To accomplish this, we work with our physical body, since it is the basis for both samsara and enlightenment. Our current samsaric body is an afflicted mental formation based on our own karma from past lifetimes. The same will be true in the future, the shape of which will be based on our present motives and actions. Therefore, in order to realize enlightenment and manifest a pure form, we establish the cause now by habituating ourselves to that state by visualizing ourselves in a deity's form.

Without the creation of karma and mental formation, a body could not be achieved, because there would be no preceding cause for it. In the unenlightened samsaric state, our ignorance continually invites undesirable conditions and suffering. For the most part, negative thoughts such as attachment, hatred, pride, jealousy, and so on arise because of this body. Because we have a body, we need food, clothes, TV, computer, car, house, and so forth. We work hard to accumulate material necessities, generally creating a multitude of negative actions in doing so, and thus set up a future of suffering. Then we age, become ill, and finally die. If we don't take advantage of this precious human life to achieve enlightenment, it will merely be a basis for suffering.

On the other hand, our relationship with the pure body of the enlightened state is developed through the practice of bodhicitta. Prior to practicing deity yoga, we train this body to benefit and help others with the support of paramitas such as generosity, moral ethics, and forbearance. Here, to enhance their effectiveness, we combine those practices with deity, or *yidam,* practice by visualizing being generous and so forth while manifesting the body of a deity. This is what Jigten Sumgön is referring to in the phrase *one's body, the king of deities.* A king has complete authority to rule over his territory. Likewise, the yidam rules his mandala in a positive way and thereby transforms all negativity and confusion into the enlightened state.

The enlightened body is stabilized on the *unchanging ground* of buddha nature. The nature of the deity is that of a buddha. When, by means of the arising stage instructions, we manifest our whole being as the yidam, we come to recognize our own buddha nature by seeing the deity's nature. This allows us to realize the true nature of mind. Our whole being, including our mind and this body form, becomes the sambhogakaya form of the deity. The ordinary body has gone nowhere, but the mind is in the enlightened state of Chenrezig, Tara, Chakrasamvara, or any other deity. The deity has also come from nowhere, just the enlightened state. As soon as we release the visualization, that state disappears and we return to our ordinary body. But the deity is not completely gone—our ordinary state of mind simultaneously abides with the enlightened state of mind. Therefore, we need to hold this enlightened state in our awareness until we become inseparable from it.

When we arise in the state of the yidam deity, we establish the three qualities of clarity, purity, and divine pride.

The quality of clarity occurs when we clearly see the deity as being inseparable from appearance and emptiness. This is like seeing the moon's reflection on water or seeing a rainbow. We can see a reflection or rainbow very clearly yet cannot grasp or hold on to one. In the same way, when we visualize clearly, we can see the clear nature of the deity—the color, attributes, and marks rather than a body of substantial blood, bone, and flesh.

The perfection of excellent qualities such as the five wisdoms, the six perfections, and the embodiment of the three kayas manifests through the quality of purity. These qualities of the Buddha will not appear until we manifest as the deity. Therefore, in the arising stage, we develop purity by meditating on the appearance of the yidam. The deity's color, posture, ornaments, jewels, silken robes, and so forth, are all expressions of the various qualities of wisdom and compassion. So when we become the deity, recite mantras, perform purification, and practice the other essential elements of a sadhana, the enlightened qualities effortlessly manifest. The phrase *retinue of dakinis* refers to the assemblage of these excellent qualities that manifests when we practice successfully.

The third quality is divine pride, through which we build confidence in our pure nature. Our basic nature is that of the yidam deity, or the Buddha. This is not an intellectual concept, an artificial construct, or an imputed state. In actuality, it is our samsaric existence that is artificial, because it is confusion based on negative thoughts. All negative thoughts are fabricated and contrived through delusion, and whatever is created through delusion is artificial. We have successfully constructed the dimension of samsara through confusion based on great ignorance, and because of this, suffering is never-ending. Now that we have a precious human life and the Buddha's complete teachings, it is time to deconstruct samsara with these authentic, enlightened instructions and methods. Our genuine nature is the enlightened state, so it is there that we must build our confidence.

In the samsaric state we have a false feeling of reality; in actuality, samsara is a delusion that must be purified. But when we rest our mind in the natural state, which is imbued with bodhicitta, negative thoughts cannot exist. This is why we occasionally receive instructions from a spiritual teacher to rest our mind there.

After we manifest ourselves as the yidam deity in these ways, and become convinced of our identity as the yidam, we then practice the completion stage. This stage can be performed with or without signs, but in deity yoga we make particular use of the completion stage with signs or supports such as mantra recitation, purification practices for self and others, and perfecting the chakras and channels. Completion without signs consists of dissolving into emptiness or mahamudra and resting the mind in that state. All these practices are to be done with the mind of bodhicitta based on wisdom and compassion.

Vajrayana is effective because of these methods; through using them, it takes much less time to achieve buddhahood than the three limitless kalpas needed on the sutra path. With deity yoga, we have a complete method to realize the enlightened state. By first receiving the empowerment and then practicing according to proper instructions, we gradually purify the obscurations and delusions that we have accumulated for millions and millions of kalpas. The result is that this very afflicted body transforms into a pure, unafflicted body. We then meditate on that for a period of time to perfect our practice.

Chakrasamvara is one of the best-known of the major Vajrayana yidam practices so retreatants generally follow the tradition of relying on this practice. The details must be received from a retreat master.

Here, I have put together a very short, simple purification practice that can easily be fit into a busy life on a regular basis. While in the state of deity yoga, chant OM AH HUNG. These three syllables are the essence and the root of all other mantras. The white OM has the nature of the wisdom body of the Buddha, the red AH is the wisdom speech of the Buddha, and the blue HUNG is the wisdom mind of the Buddha. The white OM corresponds to the nirmanakaya, the red AH to the sambhogakaya, and the blue HUNG to the dharmakaya. Their inseparable nature is the svabhavikakaya.

ༀ OM

To practice this meditation, take a deep breath and relax your mind. Release all your stress and tension. Then manifest the form of a buddha with which you are familiar—Vajrasattva, Chenrezig, Tara, or Chakrasamvara, for example. Precisely visualize yourself in the deity's form, inseparable appearance and emptiness. Then visualize a white OM, the nature of wisdom and emptiness, radiating light from inside the crown chakra above the level of your eyebrows. Chant the mantra OM AH HUNG for one mala round or more, while white light from the radiating OM completely fills your body, purifying all the obscurations and negative karma related to the body, especially ignorance. Then your body is transformed into inseparable appearance and emptiness, like a rainbow.

ཨཱཿ AH

Next visualize a red AH, the nature of wisdom and emptiness, radiating light from the throat chakra. Chant the mantra as before, while red light radiates and completely fills your body, purifying all the obscurations and negative karma related to speech, especially desire and attachment. Then your voice is transformed into inseparable sound and emptiness, like an echo.

ཧཱུྃ HUNG

Then visualize a blue HUNG, the nature of wisdom and emptiness, radiating light from the heart chakra inside your chest. Chant the mantra as before, while blue light radiates and completely pervades your body and being, purifying all the obscurations and negative karma related to the mind, especially hatred and aversion. Then your mind is transformed into the Buddha's mind, inseparable clear light and emptiness.

Chant the mantra for a fourth round. From all three syllables simultaneously, the three colors of light radiate and fill the universe with compassion and wisdom. First, purify the outer universe and transform it into a pure land. Then the lights touch each and every sentient being; they purify all defilements, suffering, and negative karma related to body, speech, and mind and establish all beings in the state of buddhahood. They also become inseparable appearance and emptiness, like the moon's reflection in a lake. The lights return and dissolve into you. You feel happy because you are being purified, as are all sentient beings.

To end the session, dissolve your visualized buddha-body into the three syllables. The white OM then dissolves into the red AH, and the AH into the blue HUNG. The HUNG then dissolves from the bottom upwards and disappears into all-pervading emptiness. Relax the mind and meditate in that unfabricated state, mind itself as it is. Finally, dedicate the merit.

This practice, especially the completion or dissolution stage, provides very profound preparation for realization at the time of death. One experiences many different sensations during the dying process. After the four elements dissolve, the three subtle experiences of white appearance, red increase, and darkness near-attainment occur. Ordinary people without meditation experience will go through these three briefly without any awareness—completely unconscious, as in a deep sleep.

On the other hand, meditators who can maintain stable equipoise can recognize each stage as they pass through it. The following stage is the experience of luminosity, the original face of the mind, the direct nature of mind free from all limitations of boundary or edge. Those with no meditation experience or with no instructions concerning these practices will pass through this stage and go into the bardo state according to their karma and habitual propensities. Those who are highly accomplished in meditation practice can recognize the experience of luminosity as an opportunity to become instantly free from samsara and achieve enlightenment. If repeatedly practiced with mindfulness, this practice of dissolving the white, red, and blue syllables helps enable the practitioner to utilize that opportunity and attain realization.

At the end, if one carefully and regularly practices this and becomes used to it, one can stabilize the mind in meditative absorption. One will then experience the beneficial effects first as the purification of all the different obscurations and mental defilements. Following that, one will experience the primordial luminosity of mahamudra.

Guru Yoga

> If on the guru, snow mountain of the four kayas,
> the sun of devotion fails to shine,
> the stream of blessings will not arise.
> Attend, therefore, to this mind of devotion.

In order to study and practice Dharma seriously, an authentic spiritual master is indispensable. Even in our regular schooling, it is important to have a good teacher. Of course, this situation is interdependent. The student's attention, sincerity, and hard work must come together with a teacher's high quality, good motivation, and learned thoughts. In that way, the student will receive a good education in any subject—mathematics, science, business, social studies, physics, technology, languages, and so on. Since even in samsara we are dependent on a qualified teacher to receive a good education, it is definitely logical that to free ourselves from samsara and attain enlightenment, we must depend on an authentic and high-quality guru, lama, or teacher.

Becoming free from samsara is not an easy thing. It is not enough to read books or gain a small positive feeling through practice. We need the direct guidance of one who already understands the path. For example, Milarepa had confidence that Marpa's harsh methods were necessary, so he persevered even though they were painful. The amount of pain we suffer on the path depends on the strength and courage of our mind. Those who don't have indomitable courage supported by wisdom attach to self-cherishing, feel unbearable pain, and become derailed from the path to buddhahood. Those who have a clear picture of samsara, no matter how difficult it is, joyfully follow the path. We must sacrifice our ego in order to purify our bad habits, and sometimes it is agonizing to dismantle the beautiful castle of the ego that we have built up for such a long time. Yet, if we have the wisdom to know that the whole world exists on the basis of causality, we can come to understand that it is worthwhile to sacrifice such habits.

The ego does not exist independently—it is just a label. But that label is a habit that we have been accustomed to for a very long time. Our buddha nature, the wish-fulfilling jewel, is thickly covered by negative habits, so we have to break through their walls. In order to do so, we need *the sun of devotion* to shine. This means to surrender to our buddha nature. When we take refuge in the Buddha, Dharma, and Sangha, our mind comes closer to following in that direction. With powerful devotion, confidence, and bodhicitta, the mind becomes receptive to blessings, because they accord with our natural state. However, when we do not have devotion, the *stream of blessings will not arise,* and so we must make every effort to develop it.

In order to cultivate devotion, it is first necessary to have an understanding of the Buddha's body, speech, wisdom mind, and activities. We should take the time to learn about qualities such as the ten strengths, four fearlessnesses, eighteen unmatched qualities, and the thirty-two major physical attributes. Having some knowledge and understanding of the Buddha's qualities will help us to develop devotion to an authentic teacher. One can take historical figures like Milarepa, Gampopa, or Jigten Sumgön as root teachers. The blessings will be the same now as they were when those masters were alive, due to their cultivation of bodhicitta and their perfection of wisdom, both of which will extend to all sentient beings until samsara is exhausted. Therefore, it is very useful to read their life stories and familiarize yourself with their activities on behalf of sentient beings. This will give you a good opportunity to develop unwavering devotion.

As ordinary people with impure minds, it is difficult for us to perceive the sublime qualities of enlightened beings. Our impure vision has no means to judge the pristine qualities of the masters. Even at the time of the Buddha there were a few who could not perceive him as a sublime being, though most people saw him as someone who possessed the supreme qualities of wisdom and compassion. So, we must take personal responsibility to engage ourselves in the spiritual path. To accomplish this, the Vajrayana system provides guru yoga, a special technique through which we reveal our own mind as the Buddha's wisdom. Because it is so effective, this guru yoga practice is both emphasized and highly cherished.

In this verse, the *snow mountain* that embodies *the four kayas* is a metaphor for the guru or lama. The guru is as stable as a mountain and embodies the four kayas:

- the *nirmanakaya* (emanation form), the physical form that a buddha manifests whenever needed in any of the six realms;
- the *sambhogakaya* (pure enjoyment form), a subtle form that a buddha manifests for highly accomplished bodhisattvas;

> ► the *dharmakaya* (truth or wisdom form), the complete buddha-hood that can be comprehended by a buddha alone; and
> ► the *svabhavikakaya* (nature form), which is not a physical form but rather is the unified and inseparable nature of all buddhas' forms.

Understanding "inseparable nature" is like understanding a lit candle. One can describe a lit candle as a stick of wax with a wick, as light that dispels darkness, as a chemical process with heat and color, and so on. Each aspect can be individually examined, but they are, in fact, inseparable. In the same manner, these kayas exist inseparably in the realization of a great spiritual master. More broadly, the body of the spiritual master is the nirmanakaya, an emanation of the Buddha's body. We describe speech, the Dharma teachings that he or she imparts, as the sambhogakaya. The mind that manifests these two is the dharmakaya. Again, these three are inseparable within a single person; none can exist without the others. That aspect is the svabhavikakaya. We should see the enlightened guru in this way.

One who possesses these four kayas is free from all delusion and negative thought; thus, his entire environment becomes a mandala of the enlightened state. Because of emptiness, all activities and appearances can unceasingly manifest; the unceasing manifestation and the source of the manifestation are inseparable. When our mind begins to comprehend this, great confidence and devotion arise. In order for us to come closer to this state we must purify our negative habits, our arrogance, and our inveterate mental propensities. Sometimes purification is painful because our chronic inclination is very difficult to penetrate, quite stubborn, and difficult to release. But, when we see the benefit and outcome of this path, we become willing to sacrifice our negative habits. We need strong devotion and courage in order to progress on the path. Without them, we will not move forward.

Guru yoga meditation is such a beautiful practice. In it, we take Buddha Shakyamuni as our guru and practice by visualizing him in front of us, reciting his mantra, and praying with confidence. We make offerings, including the offering of our body, speech, and mind, and of the entire universe. Without expectation, we freely offer everything imaginable. This is a skillful way to cultivate bodhicitta and perform service for sentient beings. The Buddha's mind continually wishes for all sentient beings to be free from suffering and achieve happiness. So when we offer service to sentient beings, this is also an offering to the Buddha. Thinking in this way, it is not difficult to serve sentient beings. This is a way to practice the nirmanakaya. At the end, the guru dissolves into us and we dissolve all the delusions into pervading emptiness, the total nature of wisdom and compassion.

After that, we practice the sambhogakaya by visualizing Buddha Vajradhara at our heart level. This form of the Buddha is a special expression, skillfully designed to allow us to realize that our mind and the Buddha's mind are of one nature. Its infinite qualities can be perceived only by bodhisattvas who are highly accomplished in their realization and have reached at least the eighth bhumi. The celestial body of a Buddha, the inseparability of appearance and emptiness, pervades limitless buddhafields in a single atom, and all the buddhafields appear within that body without overcrowding it. This celestial form is also an expression of the perfect body of a buddha and is adorned by the 112 major and minor marks. The sambhogakaya is like a TV station that effortlessly broadcasts to thousands of television sets at the same time. But the difference is that a sambhogakaya buddha eliminates confusion and TV shows sometimes create more confusion! Here, we vividly visualize the sambhogakaya state and recite the corresponding mantra. After chanting the mantra, we (as the yidam) dissolve into the sambhogakaya, and the sambhogakaya dissolves into emptiness. Rest the mind there. This is a wonderful and effective practice to overcome our negative habits. These practices give us an excellent opportunity to recognize our ultimate nature without much difficulty.

Next we practice the dharmakaya meditation. Dharmakaya is the aggregate of all the Buddha's qualities, a name given to the indestructible nature of complete enlightenment. This nature is all-pervading emptiness, inseparable from luminosity. It is beyond expression, a heap of innumerable, excellent qualities, such as the ten strengths, four fearlessnesses, eighteen unequaled qualities, four immeasurables, thirty-seven branches of enlightenment, and so on. The Buddha's pervading wisdom mind is vast as space but is also not different from our own mind. We vividly visualize Buddha Vajradhara surrounded by all the buddhas and lineage gurus. We supplicate, pray, and meditate on this in order to manifest as the dharmakaya, to realize that our mind is, and always has been, inseparable from the pure primordial state. Then dissolve all the buddhas and lineage gurus into Vajradhara, after which he dissolves into you. You, as the yidam, dissolve into emptiness like a rainbow dissipates into the sky. Rest in that state. Space cannot be contaminated by clouds because when the clouds dissipate, no trace is left behind. In the same way, our mind is primordially pure and unstained. Our pure nature is only temporarily obscured by negative thoughts. When these obscurations vanish into the space of pure mind, only the excellent quality of inseparable appearance and emptiness remains.

The fourth aspect of guru yoga practice is the svabhavikakaya, or nature body. In this practice, there is no form to visualize as an object of the mind, because it is the inseparable union of the other three kayas. It is the basis of ground, path, and fruition mahamudra, which is the direct nature of our own mind. In this practice, one needs to meditate on the inseparable nature of the guru and one's own mind without wavering from that state. While maintaining that nature, supplicate and say prayers.

When Milarepa meditated in the mountains, he was alone for a long time. In spite of this, he always felt that he was inseparable from Marpa because his devotion was so powerful. Milarepa sang his vajra songs in solitude but, through devotion, was always connected to his lama. Devotion to the lama is a powerful protection from negative thoughts and nonvirtuous actions. It is also a special protection that allows us to properly practice meditation. Our awareness of enlightened beings and our knowledge of how to take care of our mind protect the mind so that it doesn't flow in a wrong direction. Through these joyous practices we develop a feeling of appreciation of how fortunate we are, and we cease feeling lonely or depressed.

So, guru yoga unites our mind with the pure and pristine wisdom mind of Vajradhara. Through this skillful practice, we can directly embrace unfabricated, luminous, and uncontrived peace and joy. Those with limited time can use the following practice. It may be short, but it contains the core essence of the four kayas of guru yoga.

A Guru Yoga That Brings the Dharmakaya onto the Path

Refuge and Bodhicitta
Recite three times:
Vajradhara Lama, embodiment of the Three Jewels,
I take refuge in you, and will until I attain enlightenment.
Sentient beings, victims of confused-projection suffering,
and I generate bodhicitta in order to establish all sentient beings
    in the nonabiding state.
KÖN CHOG KÜN DÜ LA MA DOR JE CHANG
CHANG CHUB BAR DU MI DRÄL KYAB SU CHI
TRHUL NANG DU KE NAR WA'I DRO WA NAM
MI NE SA LA GÖ CHIR SEM KYE DO

Visualization

Lord Vajradhara Jigten Sumgön sits on a seat of the ten strengths,
four fearlessnesses, and eighteen unmixed dharmas,
with the radiating light of the major and minor marks of love,
   compassion, and bodhicitta,
and nonconceptual enlightened activities equally reaching all
   migrators.

DOR JE CHANG WANG JIG TEN SUM GÖN SHAB
TOB CHU MI JIG MA DRE DÄN LA SHUG
JAM TSE SEM CHOG TSHÄN BE Ö SER TRHO
TRIN LE TOG ME DRO WA'I THA DANG NYAM

Mantra recitation

OM AH RATNA SHRI SARWA SIDDHI HUNG
Accumulate many recitations

Blessing supplication

Recite at least three times:
You are the buddhas Nagakulapradipa and Dipankara of the past,
Maitreya of the future, and Shakyamuni of the present.
The reincarnation of Nagarjuna, the peerless Ratna Shri—
Jigten Sumgön, I supplicate you.

DE DÜ LU RIG DRÖN DANG MAR ME DZE
MA ONG CHAM PA DA TA SHAK YA THUB
LU DRUB LAR TRUL NYAM ME RIN CHEN PÄL
JIG TEN SUM GÖN SHAB LA SOL WA DEB

Empowerment and Dissolution

Light rays emanate from the lama's body, speech, and mind and
   dissolve into my four places,
thereby purifying the four obscurations, bestowing the four
   empowerments, and planting the seeds of the four kayas.
The lama then dissolves into myself.
My mind is natural luminosity-emptiness.

LA MA'I KU SUNG THUG LE Ö SER TRHÖ
DAG GI NE SHIR THIM PE DRIB SHI DAG
WANG SHI LEG THOB KU SHI SA BÖN TRÜN
LA MA RANG THIM RANG SEM SÄL TONG NGANG

Rest in the mind itself as-it-is.

Dedication

Through both the innate virtue and the virtue accumulated in the
three times by all in samsara and nirvana,
may I and all sentient beings filling space, none left out,
realize the coemergent ultimate reality
and attain the final state of nonabiding in existence or peace.
KHOR DE DÜ SUM SAG YÖ GE TSHOG KYI
DAG DANG KHA NYAM SEM CHEN MA LÜ PA
DÖN DAM LHÄN CHIG KYE PA'I DÖN TAG TE
SI SHIR MI NE THAR CHIN SA THOB SHOG

Mahamudra

> If from the sky-like expanse of mind's nature
> the clouds of conceptual thought are not blown away,
> the planets and stars of the two wisdoms will not shine.
> Attend, therefore, to this mind without conception.

This verse contains the presentation of mahamudra itself. The phrase *from the sky-like expanse* refers to space, free of all limitations, as a metaphor for our mind, free of all delusion. Sky or space has no boundary, limit, or physical form, but it is nonetheless the foundation for all form, even planets, galaxies, and stars. The sky does not depend on the elements, but the four elements all depend on the fifth element of space. The blue of the sky is not the sky itself. We call that blue color "an ornament of the sky." Neither are clouds the sky. We can see the sky but there are no words to describe this boundless space. Even though space itself is free of any form, color, shape, and so forth, nothing could manifest or function without space. All phenomena manifest from space and dissolve back into space-like clouds.

It is the same for our mind. In samsara and nirvana both, all experiences, projections, and objects are just the dexterous movement of mind's play. The buddha mind is the basis from which all experiences manifest. Our body, the five skandhas, the twelve links of interdependence, the eighteen elements, and all our negative and positive thoughts manifest from that state. They all depend on the pure buddha nature, but buddha nature does not depend on them. It is totally free and limitless. However, in the beginning we have no idea what our mind looks like; we can't see it because we are so lost in delusion.

When clouds cover the sky, we cannot see the pure nature of space. Likewise, when conceptual thoughts occupy the mind, we cannot see the pure nature of the mind. To see whether this is true, we can meditate so that the mind becomes relaxed and peaceful, and then there is room to develop compassion, love, and bodhicitta. But when our mind is occupied by *conceptual thoughts* and negative thoughts, there is no space to develop good qualities. Our mind becomes full of suffering and we cannot disentangle ourselves from confusion. Focusing attention on one small negative thought can give rise to another negative thought, and then another, until the mind is fully occupied with afflicting emotions. This is the same as watching the sky fill with one small cloud after another until the whole sky is blocked from view. When our mind emphasizes positive, calming, and relaxing thoughts, it leaves no space for negative thoughts to arise. Then we can maintain a peaceful, harmonious mind regardless of external conditions. This becomes a matter of how much we habituate ourselves to the Dharma teachings.

Mahamudra meditation practice encompasses four progressive yogas. The first, the one-pointed state of mind, comprises nine stages in the desire world, four in the form world, and four in the formless world. Any one of the four form-world meditative states makes a perfect foundation for special insight. The second, free from elaboration, occurs when the mind is in a state of total absorption or equipoise. This creates an excellent opportunity to comprehend the total nature of emptiness. That state is called "free from elaboration." The third, one taste, consists of concurrent equipoise and special insight. One who continues in that practice with mindfulness will experience that the empty natures of samsara and nirvana, of suffering and joy, cannot be differentiated. The fourth, nonmeditation, is the continuation of concurrent special insight and equipoise in which these are fully perfected. The mind then is fully revealed in all-pervasive luminosity. There are no meditation sessions that can be distinguished from post-meditation, and so it can be said that the dharmakaya, or enlightenment, has been achieved.

Within the context of these four stages of yoga, mahamudra practice is often explained in terms of ground, path, and fruition. Ground mahamudra is the buddha nature that every sentient being has. Whether they realize it or not, the potential for enlightenment intrinsically pervades everyone. The inseparability of samsara and nirvana is unfabricated by its nature. This is the same buddha nature with which all sentient beings are inherently endowed. Every individual must recognize this potential, the possibility for enlightenment, and then practice path mahamudra in order to actualize that state. This encompasses the purification practices that help us to eliminate adventitious defilements. Thus, it serves to purify our obscurations, gather the two accumulations, and perfect wisdom. Through these steps, one will achieve the fruition mahamudra, which is the result of these practices—the attainment of buddhahood.

Ground mahamudra. Ground mahamudra shares the same nature as samsara and nirvana. For example, the sky has the same nature, whether cloudy or free from clouds. Sky itself is free from defilement and obstruction. This is also true of samsara. If we empirically investigate samsara, we cannot find any permanent phenomenon, not even so much as a subatomic dust particle. Sentient beings are confused about the nature of samsara, both in its physical and mental aspects, due to their fundamental ignorance. But that ignorance itself has no legitimate basis. Sometimes ignorance and afflictions seem to be very powerful and real, but if we apply wisdom and investigate them within the context of emptiness, we find they have not even a trace of firm existence. They are adventitious defilements, like clouds in the sky. So whether we attain buddhahood or remain as sentient beings in samsara, the nature of the luminosity of the mind is no different. The luminous mind is never afflicted. If we understand this ground, we are inspired to go through the path that can purify all obscurations and reveal the absolute nature of enlightenment, total peace.

Path mahamudra. With the inspiration and guidance of an authentic spiritual master, the disciple is encouraged to develop the indomitable courage to face the obstacles and difficulties of the path. One receives instructions on such topics as the four foundations (also called the four thoughts that turn the mind), the preliminary meditation practices (ngöndro), and especially the fivefold path of mahamudra. Then one must study their meaning and actually follow the path of meditation practice step by step—joyfully purifying the gross and subtle obscurations and developing mental stability and calm. Through these methods, one holds in one's hand the complete means to dispel all the temporary obscurations and realize the ground mahamudra.

To allow great wisdom to arise, there are five consecutive paths to practice: the path of accumulation, the path of preparation, the path of special insight, the path of meditation, and the path of perfection. But first we must study the teachings in order to understand thoroughly that the nature of samsara is impermanent, is made up of composite phenomena, is the result of causality, and is of the nature of suffering—in short, a state that brings no satisfaction. With the support of a good understanding of samsara, we can develop the insight that will allow us to see everything as a rainbow or scarecrow.

All sentient beings are confused and victimized by delusion. This empirical fact gives us reason to develop bodhicitta, the nature of wisdom and compassion. We practice the yidam deities that transform us into the enlightened state, the guru yoga which develops confidence and trust, and place the mind correctly in mahamudra meditation. There are different methods to bring the mind into the right place, to rest in one-pointed concentration, and to abide calmly in tranquility and equipoise. For example, we can take the breath as the object of our meditation by counting it or resting with it. When this practice has progressed, we can maintain the meditation without relying on an object.

The fundamental basis for special insight depends on samadhi, also called "equipoise meditation," or "absorption." One may face many different types of impediments, such as strong attachment, anger or resentment, dullness, jealousy, and so on. To counteract these obstacles, contemplate objects such as a beautiful flower, with the understanding that they have no essence. Like bubbles in water, they come and go and are mere manifestations. When one becomes convinced of this, one sees that there is no benefit to attachment or anger. Otherwise, the allure of appearances will so entangle us that we suffer helplessly. Contemplating the many levels of suffering experienced throughout the world can also help us free ourselves from attachment and anger. These methods help us to meditate and achieve the equipoise absorption that is the foundation for mahamudra realization. There are nine different stages of calm abiding (shamatha) to develop, and then one can learn the four samadhi, and the four formless states. In order to practice mahamudra formally, it is an indispensable prerequisite to have the experience of full absorption or meditative equipoise. Without completely calm abiding, there is no basis from which to realize and stabilize mahamudra meditation.

Fruition mahamudra. On the basis of ground and path mahamudra, after purifying the afflicting emotions and subtle obscurations to enlightenment, and after perfecting the two accumulations of merit and wisdom, one achieves the fruition of one's efforts—buddhahood. A buddha has two basic forms: dharmakaya (wisdom body) and rupakaya (form bodies). The wisdom body is the ultimate cessation of suffering and all causes of suffering. It signifies one's own benefit, that one is free from suffering, and that one has perfected the infinite excellent qualities. The form bodies are the perfection that fulfills the wishes of sentient beings. Until the end of samsara, these infinite manifestations will arise effortlessly according to the needs of individuals.

Two categories of wisdom are achieved. The first, primordial wisdom, is the mind that realizes the nature of every aspect of phenomena, as they are, in the unfabricated state. That wisdom is achieved through the equipoise absorption called "vajra-like" meditation. The second category, wisdom awareness, occurs within this state and is the knowing of all phenomena, their meaning, the definition of words, and achieving confidence in expressing the causality of phenomena. This wisdom is achieved when all the obscurations are fully exhausted and cease to exist. These *two wisdoms* are actualized when our mind is pure and clear of conceptual thoughts.

In the beginning, when you are just getting used to mahamudra practices, let the mind rest in the nonreferential state, free of all objects. Make your mind completely independent, rather than dependent on or reactive to objects, and become stable in that state. Once you are stabilized, various experiences may arise, such as great bliss, clarity, and the state of nonthought. Some practitioners mistake such experiences for enlightenment. If you experience any of these states, incorporate special insight so that your meditation results in mahamudra realization. When you look at the mind, there is no object to observe and no observer realizing the nondual state. In this state you can achieve great joy and freedom from all fears. This fearless, unafflicted joy is free from boundaries. The time will come when you no longer need to meditate because all experiences will have become seamless meditation. At that point, your meditation practice will be perfected.

You can become very eloquent by reading many books, but reading will do you no good if you don't practice. Of course, reading some profound philosophical texts will give you very important information, and through that, you will be able to theoretically establish the view. But without meditation practice and experience of the view, learning alone won't free you from samsara. As far as mahamudra realization is concerned, there is nothing special about being a scholar. One can have vast information about samsara and nirvana but remain in the ordinary, afflicted state. But if you practice well, you will die peacefully, joyfully, without regret, and free from samsara. That is the purpose of Dharma study and practice. Negative thoughts bring suffering, but negative thoughts can also be the basis for Dharma practice. If you didn't have negative thoughts, there would be no purpose for practice. Great bodhicitta arises in the midst of strong afflicting emotions in the same way that a beautiful flower grows in the midst of a compost heap. We only need to utilize the precious Dharma teachings for this to happen. But if we don't learn how to utilize the compost, it is just more useless dirt. *Attend, therefore, to this mind without conception.*

Take a few moments now to relax the mind. Take a deep breath; exhale all your physical and mental tension. Remain in a natural position, like a cotton ball. Breathe freely in and out, observing the breath. Free the mind of objects. Let all delusion dissipate within the space of mind. Abide there without any fabrication or effort.

DEDICATION

> **If the wish-fulfilling gem of the two accumulations**
> **is not polished by aspiration,**
> **the results we have hoped for will not arise.**
> **Attend, therefore, to this final dedication.**

The enlightened master Gampopa reasoned that since we have had countless prior lifetimes, along the way we must have done some positive deeds, attended a spiritual master, gathered great accumulations, and done meditation practices. Why then, he asked, are we not yet free of samsara? It is because we lacked the important practice of dedicating the merit gained for those actions. If our merits are dedicated to this life's success, good health, fame, or business, that merit will have been consumed and exhausted as soon as we experienced these results. This approach will not lead us to the final goal. The wise will invest their merit for the optimal goal, to achieve complete buddhahood for themselves and others. Thoroughly practicing dedication is a very special aspect of the Buddha's teachings and one that Jigten Sumgön particularly emphasized.

Dedication is like putting your money in the bank. When you put money in the bank, it earns interest that comes back to you whether you are aware of it or not. In the same way, when you earn merit and dedicate it to enlightenment for the sake of others, you get the benefit whether you are aware of it or not. Even if we create just a small amount of merit, virtue, or wisdom, it will increase if it's dedicated for the benefit of all. It is said that our merit increases by the number of sentient beings that are in this world, and thus it can grow infinitely.

The *two accumulations* are the accumulation of merit and the accumulation of wisdom. The accumulation of merit can be created by giving food, clothes, or wealth, for example. The accumulation of wisdom can be gathered by the practice of giving Dharma books, pens, paper, and Dharma teachings. If food, clothes, and so forth are given with wisdom and special insight, then that practice can also become the accumulation of wisdom. When we properly study and practice Dharma, we gather merit. When we practice generosity, moral ethics, forbearance, and so forth, we gain merit. Then, when we come to know the meaning of the Dharma teachings, that becomes wisdom. So merit and wisdom go side by side, hand in hand; each helps the other to develop. By using this skillful method of merit and wisdom, we have a complete path to purify all the adventitious defilements and gather all the excellent qualities of the Buddha. They are like a *wish-fulfilling gem* that grants all our wishes for happiness.

Aspiration refers to our intention or wish to attain enlightenment. To attain this aspiration, we should be sure to dedicate whatever virtue and merit we generate. We can think, "May this become a special cause for all sentient beings to become free from suffering and achieve complete enlightenment." In that way, we do not become attached to our accomplishments. We just give them away to other sentient beings for their benefit so that they may attain enlightenment, buddhahood. This is the meaning of the phrase *polished by aspiration.*

If we dedicate our virtue for the benefit of all sentient beings, it will never be wasted because it has been "sealed" for enlightenment. But if you dedicate with a wish to be free from physical sickness or to overcome some small obstacles, that result may come about instead. You may have good health for a while, but then the benefit will be exhausted. We can waste our good deeds in this way, which is why we aren't free from samsara and haven't attained enlightenment. Now we know how to dedicate, so from now on, we can dedicate for the benefit of others rather than just for ourselves, for this life, or for samsaric happiness. In this way, the benefit will last until we attain buddhahood.

When we know how to dedicate, the results we hope for will definitely arise. Without dedication, our merits can be undone by regretting the good we have done and can be destroyed by strong afflictions such as anger or rage, or by touting our good deeds out of pride. However, if we seal the merit and wisdom with dedication to enlightenment, then these impediments cannot destroy them. For this reason, dedication is regarded as crucial, powerful, and necessary. Dedication practice is as important as the initial cultivation of bodhicitta and the main session of meditation practice.

Not only can we dedicate our own merit and wisdom, we can also dedicate all the virtue, merit, and wisdom created in the three times by all other sentient beings and by all the buddhas and bodhisattvas. Gather all this merit into your enlightened mind and dedicate it. This is possible because of bodhicitta; therefore, the development of bodhicitta is the most important step to take when beginning a spiritual practice. Bodhicitta is also important in yidam practice, guru yoga, and mahamudra. Relative bodhicitta is important in mahamudra because without it there is no way to achieve ultimate bodhicitta or enlightenment. To open the door of ultimate bodhicitta, the key is relative bodhicitta. If we know how to practice bodhicitta, then we really know how to practice Dharma. The wish-fulfilling gem is *polished by the aspiration* to attain enlightenment because of dedication supported by bodhicitta. We also must have bodhicitta to dedicate properly because without it, we will have no basis on which to dedicate the vastness of meditation practice.

After reading a Dharma book, saying prayers, or meditating, bring your mind again to the spot where you presently are. Relax and calmly abide there. Visualize all the enlightened beings in front of you as witnesses to your accomplishment of dedication practice. Then, with a sincere mind, recite the following prayer in a contemplative manner:

> Glorious, holy, venerable, precious, kind root and lineage lamas,
> divine assembly of yidam deities and assemblies of buddhas,
>   bodhisattvas,
> yogins, yoginis, and dakinis dwelling in the ten directions:
> please hear my prayer!
>
> May the virtues collected in the three times
> by myself and all sentient beings in samsara and nirvana,
> and the innate root of virtue
> not result in the eight worldly concerns, the four causes of samsara,
> or rebirth as a shravaka or pratyekabuddha.

May all mother sentient beings,
especially those enemies who hate me and mine,
obstructers who harm, misleading maras, and the hordes of demons
experience happiness, be separated from suffering,
and swiftly attain unsurpassed, perfect, complete, and precious
    buddhahood.

By the power of this vast root of virtue,
may I benefit all beings through my body, speech, and mind.
May the afflictions of desire, hatred, ignorance, arrogance, and
    jealousy not arise in my mind.
May attachment to fame, reputation, wealth, honor, and concern for
    this life not arise for even a moment.
May my mind stream be moistened by loving-kindness, compassion,
    and bodhicitta
and, through that, may I become a spiritual master
with good qualities equal to the infinity of space.
May I gain the supreme attainment of mahamudra in this very life.
May the torment of suffering not arise even at the time of my death.
May I not die with negative thoughts.
May I not die confused by wrong view.
May I not experience an untimely death.
May I die joyfully and happily in the great luminosity of mind's
    nature and the pervading clarity of dharmata.
May I, in any case, gain the supreme attainment of mahamudra at the
    time of death or in the bardo.

6. The Song That Clarifies Recollection

Once, when Jigten Sumgön was residing at Drigung Thil, he gathered together about thirty of his students in a meadow behind the monastery and asked them to perform displays of their miracle powers. All but one were able to comply with their guru's request, and this disciple, Rinchen Drak, died suddenly from shame when he could not perform. When the undertakers tried to dismember his corpse to feed it to the vultures, the body resisted the knife. Jigten Sumgön placed his walking stick on the heart-center of the corpse, and sang this song:

I bow at the feet of glorious Phagmo Drupa.

Listen, Rinchen Drak, my son.

Ka! At the time of death
worldly activities are a lie.
The eight worldly dharmas are like the colors of a rainbow—
think, can you put your trust in them?

When you see the separation of gathered friends,
the affection of relatives and friends is a lie.
Heartfelt words are like an echo—
think, can you put your trust in them?

When you see the growth and decline of the four elements of the body,
the illusion of strength and ability is also a lie.
The autumn flower of youth—
think, can you put your trust in it?

When you see the gathering and consumption of wealth,
clinging and painful accumulation are also lies.
Food and wealth are like dew on a blade of grass—
think, can you put your trust in them?

When you see the suffering of birth and death,
the happiness of the assemblies of gods and men is a lie.
The joy and suffering of the wheel of samsara—
think, can you put your trust in it?

To the tree, the father, bodhicitta,
the bias of disciples is a lie.
Nonvirtuous and misleading friends—
think, can you put your trust in them?

When you understand that all sentient beings are your parents,
attachment to self-cherishing is a lie.
The shravakas' vehicle of self-liberation—
think, can you put your trust in it?

When you become convinced of the cause and result of karma,
the instruction of non-effort is a lie.
Thunder without rain in an empty sky—
think, can you put your trust in it?

For the guru who has the realization of power and blessings,
the obstacle of maras and error is a lie.
Chattering prayers like a parrot—
think, can you put your trust in that?

When you realize the nature of your mind,
the three limitless kalpas are also a lie.
The deceptive vehicle of relative truth—
think, can you put your trust in it?

In the Gathering Relics cemetery,
are you sad, son, at being alone?
Since nothing lasts and all must die,

Rinchen Drak, do not be attached.
If your mind is still attached,
transfer it to your guru's heart.

Rinchen Drak's body was then cut open and found to contain numerous relics in the form of small, multi-colored pills. There were so many of them that they had to be swept together with brooms.

INTRODUCTION

"THE SONG THAT CLARIFIES RECOLLECTION" contains vast and profound spiritual teachings. Such songs are called *doha* in Sanskrit. Though in English we translate this word as "song," we should not think of this kind of composition as an ordinary song. *Doha* arise spontaneously from the enlightened mind at just the moment they are needed. Teachings given in this manner come directly from the wisdom of the singer's realization. A well-known example of this is the *Hundred Thousand Songs of Milarepa*. Of course, Milarepa didn't sit around in a cave pondering how to compose spiritual songs—far from it. He uttered each of those teachings at the exact moment it would be most beneficial to an individual.

Sometimes we chant such verses with a special melody, and in this way they resemble ordinary songs. In Tibetan two different words are used to distinguish ordinary songs from songs of edification. The song we are studying here is an example of the latter. Its insight, wisdom, and blessings point to the means by which we can dispel the root cause of our suffering.

The background of this particular song tells of a special occasion while Jigten Sumgön was residing at Drigung Thil monastery. The weather was clear and the sun was shining, so he and about thirty very close disciples walked behind the monastery to a peaceful and pleasant hilltop meadow. Jigten Sumgön sat down on the grass gazing at the nature of space with full delight and amusement. He requested his disciples to display their miracle powers as a test of their progress in meditation. All but one were able to comply with their master's request and demonstrate their ability. One disciple, at the very instant of the request, went to India and brought back an *arura,* a fruit with strong healing power, and offered it to Jigten Sumgön. Some levitated and remained sitting cross-legged in the sky above the meadow. Others simply vanished into the sky like a cloud, leaving their vajras and bells hanging in the air, and then reappeared. Still others flew about in the sky. Even Jigten Sumgön's personal cook, an elderly monk, was able to hang his ladle and tea strainer on a sunbeam. Everyone succeeded in exhibiting their power except for Rinchen Drak, who hesitated and then suddenly died of embarrassment at his inability to perform.

When the undertaker brought Rinchen Drak's corpse to the sky burial site and tried to dismember it, the body resisted the knife. This information was conveyed to Jigten Sumgön, who directly perceived what was happening. He went there and placed the tip of his walking stick over the heart chakra of the corpse and sang this song. Jigten Sumgön had given these teachings to Rinchen Drak and the other disciples before, but at his death Rinchen Drak could not recall them. So Jigten Sumgön reminded him of these teachings step-by-step in a complete way so that his death could become a way for him to free himself from samsara and achieve enlightenment.

COMMENTARY

I bow at the feet of glorious Phagmo Drupa.

Phagmo Drupa (1110–1170 C.E.) was Jigten Sumgön's principal teacher and the guru who transmitted to him the teachings of the combined lineages of Milarepa and Atisha.

Listen, Rinchen Drak, my son.

Here, *son* means heart-son, a spiritual child whom the guru nourishes with his guidance. Jigten Sumgön was calling Rinchen Drak to pay attention to the teachings that follow. While giving teachings, Jigten Sumgön would sometimes say, "This Dharma I give you is more valuable than my heart. If you open my body and take out my heart, you will see that it is just a piece of flesh. But this teaching is infinitely precious; therefore all of you should study and practice it."

Ka! At the time of death
worldly activities are a lie.
The eight worldly dharmas are like the colors of a rainbow—
think, can you put your trust in them?

Ka is an exclamation used in Tibetan to get another person's attention, something like "Hey!" in English.

To say *worldly activities are a lie* is to say that they have no meaning. They cannot be relied upon because they are transitory. In samsara, all human achievements and pleasures are momentary and without essence, like a dream or a magician's show. There is no one in this world who is not subject to death. Contemplate this repeatedly and frequently, and transcend your attachment and resentment. At the time of death we have to leave everything behind, including our belongings, Dharma centers, beloved Dharma brothers and sisters, and the precious Dharma books that one has translated, written, or bought. One's life span is exhausted, one's breathing stops, one's body becomes a corpse, and one's consciousness leaves the body. That is the end of an individual's life, vanishing *like the colors of a rainbow* that appear precisely but don't last. In this case, Rinchen Drak is experiencing this. His precious guru reminds him of his previous realizations so that he can die joyfully by revealing his own nature.

Here the word *dharma* is used in a general way to mean phenomena. It refers to all the events of our experience, everything in this world of samsara. The *eight worldly dharmas* are our concern with

- gain and loss;
- pleasure and pain;
- fame and disgrace; and
- praise and blame.

Regarding the first pair in this list, gain and loss, it is obvious that we're almost always concerned with gaining one thing or another and then guarding it against loss. Much of our time and energies go into acquiring materials and protecting them out of fear of their loss.

The next pair is pleasure and pain. Pleasure is mostly related to sensual pleasure, such as beautiful forms as an object for the eye, pleasant sounds like music for the ears, fragrant odors for the nose, delicious cuisine for the mouth, and smooth textures for the body. To fulfill our need for sense pleasures, we participate in entertainments such as picnics or movies and end up uselessly consuming our energy. We try to avoid pain but it follows us like our shadow. Our life plays out in a struggle between pleasure and pain. Yet pleasure and pain are no more substantial than the colored bands of a rainbow, which are beautiful and vivid but have no essence. The more we try to capture a rainbow, the farther away it moves from us. Pleasure and pain are likewise insubstantial. We are uneasy because we know that at any moment our situation might change and our pleasure could turn into pain. We fear pain and will go to great lengths to avoid it but, of course, we cannot. These are just hooks and traps for ordinary, unenlightened beings.

Fame and disgrace make up the third pair in the list of the eight worldly concerns. We want everyone to think well of us. We work hard to acquire a good reputation, sometimes even to the point of risking our own life. It's really very strange that, in order to protect a good reputation, some will sacrifice their lives, yet one hears of people doing this. When you're dead, what good is fame? This is what is called confusion.

It's the same with the last pair on the list, praise and blame. We crave hearing praise like, "Oh, you're so good, so wonderful. You're such a great person, you are so wise, you know Dharma so well that perhaps you are enlightened." We detest harsh words of criticism and rebuke. Though they contain no sharp blades, harsh words can cut the heart. All praise and blame are sounds that are insubstantial like an echo. Yet worldly people pursue them and dedicate their entire lives to such concerns as if they would permanently free them from suffering. This way, we wander helplessly through hope and fear in unending samsara.

Jigten Sumgön then asks us to contemplate well whether we can *put our trust* in any of the eight worldly concerns. Can we rely on them? Can we really get anything out of them? Do they have any real substance? Meditate and contemplate these topics carefully. Purify your mind's attachment and aversion to these things. Bring the mind into the freedom of the Dharma-expanse. If we encounter gain, pleasure, fame, and praise in our life, we should look upon them without attachment. When we have loss, pain, disgrace, and blame, we should regard them without fear.

> **When you see the separation of gathered friends,**
> **the affection of relatives and friends is a lie.**
> **Heartfelt words are like an echo—**
> **think, can you put your trust in them?**

Here, Jigten Sumgön is speaking of very close friends and family, those connected by bonds of kinship and love tainted by attachment. In the course of life, we acquire dear friends and family and, due to causes and conditions, must eventually part from even the dearest of them. Whether circumstances seem good or bad, regardless of our wishes, sometimes people go out of our lives. In particular, we cannot prevent them from dying. This doesn't mean that we shouldn't have affection for relatives and friends. We should do whatever we can to support their life and especially to connect them with the Dharma. This is the best way to help, but it must be done without attachment. Attachment will bring only suffering. No matter how much affection we feel, no matter how close our relationship, it can't last long. In reality, there is no substance upon which this affection can rest; there's no essence there. Ultimately, affection related to attachment becomes a cause of suffering and pain. That's why the affection of relatives and friends is called *a lie*. Instead of these worldly attachments, one should develop affection for all sentient beings through bodhicitta, and cultivate that mind successfully. Bring these friends and family, all sentient beings, toward enlightenment. This is affection based on wisdom and reason; it will bring absolute benefit for oneself and others.

If you go into a large cavern and shout, the sound comes back to you. When we hear this kind of sound, we know that it's just *an echo* with no particular significance. We're indifferent to it and don't react the same way we would to an intentionally spoken word. Jigten Sumgön, using the simile of an echo, is suggesting that we ought to regard all words of emotion with this same attitude. For instance, if an echo said, "You are a rotten person," would you take it seriously? I doubt it. Nor would you care if it said, "You're really terrific." Either way, it wouldn't provoke much of a reaction. All sound is like that in actual fact. Even *heartfelt words* are just so many echoes. This is not to say that human beings don't feel genuine affection for each other because, of course, we do. But relationships are impermanent and should not be grasped as ultimately real. This is a practical realization, truly helpful whether we hear a pleasant or unpleasant sound. Highly accomplished teachers who have the realization of mahamudra are not much affected by these illusory, samsaric manifestations, whether positive or negative. So their minds remain fully tranquil and peaceful no matter what happens.

We are often deeply bewildered and, in our confusion, cling with strong emotional ties to others. In so doing, we create more suffering and confusion for each other instead of helping. When we have to part from loved ones, the result is great sorrow and grief, but this does not bring much benefit for ourselves or others. If we can come to truly understand the reality of our situation, we can prepare for this inevitable loss. This is when our heart opens and we relax, allowing us to perceive things as they truly are. These lessons can help us avoid a lot of suffering and keep us from falling again and again into the same predicament. Meditating on these things can be so helpful. We should reflect on them daily as Rinchen Drak did.

When you see the growth and decline of the four elements of the body,
the illusion of strength and ability is also a lie.
The autumn flower of youth—
think, can you put your trust in it?

Our bodies are composed of *four elements:* earth, water, fire, and wind. The solid portion of flesh, bones, and so forth, is the earth element. Blood and other bodily fluids are the water element. The heat of our body, produced by digestion and other physiological processes, is the fire element. Breathing in and out is the wind element. All four must be present in order for life to exist, and for good health they must be in proper balance, because we experience imbalances as illness. When the element of heat is too strong, for instance, we develop a fever. When the earth element is too dominant, we become lethargic and feel very heavy. When the wind element predominates, especially in the upper part of the body, we can't sleep and the mind becomes restless. Usually earth, wind, fire, and water are incompatible, but inside our bodies they work together. The human body is amazing in its power to reconcile and harmonize these conflicting elements.

Especially when we are young, we believe that we will always be strong and healthy. In reality, however, all assertions of health, *strength, and ability* are a kind of fiction because the body has no essence, no inherent existence, no separate fundamental core. An *autumn flower* is very fragile. In the morning it blossoms so beautifully, especially in the high mountains, but when frost or snow falls the next day it withers and falls to the ground. Contemplate this way: remind yourself how fragile this body is and then sincerely practice Dharma.

Late in 1981, during my three-year retreat, our retreat master, Khyunga Rinpoche, fell ill. His illness grew worse and worse. We all began to worry and said many prayers for his good health and long life. Still, he continued to lose weight. One day we mentioned it to him; we just couldn't help it. He replied by reciting this verse. Even though his body was deteriorating and he was physically uncomfortable and weak, he was not worried about anything. He was like a lotus flower unstained by the mud, and his mind was totally in the state of mahamudra. His mind was clear and confident because he didn't rely on such things as flesh and blood and breath. The Buddha, Milarepa, and many other enlightened beings left their bodies. So repeatedly contemplate and recollect, "One day I, too, will have to leave this body that I cherish and am so attached to." At the final departure from this life, no matter how wonderful our friends and family are, or how much wealth we have, we must leave it all behind. Considerable mental agony, confusion, and physical pain will arise at that time unless we are prepared. So meditate, "From today onward I will apply myself to the practice of bodhicitta, which is the nature of compassion, wisdom, and emptiness."

If we meditate on this subject well, returning to it again and again, we will not be disturbed one way or another whether we maintain good health or lose it. The real subject of this meditation is change, impermanence. Everyone and everything is included in this subject. We must all learn to dwell in this realm of transience, because there is no other reality. By accepting and understanding this condition, and thereby building mental strength, we will dispel our confusion and fear.

Dharma practice will give us an opportunity to experience confidence and fearlessness within the sphere of dharmakaya. For this reason, we must make time to practice and realize this freedom.

One of the most important reasons to practice Dharma is its benefit at the time of death. Our understanding of impermanence will allow us to die peacefully and joyfully in the great luminosity of the mind. Otherwise, confusion, fear, and attachment will arise at the time of our death. So, from now on, it is clear that we must put bodhicitta into heartfelt practice. Live with bodhicitta so that you can die with bodhicitta. Therefore, we have a choice whether to die with frustration or fulfillment and joy.

> **When you see the gathering and consumption of wealth,**
> **clinging and painful accumulation are also lies.**
> **Food and wealth are like dew on a blade of grass—**
> **think, can you put your trust in them?**

We need *food and wealth* in this world to support our lives and to bring happiness and joy to society. Wealth can also solve many social problems and relieve poverty or famine. For these reasons, wealth is fundamentally useful. Those who are ordained, monks and nuns, have to study philosophy and related subjects, and need to go into retreat for many years without interruption. For this, they need support for food, clothes, and utilities. But when we are over-concerned and attached to wealth, when we focus on excessive accumulation, this can be a cause of suffering as we run after wealth and become a slave to it. We become confused, believing that happiness and joy will come from wealth, and that wealth will solve all our problems. What is the benefit of being entrenched like this?

There are many cases today where someone is very rich one day and loses everything the next. This is heartbreaking for them! Wealth is like the drops of dew seen on the grass at dawn. After a few moments of sunshine they are gone. There is no essence in impermanent, transitory wealth. Can you trust something so ephemeral? People risk their lives for wealth, but what good is wealth without life? There is no benefit to be gained by attachment to things that have no essence. We act out of ignorance when we do this. Whatever wealth we have, it should be utilized properly, especially to develop good conditions for Dharma study and practice so that we can free ourselves from suffering.

And what of life itself? There is nothing we cherish more! However, when we look closely at our situation, we might see that instead of having wealth support life, our life is devoted to serving wealth. What good is that? Such activity is merely an effort to appease our afflicting emotions. It doesn't really enhance our lives. We are confused about what is important. We have forgotten what is really valuable and, as a result, the truly crucial things of life have become trivial, and the meaningless have become important. The result of this confusion is that we continue to suffer year after year, and life after life. We need decisive wisdom and courage to make wise choices between this life's temporary happiness and complete freedom from samsara.

> When you see the suffering of birth and death,
> the happiness of the assemblies of gods and men is a lie.
> The joy and suffering of the wheel of samsara—
> think, can you put your trust in it?

We experience intense suffering at the time of *birth* that we don't remember, but fear of *death* is quite common. Especially when we are seriously ill, we try everything to find a way to avoid death. We don't see the suffering that accompanies death itself, though, because after the dying person stops breathing they can't answer our questions about dying and what it's like to be dead. We can only see the suffering of aging and sickness because these are clearly apparent.

Much happens in death that we can't observe. But there have been great masters who, able to see the entire situation clearly, have described in detail what happens between death and rebirth. Because of these teachings we can be sure that there are different levels and stages of suffering in the intermediate state between death and rebirth, and that each of us will have to experience them. If there has been no experience or realization of the Dharma, it will be like going into a totally unknown place. There is no way to become familiar in advance with the route or the destination unless we have a calm and clear mental state. Otherwise, we will be tossed about by the karmic winds of our own bewilderment and terror.

We could say that the happiness of our human life is not real happiness. It is merely a momentary, illusory happiness; it disappears like the dissipation of a beautiful rainbow. It is not happiness based on reason but rather on duality and delusion. In samsara, happiness and suffering constitute a cycle. Our human condition alternates between pleasant and unpleasant feelings. We experience happiness, then suffering, then happiness, then suffering, and so on. Day and night this wheel turns. Thus we experience fear and hope in our daily life. Whether one is a businessperson, politician, lawyer, medical doctor, or taxi driver, life plays out between hope and fear for all alike.

Ask yourself whether you can rely on this for ultimate happiness. When you experience happiness, can you count on it to stay? Can you expect to keep it? You cannot. It is merely the product of causes and conditions, and is sure to change because it is impermanent. This is the nature of samsara. Dharma study and practice can give us an absolute solution to this complex and hidden problem. They will uncover our inner reality and wisdom, which are complete joy and happiness. So, it is empirically logical that we follow this path. We also need inspiration and dedication toward this goal. Then there is a chance for the Dharma to take root deep in our heart.

> To the tree, the father, bodhicitta,
> the bias of disciples is a lie.
> Nonvirtuous and misleading friends—
> think, can you put your trust in them?

This metaphor compares *bodhicitta,* which is without bias, to a sheltering *tree* and a protecting *father.* Jigten Sumgön is not referring to an ordinary tree but rather to a wish-granting tree. In mythology, it is said that such a tree impartially fulfills the wishes of everyone near it. The fruits are jewels from which wishes are fulfilled. The thick leaves flutter to make a pleasant, soothing sound that cheers those who are sad or depressed. Its breezes cool in the summer and shield one from cold and rain. Likewise, bodhicitta impartially enriches those destitute of compassion and wisdom. Bodhicitta protects from all fear and suffering, life after life. There is no danger of it being stolen; it can only be destroyed by one's own disturbing emotions. Similarly, in a family the father is usually responsible for taking care of everyone. Likewise, bodhicitta takes care of all sentient beings.

Bodhicitta bestows benefit on all sentient beings, regardless of who they are. If we have a *bias,* a preference for one being over another, this reveals that we have not yet realized bodhicitta. Bodhicitta is the foundation of the enlightened attitude and, from that perspective, *the bias of disciples is a lie.* This doesn't mean bodhicitta is indifferent or naïve. Bodhicitta is explicitly precise with objective discernment. It has no prejudice, but rather is a compassionate mind that extends to all sentient beings.

The ultimate purpose of training in bodhicitta is to realize the basic nature of samsara, which is emptiness; to open the wisdom mind; and to overcome confusion. With that explicit, precise, and prudent wisdom, we can see the cause of suffering in samsara and the cause of enlightenment. It allows us to use reason to abandon all the causes of suffering and bring the causes of enlightenment into our hearts.

When we accomplish this, we will know how to act skillfully in every situation, freeing both ourselves and others from suffering. In contrast, *nonvirtuous and misleading friends* encourage our self-cherishing and lead us to abandon the welfare of others.

> **When you understand that all sentient beings are your parents,**
> **attachment to self-cherishing is a lie.**
> **The shravakas' vehicle of self-liberation—**
> **think, can you put your trust in it?**

This doesn't mean that all beings are literally our *parents* in this life, but that they have been our parents in one lifetime or another since beginningless time. To get an idea of what we mean by "beginningless," consider which came first, the chicken or the egg. Generally speaking, we receive the greatest kindness from our parents. They show greater concern for us and do more for us than anyone else. From the day of our birth, year after year until we are grown, they nurture our physical and mental growth. They see to our needs without expecting anything in return. If a friend gives us a cup of tea we think she is kind and generous. In comparison, our parents have done much more for us and have spent countless thousands of hours and dollars caring for us. They are, therefore, the kindest of all people to us and nothing can compare to that kindness.

Sometimes we might experience differences with our parents. They may be mean and unkind. In reality, they don't want to be mean or to treat their children unkindly. Their disturbing emotions control them and don't allow them to do the right thing. Even animals and small bugs will sacrifice their lives for their offspring. But when their minds are dominated by clouds of afflictions and defilements, they have no choice but to create suffering. Their positive motivation and clear mind are obscured by these counterproductive emotions. So, to bring about real inner peace and happiness, we need to study bodhicitta and practice it sincerely to solve social problems. There really is no alternative. Enlightenment is not just for a few Buddhists; it is for the whole world.

Sometimes it happens that we might have a stronger connection with a close friend, another relative, or a teacher, than with our biological parents. If this is the case, we should use that relationship as our example and see ourselves enjoying that same kind of relationship with all sentient beings. Really practice that! Start from there and mentally practice repaying the kindness that we have received from them. Then expand this thought to all sentient beings. Our study and practice of Dharma teachings also depends on others' kindness. Through the spiritual master's skill and kindness, for example, we gain the opportunity to learn and practice the different steps of Dharma. So it is critical to observe carefully, and through that we can dismantle self-cherishing and build the altruistic mind to achieve ultimate bodhicitta.

Attachment to self-cherishing is a lie. Why is self-cherishing called a lie? Imagine that your parent, or whoever has shown you especially great kindness, is nearby and suffering great torment. Could you ignore their suffering and concentrate on your own business? That would be impossible; you would have to respond to their plight. The kind of self-cherishing that ignores others' pain will only make our own afflictions stronger, and we will suffer because of this.

The *shravakas,* or hearers, cannot bear the suffering of samsara for themselves, but they are not so concerned about others. They are strongly motivated for their own liberation, whereas bodhisattvas cannot bear the suffering of other sentient beings and are not concerned for themselves at all. They have transcended attachment and always sacrifice themselves for others. Therefore, we should abandon deceitful attachment to self-cherishing and self-liberation. Instead, we should engage in the bodhisattva's path.

> **When you become convinced of the cause and result of karma,**
> **the instruction of non-effort is a lie.**
> **Thunder without rain in an empty sky—**
> **think, can you put your trust in it?**

Here, the *instruction of non-effort* refers to a school of thought that asserts that within the state of emptiness nothing exists. There is no virtue or nonvirtue, nothing to accept or reject, because they are of the nature of emptiness. The exhaustion of mind and phenomena is the ultimate goal to achieve. The teachers who explain this doctrine have reasoned that since all phenomena of samsara and nirvana have the same taste from the ultimate perspective, there is no need to maintain moral discipline. In the state of one taste, no one thing is better than another; there is no objective reality to call good or bad. Therefore, they think it makes no difference whether one avoids negative actions or cultivates positive actions. The instruction to their students is that of non-effort. Since everything is the enlightened state, they say, one should just effortlessly abide in that state. Due to gross afflictions and a lack of realization of emptiness, they thus disavow causality. That makes this a very dangerous teaching that leads to carelessness and a complete absence of mindfulness.

Without realization, and in the name of high view, they make this error due to a lack of experience with insight. Such a dull mind has no discernment or awareness regarding infallible causality. According to the actual mode of abiding of all phenomena, results manifest unerringly according to their causes. The Buddha himself taught that even the realization of emptiness does not negate the operation of cause and effect.

To claim that in the realm of emptiness there are only random and inexplicable events, without wholesome deeds to accept or unwholesome deeds to reject, creates noise with no meaning—like *thunder without rain*. Great masters, those who have fully realized the teachings, are much more scrupulous than the average practitioner in matters of moral discipline. Because they are aware of every wholesome and unwholesome impulse that arises, they take great care to avoid even the smallest negative action and take advantage of every opportunity to perform even the smallest positive action. In contrast, those who have only studied about the view of mahamudra and emptiness have no realization. Without direct experience of the teachings, they just make a meaningless racket with their chatter.

All causalities function in the context of emptiness. Emptiness and phenomena cannot be separated; they are indivisible. So even within emptiness we cannot ignore causality. Even though the nature of causality is empty, without inherent existence, the results of whatever wholesome or unwholesome deeds we have created will come without fail. This is a universal truth that transcends all belief systems. As Dharma practitioners we must learn to be honest with ourselves and take care to examine our actions. When Gampopa was about to depart, his teacher Milarepa advised him:

> Even if you have no need to worry about falling into the lower realms be heedful not to commit the slightest misdeed. Even if you possess unshakable confidence in your eventual achievement of the awakened state, nevertheless take care to accumulate even the smallest increment of positive karma when the opportunity arises.

For our own benefit, we must learn how to be sincere and honest with ourselves and make every effort to act ethically. This will result in peace and happiness in our own lives, and from there we can extend help to others.

**For the guru who has the realization of power and blessings,
the obstacle of maras and error is a lie.
Chattering prayers like a parrot—
think, can you put your trust in that?**

The realization of power and blessings is true actualization of bodhicitta based on the accumulation of wisdom, merit, understanding, and blessings. When these qualities are in full power, especially the full realization of bodhicitta, there are no further obstacles. For one who has mastered the practice of bodhicitta, the nonduality of compassion and emptiness, any obstacles that arise become a part of meditation or the path. Such a bodhisattva has great skill and mental capacity to bring all positive and negative experiences onto the path to enlightenment.

Because obstacles arise out of the ordinary state where ignorance predominates, *maras* are powerless once enlightenment is achieved. When the mind is weak, there can be many hindrances and impediments. But when one has realization of both relative and absolute bodhicitta, no matter what kind of powerful obstacles there may be, they all become an aid that enhances peace. This is like a blazing fire that consumes everything in its path; even water can be an aid to such a fire. So one needs courage, devotion, and dedication to transform obstacles and problems into the path based on bodhicitta. When we have that skill, there is no need to ask for prayers to overcome obstacles.

When we have hope and fear, we say prayers to overcome obstacles and ask others to pray for us. Realized, enlightened beings don't depend on prayers. The point is that if we want to develop the mind, we must focus and train our mental abilities. How else could we realize wisdom and compassion? To neglect these qualities of mind and just recite prayers is actually to lose ground. Prayers support our meditation practice, but we shouldn't think that prayers alone will solve our problems. We also need action to understand and know Dharma, to practice it, and to embody bodhicitta.

> When you realize the nature of your mind,
> the three limitless kalpas are also a lie.
> The deceptive vehicle of relative truth—
> think, can you put your trust in it?

A *kalpa,* or eon, is equivalent to the time that it takes a world system to begin, maintain itself, dissolve into space, and then lie fallow. This is an inconceivably long period of time. The Buddha practiced for *three limitless kalpas* before attaining enlightenment. But once we fully realize the nature of mind, we don't have to wait three limitless kalpas before awakening. Then it's actually possible to achieve enlightenment in a single lifetime. Take Dharma Lord Gampopa as an example. After thoroughly studying with Kadampa teachers, he went to see Milarepa, from whom he received further teachings that he practiced day and night. On different occasions during these meditation sessions, he perceived Buddha Shakyamuni together with a thousand buddhas, and he also had a vision of the Hevajra mandala and many other deities. He reported these experiences to Milarepa, who said, "You have seen the Buddha's nirmanakaya and sambhogakaya. Now soon you will see the dharmakaya. So go back to Central Tibet and meditate without interruption." As his teacher instructed, Gampopa returned to the vicinity of his birthplace. After strict retreat for six consecutive years, he fully revealed the dharmakaya by realizing the absolute nature of mind and he attained enlightenment. Because of this, his activities of benefiting beings became incomparable, surpassing even those of other great teachers.

If we do not awaken in one lifetime, it is also possible to awaken within several lifetimes. It's a matter of which method we use and how much effort we put into practice. In this regard the Vajrayana is very special, because it emphasizes study and practice hand-in-hand. Through unbroken practice and continuously renewed experience, the teachings are kept pure. Today the great masters can still point directly at the nature of mind, enabling us also to recognize it and then practice in accordance with their instructions. This tradition, called the Practicing Lineage, is very effective because the practitioners are conditioned to have strong renunciation and invincible dedication to enlightenment.

We wander for ages in the realm of relative truth, unable to get out because we are deceived by it and fail to understand its fundamental nature. Once we can consistently and correctly discern phenomena and can identify positive and negative karma, samsara, and bodhicitta, we will no longer have to spend much time studying these things. We can then focus on the nature of mind, which is within us and is the heart of the teachings. To do this one needs a powerful yearning for enlightenment, little entanglement in samsaric self-interest, and a firm foundation of meditative equipoise.

In this life, all experience is ruled by the mind. Whether a thought is positive or negative is determined only by the mind. Peace and happiness depend on mind. The suffering of undesirable conditions is the result of our actions and is a perception of mind. From every direction, all phenomena lead back to mind. It's inevitable, then, that at a certain stage in our practice, the mind becomes the main focus of our meditation. Generally, we neglect the mind in the course of everyday life. We effortlessly attend to external things due to our habit from a long time, thinking, "If I only could get such and such thing, then I'd be happy." We are consumed with the projection of objects instead of being inwardly oriented. We usually think that our well-being depends on external objects, and that if we don't get certain things, we suffer. Instead of continuing in this way, we should attend to mind, because that is the essence of the practice. Through this, if the mind is directly and perfectly revealed, we will have an opportunity to experience the complete satisfaction of peace and joy without relying on any other objects. We will have gained the objective of our meditation practice, and our mission will have been accomplished.

> In the Gathering Relics cemetery,
> are you sad, son, at being alone?
> Since nothing lasts and all must die,
> Rinchen Drak, do not be attached.
> If your mind is still attached,
> transfer it to your guru's heart.

In this verse Jigten Sumgön is speaking to his disciple Rinchen Drak. Although clinically dead, Rinchen Drak's *mind was still attached* and he is grieving on account of it. With this compassionate song, Jigten Sumgön causes Rinchen Drak to recollect all the teachings he had learned and to fully and directly realize them. He could now release all his entanglements and achieve enlightenment.

This song is so precious and full of blessings. The power of the teachings contained in it cannot be overestimated. In this one short song, Jigten Sumgön teaches all the essential doctrines and practices. What skill he had! His words are incomparably profound and effective and, because of this, it is called a "vajra" song.

Of all the things that are dear to us, none lasts very long, and everyone who is born will eventually die. Everyone we meet in our life eventually separates from us, everything we accumulate eventually disperses, and whatever is constructed eventually disintegrates. This being so, Jigten Sumgön advised Rinchen Drak to release his attachment. He instructed Rinchen Drak *to transfer his mind* into the heart of Buddha Vajradhara, and here Guru Jigten Sumgön performed a transference of consciousness, called *phowa* in Tibetan. This was not the ordinary phowa, but rather one called Dharmakaya Phowa, in which Jigten Sumgön introduced the nature of his mind as inseparable from Jigten Sumgön's own mind. In that moment Rinchen Drak was able to see his own enlightened nature and was liberated. Rinchen Drak's body was then dismembered, and numerous precious relics were found in it. So, in the end, Rinchen Drak did display miraculous powers. His body was no longer an ordinary body but had become a vessel containing treasures.

There were so many relics from this incident that they had to be gathered up with a broom. The charnel ground where this miracle occurred was originally called Horse Running Platform, but after this incident was known as *Gathering Relics* Platform. Since this place had become a popular location to bring corpses for sky burial, Jigten Sumgön created a special place there for the benefit of future generations. He opened a mandala called Purification of the Lower Realms and placed it under a large slab of stone that is still there today. Also under that slab, he created a light that will burn until the end of this kalpa and benefit anyone whose body is brought there, making a connection for them to be freed from birth in the lower realms.

In addition to these miracles, around that same time a dakini from the most famous cemetery in India, Sandalwood Forest Cemetery, arrived at the Drigung charnel ground bearing a big piece of rock. She said, "If the heads of corpses are placed against this stone, none of those beings will fall into the lower realms." The rock is still there at the charnel ground. All the corpses brought there are dismembered and given to the vultures, without a trace being left. This practice is environmentally and spiritually clean. For these reasons, sky burial at the Drigung charnel ground remains very popular among Tibetans.

7. Vajra Song at Tsa-uk called "Tsa-uk Dzong Drom"

In order to open this secret place, and to inspire the exertion of his disciples, Jigten Sumgön went to Tsa-uk and sang this song, called "Tsa-uk Dzong Drom":

I bow at the feet of glorious Phagmo Drupa.
By the great kindness of glorious Phagmo Drupa,
certainty was born in my mind.
I obtained the confidence of bodhicitta.
I, a yogin, remain in solitude.

My experience and realization come out as mere words.
Even for you disciples who are proper vessels
experience and realization are difficult.
I, a yogin, remain in solitude.

My qualities have become a source of wealth
that provokes attachment and aggression.
Consuming the food of Mara is a cause of many faults.
I, a yogin, remain in solitude.

My attendants are distracted.
It is not helpful to keep bad company.
There is no end to the actions of attachment and aggression.
I, a yogin, remain in solitude.

My monks are insincere.
Many don't think about the needs of this life and the next.

Feeding a retinue of cattle is a cause of many faults.
I, a yogin, remain in solitude.

My actions have been [only] for this life.
I [only] aspire to worldly dharmas.
This deceives faithful disciples.
I, a yogin, remain in solitude.

A phantom crosses a mirage river.
Dream bees sip a sky lotus.
The son of a barren woman plays and sings the music of gandharvas.
Those who are childish and have no experience or realization
say that one can realize the absolute truth through worldly activities.

[But] one's pure and stainless mind
abides with the precious teachings
on the mountain of nonduality.
The forest of great bliss grows dense.

The wild animals of recollection and mindfulness roam about.
They consume the grass and water of bliss, clarity, and nonconceptual
    thought.
If you desire solitude, practice this way.
I, a yogin, remain in solitude.

INTRODUCTION

WHEN WE STUDY a song or text like this, it is important to first
cultivate the mind of enlightenment, or bodhicitta. We can easily see
the benefit of such studies for ourselves, but it is more important that we
study these precious teachings for the benefit of our families, society, country, and all other sentient beings in samsara. Through our Dharma studies
and practice we can develop the wisdom of knowing how to benefit others.
This is the real reason to study and practice the precious Dharma. The Buddha taught this, and we must sincerely try to develop this altruistic thought
by understanding that we are all interconnected within the framework of
causality.

The author of this short song was Jigten Sumgön, whose life story is briefly recounted in *Great Kagyu Masters, Calling to the Lama from Afar, Prayer Flags,* and the later chapters of this book. He may not be as widely known today as other masters; nevertheless, he was one of the greatest teachers ever to come into this world. Jigten Sumgön presented the Dharma in an all-encompassing manner that demonstrated it to be more than a narrow system to be followed by rote. He shows each and every one of us how to be true to ourselves and sincere toward other sentient beings. His way of teaching was empirical, explicitly precise, and based on the real understanding of samsara and nirvana that transcends distorted tenets.

By way of a short introduction to Jigten Sumgön's teachings, we can examine positive and negative karma. Jigten Sumgön taught that karma is not simply a notion belonging to one tradition. Rather, it is the actual constitution of the universe and the complete nature of samsara and nirvana, both the unenlightened and enlightened states. Samsara is established by our state of delusion and the resulting negative thoughts that give rise to negative karma. Because of this, we wander round and round, endlessly creating additional negative karma. This repetitive pattern applies to the minds of all sentient beings, not just in one culture or to a particular type of person.

Due to our karmic imprints, we continually wander in delusion from rebirth to rebirth in different realms, depending on the causes we have created. There are six realms of relative existence in which sentient beings take rebirth depending on the intensity of their negative or positive karma. And within each of these, many different levels of suffering are supported by our habitual tendencies. The mind of enlightenment is a state of mind free from delusion, negative mental habits, obscurations, and karma.

Nirvana, like samsara, also consists of many levels of enlightenment, such as those of the shravaka, pratyekabuddha, bodhisattva, and buddha. Both samsara and nirvana are formations of one's state of mind. This is what Jigten Sumgön's teachings are about. Samsara is a state of confusion; its result is an endless state of suffering. Nirvana is the exhaustion and dissipation of suffering; its result is liberation from suffering.

All happiness and peace arise from the ten virtues. Three are related to the mind: (1) contentment or appreciation, (2) love and compassion, and (3) right understanding based on wisdom. Three are associated with the body: (4) not taking life, and respecting and protecting others' lives; (5) practicing generosity and openness of the mind; and (6) keeping pure moral conduct. The last four concern speech: (7) speaking the truth, (8) harmonizing speech, (9) using gentle and respectful words, and (10) speaking meaningful words. Anyone who practices these ten virtues possesses the source of peace and happiness.

At the same time, all suffering and undesirable conditions arise from the ten nonvirtues. There are also three of these related to the mind: (1) covetousness and greed, (2) aversion and resentment, and (3) confused, wrong view. Three are associated with the body: (4) taking others' lives, (5) stealing, and (6) sexual misconduct or harassment. The last four concern speech: (7) telling lies, (8) divisive speech, (9) harsh words, and (10) idle talk. Worldly actions based on these ten are the source of suffering and negative influences.

These ten virtues and nonvirtues were clearly explained by the Buddha and have application to both the secular and spiritual worlds. His penetrating teachings clarify the demarcation between the sources of peace, happiness, and enlightenment, and the sources of confusion, defilement, and suffering. Since we all are equal in wanting to experience peace and happiness and be free from suffering, we must all closely watch ourselves and act on the basis of the ten virtues. All spiritual paths and methods entirely depend on this. We have every opportunity to use our intelligence to decide which direction to choose.

Jigten Sumgön taught that genuine Buddhism is not just intellectualization or theoretical knowledge. Instead, he said, the main point is how much we practice and actualize what we have learned. If we have not practiced, the teachings are reduced to mere academic knowledge. We may know Dharma and be able to express it eloquently, but if we lack practice, the meaning of Dharma cannot be experienced and we will have no chance to taste realization. When it comes to facing difficulties and obstacles we will remain ordinary samsaric beings. Therefore, in order to gain benefit from the teachings, we have to implement them sincerely.

We can become free from delusion and negative thoughts because these things are not permanent or substantial. Instead, they are like clouds, fog, or a magic show. When there is fog we can't see into the distance or even clearly see what is nearby. But clouds and fog are temporary and insubstantial. In the same manner, when our mind is clouded by a fog of negative thoughts and afflicting emotions, we can't perceive what is right or wrong. But if we practice and make great effort, it is just a matter of time until the delusion disappears. When we can see negative thought as nonexistent, it dissolves. It came from nowhere and it dissolves into nothing. Release from suffering, then, becomes a matter of how seriously and sincerely we practice. No matter how thick the samsaric habit, it can still be erased because it is just an adventitious defilement. In addition, our essential nature is that of a buddha, so we have within ourselves the complete potential for enlightenment.

This is the purpose of having a precious human life. We work hard to bring happiness and peace into our lives, but there is no way to achieve real peace through material goods alone. Perhaps we can accomplish a little artificial joy and happiness, but these don't last long. Truly substantial and lasting happiness and peace can be established only by exercising our inner mind with the precious Dharma teachings. This is the purpose of our meditation practice, and this is what Jigten Sumgön taught. Mental afflictions and neuroses can be pacified only through the Dharma. Dharma is the ultimate remedy for confusion.

In order to open this secret place, and to inspire the exertion of his disciples, Jigten Sumgön went to Tsa-uk and sang this song, called "Tsa-uk Dzong Drom."

Jigten Sumgön came to Drigung when he was thirty-seven, as prophesied by his guru Phagmo Drupa. There, he established the monastery that he named Jangchub Ling (Center of Enlightenment). Later it became popularly known as Drigung Thil, a place for enlightenment. He presided there for about thirty-eight years and taught Dharma to the many disciples who gathered there from throughout Tibet. He explained the meaning of Dharma at many different levels according to the disposition and mental capacity of the various individuals in order to free them from samsara. He particularly emphasized retreat practice so that disciples could experience the teachings for themselves.

Among his numerous disciples, a few didn't conduct their lives according to Dharma. Therefore, to open Tsa-uk for future Dharma practitioners, and also to inspire these disciples to practice more sincerely, Jigten Sumgön left for Tsa-uk without notice. Although he had gone without notifying the monks, they later found him and followed him out there. Each monk brought a rock, which they piled up to make a large, auspicious throne. Jigten Sumgön sat on that throne and sang this song on this occasion.

I heard the story of this sacred place long ago and had developed a strong aspiration to visit there and receive its blessings. Finally in July 2004, I had a chance to go there with a small group of people from Sweden and the U.S.

It was during the Monkey year anniversary teachings at Drigung, which happen every twelve years. Usually, the ceremonies last about two weeks, but that year they lasted only three days. Nevertheless, almost 300,000 participants filled the Drigung valley.

I inquired about Tsa-uk from many different people, asking about its location, the distance from Drigung Thil Monastery, and so forth. Everyone gave a different answer, which confused me and discouraged us from going there. Fortunately, in the end, a monk from Tsa-uk approached me and when I expressed an interest in visiting his home region he said, "Let's go tomorrow!" So, we all decided to go.

We left in the early morning and drove for some distance in the mud and dust of a rough road. The valley was breathtakingly beautiful, filled with bushes and beautiful flowers. It held a serenity that was intensely pacifying to our being. After the road faded out, we had to continue on foot. We crossed streams of glacier ice melt, which pierced our feet with cold. The rocky, snow-covered mountain was very high, and below we could see forests and fragrant grasslands with flowers and springs.

Jigten Sumgön's cave at Tsa-uk is a very sacred place. It is special because of his activities there, and also because many lifelong retreatants have gained realization there over the intervening years. When he first saw the cave, he thought that it was a little small, so he pushed the ceiling up and the walls out. Then he said that the cave was a little dark, so he made a window by putting his hand through the rock. Then he said the cave was somewhat plain, so he made a place to hang his bag and other things. Today, the area houses a small monastery with a few monks. The monks showed us Jigten Sumgön's imprints in the rock—hand, foot, and body prints made as easily as those of a child playing in the mud.

Tsa-uk is still an ideal place for retreatants, with an unobstructed view and fresh air. Just below the cave is a spring that was revealed by Jigten Sumgön for the retreatants in that vicinity. It rained off and on the day we were there. Even though there is a roof over the entrance to the cave, I noticed that water was leaking inside, so I made a small donation to improve the roof.

COMMENTARY

> I bow at the feet of glorious Phagmo Drupa.
> By the great kindness of glorious Phagmo Drupa,
> certainty was born in my mind.

I obtained the confidence of bodhicitta.
I, a yogin, remain in solitude.

Phagmo Drupa was Jigten Sumgön's principal teacher. Jigten Sumgön had received teachings such as lamrim, mahamudra, and Vajrayana instructions from several other great masters, but it was Phagmo Drupa who introduced him to the buddha mind. And it was from him that Jigten Sumgön received the complete lineage teachings of the Buddha.

Sometimes Phagmo Drupa scolded Jigten Sumgön, but in a very compassionate and skillful way with *kindness* rooted in his mind. No matter how harshly Phagmo Drupa spoke, his main focus was to inspire his students to practice the Dharma. All the Buddha's teachings were imparted to Jigten Sumgön and many of his other great disciples in this way. Because of his direct, pure, and penetrating style of teachings, many of Phagmo Drupa's disciples achieved enlightenment in a single lifetime.

It is through practice that practitioners can become free from confusion and deeply root the Dharma teachings in their hearts. When that happens, there is no doubt that a person will become free from samsara. Becoming free from samsara does not result from just having an expectation or wish. We can become liberated only by studying and practicing the Dharma teachings. Bringing the Dharma teachings into our heart, striving to implement them, and making an effort to maintain those teachings in our mind—*that* is called Dharma practice. There is no special place to go to become free from samsara. It is a journey of the mind, a mental journey that is taken through the study and practice of these precious teachings. These songs of Jigten Sumgön are pith instructions. They are the essence of the teachings, brought to a single point. This is the *great kindness of the glorious Phagmo Drupa.*

Phagmo Drupa gave these teachings out of great wisdom and compassion, and Jigten Sumgön practiced them sincerely. Jigten Sumgön said in this verse that *certainty was born in my mind,* meaning that he had direct realization of these teachings. This is important, because only when you are fully experienced in the Dharma can such certainty arise. When there is no certainty, even though we may have vast intellectual knowledge of the teachings, fear, doubt, and hesitation will remain. The cloud of afflictions will pervade the sky of clear mind.

Jigten Sumgön *obtained the confidence of bodhicitta,* meaning that he embodied bodhicitta. Bodhicitta is the nature of his mind and embraces every sentient being. Not one is excluded. Bodhicitta is the perfection of the mind freed from all delusions. This is the mind that has unlimited wisdom and compassion, like limitless space. That mind was born in Jigten Sumgön's heart when he attained complete buddhahood, because buddhahood and complete perfection of bodhicitta are one and the same.

Jigten Sumgön is *a yogin*, which means an accomplished practitioner. Sometimes we use the term "yogin" for people who are married lamas, but that is not necessarily the case. Anyone can become a yogin, whether fully ordained or lay. He *remains in solitude* means he was inspired to practice Dharma wholeheartedly and to purify all his mental afflictions, which are the root cause of suffering. We, too, can reveal our inner, innate nature and experience it directly, as he did.

There are different types of *solitude:* physical solitude and mental solitude. Physical solitude occurs when you go to a mountain, or some other secluded place, and physically remain there without engaging in samsaric activities. Mental solitude means having a mind free from negative thoughts. With mental solitude, it doesn't matter where your body is; you can be in the market or at an assembly and your mind will remain in the solitary state. But in the beginning, it is necessary to protect the mind in order to achieve mental solitude. It is initially useful to put your body into solitude until your mind becomes accustomed to that state. Once the mind is free from negative thoughts and you become accustomed and habituated to that state, the mind has infinite capacity to generate enlightenment. A single-pointed mind can capture both equipoise and special insight. In a busy and mentally distracted state, the mind is fragile and doesn't have the ability to implement these practices, leaving us doomed to delusion. But freed from the bonds of negative thoughts, the mind awakens. Because of this, you can experience the whole of samsara as a state of enlightenment. This is the essence of the Dharma teachings.

> My experience and realization come out as mere words.
> Even for you disciples who are proper vessels
> experience and realization are difficult.
> I, a yogin, remain in solitude.

Experience is the understanding gained in the process of progressing on the path. As you study and practice, a variety of experiences arise as signs of progress. For instance, if we study the five paths, the ten bhumis, and so on, within each of these are many types of experiences. All of those experiences are of a relative nature. They manifest due to the purification of the mind and the development of good qualities; through this, one can achieve realization. Realization of dharmakaya is the fully enlightened state, the unchanging nature. The realization of enlightenment cannot change because it is the ultimate state; there is nothing higher to achieve. But even within that state, different experiences can manifest. Jigten Sumgön is saying that he taught these teachings out of his own *experience and realization,* not just through intellectual understanding, so they are pure and precious. But if you don't practice and experience them, they are *mere words.*

Jigten Sumgön then mentions those *who are proper vessels.* The first quality of such a disciple is great honesty, based on bodhicitta, toward oneself and others. The second quality is the power of intelligence, the mental capacity to capture both the vastness and the profundity of the teachings. The third quality is great courage, inspiration, and the interest to study and practice these teachings. As proper vessels, whatever Dharma study and practice we do can become a cause to free us from samsara and, thus, bring about benefit both for ourselves and others.

Jigten Sumgön is saying that even for those who are proper vessels, sometimes it is still *difficult* to give up negative habits and to understand and realize the teachings. Our negative habits are deeply rooted, and they insidiously pollute our mind with harmful mental tendencies that take a long time to remove. These negative habits are so entrenched that sometimes we can feel frustrated. We want to purify our negative thoughts and we want to purify our delusions, yet it seems like nothing happens. This is like discovering a big rock inside your house. You would like to get rid of it, but if it can't be moved, it's just a source of frustration. As Dharma practitioners, we want to practice well and bring the Dharma teachings into our heart, but sometimes the negative habituated thoughts that manifest in our mind are so strong that we may feel our Dharma practice is going nowhere. Even sincere practitioners may have that feeling. Therefore, Jigten Sumgön is reminding us that we must consistently persevere in our practice. We should repeatedly practice with confidence, inspiration, and courage whatever teachings we have received. Progress is inevitable because afflictions are impermanent; it's just a matter of time.

My qualities have become a source of wealth
that provokes attachment and aggression.

Consuming the food of Mara is a cause of many faults.
I, a yogin, remain in solitude.

During the time of Jigten Sumgön, the Drigung Thil Monastery became one of the richest ever to have existed. Because of Jigten Sumgön's great wisdom and compassion toward all sentient beings and his limitless activities, many offerings were made to the monastery by his hundreds of thousands of disciples and their patrons. In addition to the great offerings made by human beings, many nonhuman beings, such as gods and nagas, also made offerings. Enormous *wealth* was effortlessly gathered there.

If wealth is not used in the right way to benefit sentient beings, it *provokes attachment* and jealousy. When wealth, power, or authority provoke attachment, aggression and pride in others, we can see how much attachment, aggression and hatred we ourselves harbor and have an opportunity to purify these things. We have many limitations, and it is important that we recognize them, acknowledge them, and make efforts to more sincerely and effectively practice Dharma. If we do recognize and acknowledge our limitations, we will better know how to handle the obstacles and problems we encounter.

Many people believe that wealth and power can bring happiness and joy. If used wisely, skillfully, and in accord with Dharma, they can indeed benefit many people for this life. But if these people become attached to power and indulge that fixation, then material goods will be merely a source of confusion and suffering for themselves and others in society. Collecting material wealth and power will not give us satisfaction. The more we have, the more we will want. Jigten Sumgön gives us the wisdom to develop inner wisdom and wealth, and to avoid the frustrations of indulging in pointless accumulation.

Jigten Sumgön admonishes us to be of service. The more we live in service to others, the greater benefit we will bring. Dharma is the ultimate source of peace and joy, not of authority or power.

Dharma centers are established as places for people to come to study and practice the teachings. They are not places to seek advancement, power, or authority over others. When it is useful, we should present our ideas; but when this is not useful, we should remain quiet. We should present an idea only if it is constructive and not because we want prestige or power. It is important to recognize that we do not really benefit others through power or authority. These things will inevitably come to us, even if we don't want them, when we have a sincere motivation. So it is important to reflect on the Dharma teachings, use the Dharma as a mirror to show us our limitations, and purify these inveterate propensities.

Mara is a personification of the *cause of many faults*. The *food of Mara* refers to wealth that is infused with self-aggrandizement. There is no benefit in the food of Mara. So when we find ourselves tempted by it, it would be better for us to stay in solitude, to apply Dharma in the mind, and to remain still and quiet. This will bring the peace and joy for which we are searching. The Buddha said that he gave these teachings in order to dissolve confusion, delusion, and conflict. He explained that in samsara there are already enough causes of suffering, so if the Dharma teachings only become another cause of problems, it might be better not to give them. We should repeatedly remind ourselves that the purpose of our study is to solve our own problems, which, in turn, becomes a way to solve the problems of others. It is each individual's own responsibility to practice sincerely for themselves. Then, through individual practice and progress on the path, we will become able to share our wisdom and skillful means sincerely with others.

> My attendants are distracted.
> It is not helpful to keep bad company.
> There is no end to the actions of attachment and aggression.
> I, a yogin, remain in solitude.

Jigten Sumgön's attendants and disciples were known to be great practitioners. Even so, there were some disciples who needed to be reminded to do better and not allow their thoughts to scatter. His disciples felt that they had a wonderful, great teacher—like the Buddha himself—but he didn't want this to make them lazy or to think that they could just relax and not sincerely practice. So he says *my attendants are distracted*. Some of them strayed from Dharma study and practice and toward external objects. When the mind is distracted, we think about things such as how to make ourselves attractive, rich, or powerful. Instead of entertaining such thoughts, we should dwell on how to receive the teachings, how to practice Dharma successfully, and how to apply it in our heart. We should be thinking about how to make the Dharma teachings a part of our lives and how to free ourselves from samsara. We need to remind ourselves repeatedly that all composite phenomena are impermanent and that samsara is a state of suffering.

When the mind is distracted, keeping *bad company* invites all kinds of confusion and delusions. Constantly disparaging others with attachment and aggression destroys peace of mind. No matter how much Dharma we know, it becomes useless if it is not implemented. It is insignificant how much we know intellectually. What matters is whether we have practiced Dharma. If we have not, then even if we receive the same teaching many times or receive the most profound teachings, such as mahamudra or highest yoga tantra, this will not help. Dharma is not magic. However, if we have practiced and applied Dharma in our daily life, then each word of Dharma, every sentence, becomes rich, fresh, and alive.

We create negative karma through actions of attachment and aggression. Karma is the ultimate tyrant because it doesn't deviate from its result or give us a chance to choose—we just have to go along with it without choice. Whatever we do based in ignorance, whether samsaric activities or Dharma activities, the result is the same—negative karma. Actually, if we create negative karma in the name of the Dharma, the results may be even worse. At that point, it would be better to stay in solitude.

There are many activities we can do in samsara. But we don't have enough time to do everything, so we must make choices. Dharma should be used in a good way to solve conflicts or clarify delusions. If, instead, Dharma teachings are abused and used as a source of conflict to empower ourselves, then they have no purpose, and it would be better for us to stay in solitude. Without Dharma, we will continue to wander in delusion, from one lifetime to another. It is imperative that we awaken. Just as we go to sleep and awaken in the morning, we must also awaken from the sleep of ignorance. We should reveal our buddha nature.

> My monks are insincere.
> Many don't think about the needs of this life and the next.
> Feeding a retinue of cattle is a cause of many faults.
> I, a yogin, remain in solitude.

This verse doesn't mean that Jigten Sumgön's monks didn't have good Dharma understanding or good practice. He wanted his monks to have the best scholarship and practice so that they could attain enlightenment. But, the mind sometimes wanders to samsaric attachment and is concerned with samsaric benefit. When our minds are distracted with affairs that only concern selfish aims, and when we are not concerned about the causes we are creating, we are not using this life to its best effect. That mind becomes disingenuous. Every word that we study and all our practice should be used to free our mind from negative thoughts, free our life from samsara, and attain enlightenment. We have precious human lives that possess every potential and opportunity to pursue the methods and teachings of the Dharma. If we squander this rare opportunity, we will not fulfill our life's purpose.

In *The Jewel Ornament of Liberation* Gampopa says that throughout samsara, from the topmost god realms to the depths of hell, nowhere is there any absolute peace and happiness to be found. There is artificial happiness, peace, and joy, but this is temporary, transitory in nature, and pervaded by suffering. It doesn't make sense to attach ourselves to samsaric happiness and peace while we are professing to study and practice the Dharma. With no attachment to samsaric happiness, the mind can be fully involved in the pure Dharma teachings.

Gampopa also taught that, in order to counter attachment to this life, we should contemplate the impermanent and ephemeral nature of phenomena. Look back and reflect on your life and see how much suffering and how much joy and happiness you have experienced. From the vantage point of this present moment, everything that has passed seems like a dream. If we have had a happy life, it now seems like a good dream. If we have had a difficult life, it is also like a dream—a nightmare, but nothing worse. Try to see reality from this point of view. There is no benefit to being attached to our past good life, because it will not come back. There is also no benefit to holding on to resentment and rage over bad experiences because they are also past.

When we can see and accept that life is temporary and momentary, our mind will be more peaceful and more harmonious. Then when difficult things arise in life, they won't affect us so much. Even when very good things come in life, there will not be much attachment because our mind will have achieved an even and stable state.

When we have a mass of conflict and confusion, we create negative karma and are no better off than *cattle*. As human beings with precious human lives, we have a profound intellect that gives us the ability to see and understand the reality of the whole universe. Therefore, we should sincerely practice Dharma. When we lack the wisdom to acknowledge our precious human life, and don't see its great potential, it is as if our lives really were nothing special, like those of cattle. When we understand the preciousness of human life, we dare not waste even a minute. It is important to appreciate and rejoice in the great opportunity we have.

We should look at samsara as an opportunity to acquire wisdom. When we contemplate who, within the six realms of samsara, has the best opportunity to become free of samsara, it is the humans. We don't need to think of ourselves as superior, but it is useful to acknowledge its great potential so that we don't waste this opportunity. Once we gain that realization, our precious human life can then be utilized in a very productive way, and we will no longer waste time and energy on lesser concerns.

Before we begin to share Dharma with others, we must establish ourselves in the awakened state. This is crucial. Take time to reflect and digest the teachings within yourself. We must recognize that our own mind must first be firmly established in the awakened state. We need to contemplate and check whether we are really established in that state. It helps to ask, "What is my weakness?" Just look at that question and practice. Then, after a substantial time of being established in the awakened state, we can begin to share what we know with others.

Here in samsara, we are like news reporters. We acquire information and then quickly turn around and give it out to others. In Dharma, it is completely the other way around. In Dharma we must first establish ourselves in the awakened state before we can have anything to share with others. The purpose of our practice is to establish our own mind in the Dharma teachings. Once the mind is fully established in the Dharma teachings, we will reflect peace and harmony, and this automatically makes others happy when we share this wisdom with them.

> **My actions have been [only] for this life.**
> **I [only] aspire to worldly dharmas.**
> **This deceives faithful disciples.**
> **I, a yogin, remain in solitude.**

This life will go on whether it's good or bad. One day we will die, but although that may be the end of one life, it's not the end of samsara. The absolute objective of Dharma study and practice is to get out of samsara. Recalling this, the teacher and the students both have a big responsibility.

Here, Jigten Sumgön is indirectly saying that teachers should not behave in ways aimed only at securing a happy samsaric life, of gaining their own benefit. Authentic teachers, who have established themselves in scholarship and realization, inspire others to free themselves from samsara. They do not focus on creating the causes of achievements in this life. Similarly, disciples must also be careful to ensure that they are not simply feeding their egos and attachment but rather are utilizing the Dharma to uproot the causes of samsara.

> A phantom crosses a mirage river.
> Dream bees sip a sky lotus.
> The son of a barren woman plays and sings the music of gandharvas.
> Those who are childish and have no experience or realization
> say that one can realize the absolute truth through worldly activities.

These three metaphors are very beautiful poetic images, but they describe things that don't exist. Jigten Sumgön had great skill to use these metaphors to point out how reality functions. If we contemplate these images and carefully penetrate their meaning at a deep level, they will give us a vivid and clear picture. In order to free ourselves from samsara, it is indispensable to have all the necessary causes and conditions. Worldly activities cannot bring us to enlightenment, which is beyond samsara. In other words, a confused and deluded mind cannot perceive the enlightenment mind.

In order to develop the mind of enlightenment, it is very important to study all three collections of the Dharma step by step and understand their respective meanings. After studying, it is important to contemplate them using valid cognition. Some inexperienced teachers may give the impression that you can gain realization through study and investigation while remaining involved in the eight worldly concerns. That would be like a phantom crossing a mirage river, a dream bee sipping a sky lotus, or the talented son of a barren woman. In order to experience the absolute truth, the indispensable method for a practitioner is to choose solitude, establish the mind in meditative absorption, and remain in equipoise. Thus supported, special insight will kindle the mind of enlightenment.

> [But] one's pure and stainless mind
> abides with the precious teachings
> on the mountain of nonduality.
> The forest of great bliss grows dense.

On the other hand, one who fully renounces samsaric activities and who cultivates a pure motivation to attain complete enlightenment without concern for this life will transcend all delusions and obscurations. One who abides with the precious teachings of both relative and absolute bodhicitta can sustain stability in equipoise and realize inseparable luminosity and emptiness. Then, the great qualities of buddhahood will be revealed without a doubt. This type of life causes the *forest of great bliss* to grow *dense* with excellent qualities because one is far from suffering and its origin. One can then abide forever in that great forest of unafflicted bliss.

> **The wild animals of recollection and mindfulness roam about.**
> **They consume the grass and water of bliss, clarity, and**
>   **nonconceptual thought.**
> **If you desire solitude, practice this way.**
> **I, a yogin, remain in solitude.**

This verse is inspirational for those who dwell in solitude and are well established in their meditation. They are able to roam about with mindfulness and enjoy the enlightened qualities of *bliss, clarity, and nonconceptual thought.*

Successful meditation practice does not depend only on how many mantras you have recited, the number of prostrations you have done, or the quantity of other Dharma activities you may have performed. Rather, it is judged by how much mindfulness you have. We develop this through meditation, either with or without effort. At first, we have to apply many skills and methods in order to achieve calm abiding through effort. The most important thing is to look at the faults of samsara. The happiness of samsara is just a dissipating ripple, but the waves of suffering are constant. Then reflect on the good qualities of enlightenment—absolute joy and happiness. With such methods of contemplation, one can progress to meditation without effort. As we get used to meditation, less effort is required because we have become habituated to meditating. Mindfulness then enjoys free rein as the mind becomes more workable. Eventually, we can enjoy the unafflicted enlightened qualities of bliss, clarity, and nonconceptual thought in the context of mahamudra. Jigten Sumgön advises us to *practice in this way,* and we would be wise to follow him.

There are two ways to create happiness and joy: materially and mentally. The material approach is more obvious and easier for average people. But if we realistically examine this approach, we'll find that it is limited, and sometimes it backfires to cause suffering. The mental approach is more difficult, but with study and practice we can come to understand the important role of the mind. Once we are tuned in to the practice, especially meditation, we can appreciate contentment and pursue the revelation of inner qualities, wisdom, compassion, and so forth. In this way, we can experience full satisfaction by transforming confusion into wisdom.

When Jigten Sumgön sang this song and taught it to his disciples, they were deeply inspired. Those already accomplished in meditation reinforced their practice. Many made powerful commitments to go into retreat. As a result, many of the best practitioners achieved enlightenment. Even inferior practitioners fully actualized the nature of mind and became free of samsara.

8. Song of the Six Confidences

Taklung Thangpa, seeing the inconceivable increase of Jigten Sumgön's activities, sent offerings to him and said, "I have further teachings given by our guru, Phagmo Drupa; it would be of great benefit if you were to receive these." In reply, Jigten Sumgön sent offerings of his own, including this song:

I bow at the feet of glorious Phagmo Drupa.
By the great kindness of glorious Phagmo Drupa,
I experienced bliss.
I obtained the confidence of bodhicitta.

I, a yogin, realized the unity of view, meditation, and action.
There are no sessions to practice.
In non-effort I, the yogin, am happy.
This happy yogin experiences joy.
This experience of joy is the guru's kindness.

I, a yogin, realized the unity of the guru, my own mind, and the Buddha.
I have no need of superficial devotion.
In non-effort I, the yogin, am happy.
This happy yogin experiences joy.
This experience of joy is the guru's kindness.

I, a yogin, realized the unity of parents, yidams, and the six types of beings.
There is no need for the [superficial] benefit of others.
In non-effort I, the yogin, am happy.
This happy yogin experiences joy.
This experience of joy is the guru's kindness.

I, a yogin, realized the unity of the sutras, the tantras, and their
commentaries.
I have no need of written texts.
In non-effort I, the yogin, am happy.
This happy yogin experiences joy.
This experience of joy is the guru's kindness.

I, a yogin, realized the unity of this life, the next, and the bardo.
There is no boundary of death.
In non-effort I, the yogin, am happy.
This happy yogin experiences joy.
This experience of joy is the guru's kindness.

Day and night, in all six sessions, through strong devotion,
I am always with the authentic guru.
I, the inseparable yogin, am happy.
This happy yogin experiences joy.
This experience of joy is the guru's kindness.

This "Song of the Six Confidences"
I offer to the ear of glorious Taklung Thangpa.
I don't feel that the time I attended the guru was short.
He accepted me, and taught me fully.

INTRODUCTION

To FREE OURSELVES from samsara, we need to understand the
Dharma step by step, beginning with the teachings on precious human
life. We must then come to see all composite phenomena as impermanent,
to perceive the nature of suffering, and to comprehend inexorable karmic
causation. We should also understand that these are not just beliefs or part
of a cultural system but that they describe how things universally function.
Contemplate these concepts for yourself. Once you become convinced of
impermanence, the suffering of samsara, and the way phenomena are constituted, abolish any laziness concerning Dharma practice.

Many different kinds of laziness keep us from pursuing religious practice, such as the laziness of being attached to pleasure and the laziness of
staying busy with samsaric activities. Not wanting to sacrifice attachment
to samsara is also a type of laziness. Instead of focusing on how precious

Dharma is, we remain distracted by our own thoughts and ego. It would be better to take advantage of this remarkable opportunity to study and practice Dharma now, before it is too late and we regret not having done so. We study and practice in order to purify attachment to samsaric habits. We can build the courage to sacrifice self-clinging and develop compassion for all sentient beings. That is a bodhisattva's activity. We have the same opportunity to do this as anyone else, if we will only make an effort.

Taklung Thangpa, seeing the inconceivable increase of Jigten Sumgön's activities, sent offerings to him and said, "I have further teachings given by our guru, Phagmo Drupa; it would be of great benefit if you were to receive them." In reply, Jigten Sumgön sent offerings of his own, including this song.

Taklung Thangpa attended Phagmo Drupa for many years until Phagmo Drupa entered parinirvana. As one of Phagmo Drupa's foremost disciples, he received many great teachings and later founded the Taklung Kagyu lineage. He was also a particularly close vajra brother of Jigten Sumgön. When Jigten Sumgön's activities unimaginably flourished, Taklung Thangpa noticed that he had gathered hundreds and thousands of disciples. Because Taklung Thangpa had attended Phagmo Drupa much longer than Jigten Sumgön had, he sincerely thought it would be beneficial to both Jigten Sumgön and his many disciples to offer him additional teachings.

However, unbeknownst to Taklung Thangpa, Jigten Sumgön had already achieved enlightenment. All the Buddha's teachings were revealed within his enlightened mind. He was confident that no subject was hidden from him, so he replied without arrogance, "I have the complete teachings," and sent back offerings of his own accompanied by this song. This song reveals Jigten Sumgön's realization of mahamudra and the dharmakaya state. Since it was written from the perspective of buddhahood, it may be difficult for us ordinary beings to comprehend.

COMMENTARY

I bow at the feet of glorious Phagmo Drupa.
By the great kindness of glorious Phagmo Drupa,
I experienced bliss.
I obtained the confidence of bodhicitta.

Phagmo Drupa was one of Jigten Sumgön's principal teachers, the one from whom he received all the teachings of the lineage, including the ultimate instructions on mahamudra. Because of that guidance, he was successful in Dharma practice and attained complete enlightenment. Paying homage *at the feet of glorious Phagmo Drupa* indicates that Jigten Sumgön perceived Phagmo Drupa as the embodiment of all the buddhas of the three times—past, present, and future. *The great kindness* refers to Phagmo Drupa's unsurpassable wisdom and compassion, which enabled him to transmit those important teachings into the hearts of Jigten Sumgön and other disciples.

Bliss refers to the state free from all suffering, the complete realization of the all-pervading dharmakaya where nothing is hidden and one is free from all fears. There, nothing remains of suffering or its causes. This state is called "unafflicted bliss" and is not related to any type of thought. Because Jigten Sumgön diligently and sincerely practiced and fully realized the teachings, he was able to say, *I experienced bliss.*

Jigten Sumgön *obtained the confidence of bodhicitta,* meaning that he realized both relative and absolute bodhicitta when he attained buddhahood. Vast and profound bodhicitta is the consummate teaching of Buddhism. Buddhism is beneficial to every single being because of bodhicitta, the mind that embraces everyone without exception. It is not enough just to talk about bodhicitta, or to merely read about it, think about it, or express yourself on the subject. One must actually experience the mind of bodhicitta. In other words, walk your talk!

One can realize bodhicitta through diligent practice, although it may take time to fully integrate bodhicitta into daily life. First, we must train and become habituated to the relative bodhicitta that encompasses all sentient beings in the universe. That thought, in turn, gives rise to ultimate bodhicitta. Ultimate bodhicitta is based on the stability of mahamudra as well as unwavering, indomitable courage. The wisdom of ultimate bodhicitta extends to every object, its kindness reaches every sentient being, and its activities manifest according to beings' needs. In that way, all beings benefit from the protection of ultimate bodhicitta. Thus, it is called "the King of Dharma."

I, a yogin, realized the unity of view, meditation, and action.
There are no sessions to practice.

In non-effort I, the yogin, am happy.
This happy yogin experiences joy.
This experience of joy is the guru's kindness.

Jigten Sumgön emphasized the importance of right *view, meditation, and action*. Sometimes we may have the right view but do not practice meditation. Sometimes we practice meditation but our conduct is poor. And yet at other times we may have right action but an incomplete view. The three are mutually supportive: in order to achieve right view, we must meditate; to progress in meditation, we need right action; to act properly, we must have the understanding to choose the right path.

View refers to our point of view, our understanding of the world, or our frame of reference. There are many different stages of right view, from the early understanding of an ordinary person to the ultimate view of a buddha. The first, most basic correct view of reality is to see the impermanence of all composite phenomena in the relative state. This fact is how things are naturally constituted. Even rocks that appear very stable are changing every moment. Perceiving that without mistake is a right view. Perceiving phenomena mistakenly as being solid or permanent is called a wrong view. So the first stage of view is to see that everything has a transitory nature, that nothing is substantial or concrete.

Meditation is an effort to penetrate, see, and experience the view. We do not examine it as an external object but rather learn to maintain the experience of impermanence, for example, as a quality of the mind. This is right meditation.

Action involves living a life guided by the right view—in this example, living with the knowledge that everything is impermanent. Living without attachment and hatred is also right action or conduct.

We can also look at these three—view, meditation, and conduct—in the context of causality. First, understanding how cause and result function is a correct view. Creating negative karma brings us suffering; creating positive karma will bring peace and happiness. Those results are inevitable, undeviating, and inexorable. When we become fully convinced of this, we will understand causality as interdependence. Deeply contemplating this view is meditation. Our resulting proper conduct consists of avoiding all the unwholesome deeds that cause suffering and engaging in the wholesome deeds that cause peace and happiness.

Another example of essential right view, meditation, and action concerns the truth of suffering. Samsara is defined by suffering. Not one instant of pure happiness occurs there. Occasionally a little happiness appears, but that happiness is imperfect and stained by affliction. This is simply the nature of how things truly exist, and seeing that nature is right view. Then when we reflect on samsara as a state of suffering, a sense of nonattachment to samsara arises. This nonattachment is sometimes called renunciation or even revulsion. Revulsion is not a form of hatred. Rather, it consists of nonattachment to the samsaric state, based on the knowledge that such attachment doesn't bring about happiness. Living in this way is right action.

The fundamental longing of all sentient beings is for happiness and freedom from suffering. Since sentient beings are no different one from another in this respect, we must work to develop love and compassion for all of them. This is the view we try to achieve, and when we perceive it directly, that is called right view. Repeatedly reflecting on love and compassion is meditation. Living without harming others and, beyond that, actually helping others is right action and conduct.

A more advanced practice is to reflect on all phenomena as illusory. Everything is merely a manifestation of causes and conditions. Directly perceiving all phenomena as rainbows or mirages is right view. Mindfully maintaining your mind in this state is right meditation. Based on that understanding, acting without attachment or aversion is right conduct. These teachings really help practitioners purify their mental delusions and negative habits.

The highest view can be called mahamudra, dzogchen, or madhyamaka; all three have the same meaning. Each system may present a different technique for attaining realization, but the realization that one achieves is the same. There is no higher or lower, better or worse among buddhas. For all buddhas, the phenomena of samsara *and* nirvana appear and function within the framework of dependent arising. Their mode of abiding and their very nature is emptiness, and that emptiness is interdependence. Seeing that there is no separation between emptiness and dependent arising— that is the realization of right view. Habituating ourselves to this view and abiding in that state without fabrication are called meditation. We meditate in this way in order to internalize that view. Having maintained the mind in this manner, we live our life engaging in right action by accumulating great merit and wisdom, avoiding all nonvirtues, and developing all virtues without contradicting the view; this is right conduct. These three enhance realization by working together. In other words, emptiness doesn't negate virtue and nonvirtue. In fact, the realization of emptiness, the very core essence of the mind, can only be established on the basis of all six perfections.

Direct realization of all-pervading emptiness is called "self-arising awareness" and is the mind free from all elaboration. We practice to actualize that view through meditation and by living in that way. When one directly sees the nature of mahamudra, there is no difference between samsara and nirvana. The perfection of this view is called "unity," "nonduality," or "no separation." Thus, the line that says *I, a yogin, realized the unity of view, meditation, and action* means that Jigten Sumgön has achieved this highest realization.

Therefore, *there are no sessions* that he needs *to practice* because there is no separation or duality between meditation and post-meditation. A mind of such intensive awareness is completely awakened; nothing obstructs its clarity. Without obscurations, one remains in that state without interruption. The Buddha said he was always in that meditative state, whether he walked, sat, taught, slept, or ate. Also, Milarepa said, "I am in the meditation state while I walk and when I'm eating." We need to concern ourselves with accomplishing this.

In non-effort, I, the yogin, am happy. In other words, Jigten Sumgön had no need to exert any effort because he had fully accomplished the actualization of the state of nonduality. In samsara, beings are so habituated to duality that afflictions and neuroses freely flow without effort. Because we are so deeply rooted in these defilements, suffering also flows. On the other hand, Jigten Sumgön was so fully accomplished that nonduality was effortlessly natural.

The clarity of a lit candle is part of its nature; we don't have to do anything to make the light clear. Heat and color are inseparable as soon as the flame is kindled. In the same way, peace and happiness are the flavor of mahamudra. Bliss is simply an aspect of that quality of mind, so Jigten Sumgön can say *This happy yogin experiences joy.* That joy is unafflicted because it is free from the mundane. There is no space for suffering in the unfabricated state of dharmakaya.

> I, a yogin, realized the unity of the guru, my own mind,
>   and the Buddha.
> I have no need of superficial devotion.
> In non-effort, I, the yogin, am happy.
> This happy yogin experiences joy.
> This experience of joy is the guru's kindness.

The historical Buddha Shakyamuni practiced the Dharma teachings for three limitless kalpas. Throughout that immense period of time, he never stopped developing bodhicitta. Sometimes karma caused him to be reborn in the hell realms, but even there he maintained the practice of compassion. During his limitless, kalpas-long journey to enlightenment, he was sometimes born in the animal realm as an elephant, monkey, rhinoceros, or bear and so forth. Unlike other animals, he retained an acute memory so that his consciousness could be continuously suffused by compassion and bodhicitta. He also experienced the full range of human experience as a king, an ordinary worker, and a beggar. By practicing bodhicitta for three limitless kalpas, he purified all his obscurations of negative karma, afflicting emotions, and the subtle obscurations to enlightenment. The result was full buddhahood, the fully actualized awareness of the nature of mind in which nothing is hidden and all knowledge is obvious and clear.

In the Buddha's mind there is no difference between a Buddhist and a non-Buddhist, a believer and nonbeliever, or a human being and an animal; all sentient beings are equal. He said, "I traveled this path and achieved this result. If you, too, want to be free from suffering, this is the way to do it. I'm showing you the path, but it is up to you to follow it." Out of unequaled compassion and wisdom, he taught 84,000 categories of teachings in order for everyone to be able to comprehend the complete purification of obscurations.

Anyone who has the good fortune and good karma to study this path sincerely can actualize these teachings. Great masters such as Nagarjuna, Asanga, Marpa, and Milarepa are examples of those who completely actualized the teachings. They followed the path and steps of the Buddha. Jigten Sumgön also received the precious teachings through these lineage masters and followed the Buddha's steps. He studied, fully practiced, and attained buddhahood like those before him.

In this verse, Jigten Sumgön uses the words *the unity of the guru, my own mind, and the Buddha*. Here, he is saying that there is no difference between the realization of great teachers such as Marpa, Milarepa, and Phagmo Drupa and his own mind. This is true because the essence of every sentient being, the buddha nature, is equal for all. There is no distinction between the Buddha's wisdom mind and the buddha nature of other sentient beings. One is not better or of a higher quality than the other, but there are temporary obscurations that distinguish between buddhas and sentient beings. Like clouds obscuring the clear sky, our own negativity blocks our clear vision. The clouds are not the nature of the sky; they merely obscure its clear nature for a moment. Sentient beings simply need to dispel adventitious defilements with the tools of the Dharma practice that the Buddha and the lineage masters have handed down to us.

If sentient beings had no potential to attain enlightenment, no seed of buddha nature, these teachings would be pointless. However, the Buddha precisely and explicitly perceived that each sentient being has buddha nature equal to his own wisdom mind. Because of that understanding, he taught the Dharma in order to awaken sentient beings, free them from temporary bondage, and pull them out of the deep abyss of ignorance.

The Buddha's mind and our buddha nature are the same, just as the water in our kitchen and ground water are the same. The water that comes effortlessly through the tap is not different from the water underground. One has been cleaned of impurities and the other has not, but the essence of the water itself is unchanged. Because this is true, we can attain buddhahood. We just need to cultivate the mind and find an authentic lama to give us the right instructions.

We need the good judgment to perceive and follow the path, regardless of the hardships we may face. We have to deconstruct our attachments, our ego, in order to construct enlightenment. This process can be uncomfortable or even painful, but it is necessary. When Naropa met Tilopa, he didn't think, "Tilopa is a nice person. He makes me feel good." Rather, Naropa knew Tilopa had the teachings that he needed in order to attain enlightenment, so Naropa had no choice but to follow Tilopa. It is not enough to gain a pleasant feeling from the Dharma. It's also not enough to follow or reject a teacher out of emotional feelings, because you like or dislike them. Milarepa didn't remain at Marpa's farm because he liked Marpa emotionally. Rather, Milarepa realized that he had to stay because Marpa had the authentic teachings that would lead him to enlightenment.

Following the Dharma is how we cross the ocean of samsara. First we need an authentic spiritual friend or master. Through that meeting, we then can study the texts, read Dharma books, and practice the teachings they contain. Since Dharma texts are considered to be the same as the lama who wrote them, we should read them with respect, devotion, and joy. Then, after you have received teachings from a living spiritual master and developed the eye of wisdom, Dharma texts can act as spiritual masters that allow you to experience even deeper wisdom. As we gain experience, the witness of our own mind will arise and we will take our buddha nature, our own mind, as the root lama.

When we recite the prayer, "May the lama have good health and long life," we should look to our own mind of wisdom awareness and take that as the lama. We should pray that our own wisdom mind may have good health and long life. As we develop and progress on the path, we will come to have increased confidence in the wisdom mind as we reveal it. Eventually we realize that *the guru,* [our] *own mind, and the Buddha's mind* are not different. *Unity* comes when we realize there is no separation among these three. Until we have that experience, we cannot say that we and the Buddha are equal, because we are still suffering and the Buddha does not suffer; we remain deluded while the Buddha has dispelled all delusions.

Jigten Sumgön attained buddhahood and realized it to be no different from his own guru's buddhahood or from Buddha Shakyamuni's buddhahood. In the state of buddhahood nothing is hidden, all things are clear. One recollects limitless lifetimes in the past, perceives the limitless future, and so has the limitless wisdom of the past, present, and future. This is omniscience.

Because he achieved buddhahood, Jigten Sumgön declared that he had *no need of superficial devotion.* His devotion was unfabricated, and it sprang forth with no resistance because resistance is a form of mental suffering. Having achieved effortlessness through effort, he was totally free from delusion and performed activities to benefit sentient beings with true, unafflicted compassion and inexpressible joy.

Bodhisattvas who achieve the first bhumi experience great joy because the aspirations that they have been pursuing for a long time are starting to bear fruit; they are closer to buddhahood and their bodhicitta has become powerful enough that they can actually benefit others. Bodhisattvas who have achieved the first bhumi diminish the obscurations associated with ego-grasping. Ordinary beings, on the other hand, are limited in their ability to help others because their attachment to ego creates a boundary of fear. When there is no such attachment or resistance, the mind feels relaxed, joyous, and happy. Since that realization of joy is achieved through an authentic master's instructions, he says *This experience of joy is the guru's kindness.*

> I, a yogin, realized the unity of parents, yidams, and the six types
>   of beings.
> There is no need for the [superficial] benefit of others.
> In non-effort, I, the yogin, am happy.

This happy yogin experiences joy.
This experience of joy is the guru's kindness.

Here, Jigten Sumgön describes *the unity of parents, yidams, and the six types of beings,* encompassing the myriad beings of the six realms: hell beings, hungry spirits, animals, humans, demigods, and gods. Each of these sentient beings has buddha nature, and that nature contains all the qualities of a buddha. All the qualities mentioned in the *Uttaratantra*—the ten powers, four fearlessnesses, eighteen unequaled qualities, and so on—are naturally innate aspects of buddha nature. Yet, when they are veiled by temporary obscurations, they cannot manifest, like the sun hidden behind a cloud.

The Buddha taught the teachings so that these enlightened qualities could arise unobscured within each and every sentient being. For this to happen, we first need to cultivate bodhicitta and, in order to do that, we have to study and practice compassion and love. This spiritual love is unrelated to afflicting emotions such as attachment but rather is a pure thought related to wisdom and the realization of emptiness. When we exercise spiritual love and compassion, our mind extends out to all sentient beings and connects to every one of them.

In order to practice love and compassion, we apply them first to our closest connections in this life—our parents, relatives, friends, or whoever has raised us—because it is through their kindness that we survived, grew up, and have this opportunity to study and practice the precious Dharma teachings. Once we appreciate this relationship, we should contemplate how to repay their kindness, especially by working to free them from samsara and establish them in enlightenment. Thinking of the millions of rebirths we have had, we can reason that all other sentient beings have also been our parents, friends, or relatives in one lifetime or another. That gives us a genuine sense of connection, love, and compassion for all sentient beings. On that basis, we deeply wish that sentient beings, who have all been linked to us in one life or another, may be freed from suffering and have complete happiness.

Once we are firmly connected to others through love and compassion, we can cultivate bodhicitta, also called "the mind of enlightenment," and subsequently work to perfect it. The perfection of bodhicitta is enlightenment, the fully perfected mind. When we actualize the perfection of the mind, we gain the ability to perceive all sentient beings' true nature, as inseparable from the Buddha himself. The most effective means to attain this state is the tantric, or Vajrayana, system of meditation.

The Vajrayana system entails obtaining an empowerment and then practicing the corresponding deity yoga based on bodhicitta. During the empowerment ceremony our meditation is guided in a way that gives us an immediate opportunity to directly perceive samsara as nirvana and all sentient beings as the yidam, or enlightened being. Then, in order to practice Vajrayana meditation, we receive instructions on how to transform the whole of samsara into the enlightened state through the construction of a mandala, or pure reality. We envision or recreate the universe as a particular aspect of the enlightened state. Within that mandala, we see all beings, deities and sentient beings alike, as deities populating the mandala. Finally, we practice envisioning ourselves as an enlightened being, or yidam, such as Chenrezig, Manjushri, Vajrapani, Tara, or Chakrasamvara, and transforming all sentient beings into the yidam as well.

When we first engage in mandala practice, our practice remains superficial or merely intellectual. But as we practice more and more, the mind becomes habituated to, and stabilizes in, the practice. Eventually we really do come to see all sentient beings as the deity. Once we realize that their buddha nature is no different from our own and, like our own, is just temporarily obscured, we can no longer look down on any sentient being, not even small insects. This is the path to a high accomplishment like Jigten Sumgön's.

As a result of countless lifetimes of practice, Jigten Sumgön perfected the practice of seeing all sentient beings as the deity. He fully discarded any separating demarcation of practitioner, yidam, or sentient being. Therefore, he could say *I realized the unity of parents, yidams, and the six realms of sentient beings*. This buddha quality of inseparable wisdom and compassion allows his activities to manifest infinitely and reach every sentient being without effort. His benefit for beings arises as effortlessly as the light of the sun naturally pervades all the land. The sun doesn't have to think, "I have to nourish this flower or shine on that blade of grass." A buddha's activities are similarly spontaneous, so *there is no need for the superficial benefit of others*.

When we come to perceive all sentient beings as enlightened, then samsara no longer exists. Just as we respect the yidam deities, we respect all sentient beings without partiality. In non-effort, a buddha abides in a state of total happiness and joy in the mandala of buddhafields.

I, a yogin, realized the unity of the sutras, the tantras, and their
commentaries.
I have no need of written texts.
In non-effort I, the yogin, am happy.
This happy yogin experiences joy.
This experience of joy is the guru's kindness.

There are two classes of the Buddha's teachings: *sutra* and *tantra*. They form
the basis for the *commentaries,* called *shastra,* written by great Indian masters like Nagarjuna and Asanga. There are Tibetan translations of both the
Buddha's direct teachings and the great commentaries. The Buddha's translated teachings fill more than one hundred volumes called the Kagyur. The
Tengyur contains the shastra, which were translated into more than 220
volumes.

The Buddha taught in many different times and places in order to accom-
modate the dispositions and abilities of his various followers. He gave
perfect teachings that would allow each one to establish an understanding of the teachings, then practice, and finally attain realization. Broadly
speaking, the teachings are categorized into three turnings of the wheel of
Dharma. The first turning of the wheel is the earliest set of teachings and is
characterized by the Four Noble Truths. The second turning contains the
teachings on the perfection of wisdom (*prajñaparamita*), which emphasize the absence of characteristics of all phenomena. The third turning is
known as the ultimate turning, or the complete clarification of the Dharma
teachings.

The first of Buddha's teachings, the Four Noble Truths, makes clear that
samsara is suffering, that suffering is the result of causes, that cessation of
suffering is possible, and that there is a path to follow to achieve the cessation of suffering. The Buddha explained suffering in detail so that we would
understand that it is undesirable and develop an interest in becoming free of
it. For example, he spoke of three levels of suffering, from gross to subtle: the
suffering of suffering, the suffering of change, and the pervasive condition
of suffering. Each and every form of suffering is a result that comes from a
cause; these different types of suffering cannot originate without a cause
or from an unrelated or incomplete cause. Therefore, the Buddha spoke
of the origins of suffering as the negative actions that we manifest verbally
and physically, such as taking life, stealing, sexual misconduct, lying, and
so forth, and as the afflicting emotions that inspire negative actions such

as greed, attachment, aversion, resentment, wrong view, distraction, and so forth. We will all suffer helplessly so long as we continue to create these direct and indirect causes of suffering.

This being the case, we need an impeccable method to counter our entrenched negative habits. Each culture tries its best to solve the problem of unhappiness, but the usual approaches are so completely entangled in confusion that a mountain of problems remains. On the other hand, the Buddha used meticulous reasoning and analysis to investigate suffering right down to its root cause. As a result, he found a comprehensive way to tackle our problems in both relative and absolute terms. One who sincerely follows his instructions with a spacious and courageous mind that leaves self-aggrandizement behind can find both worldly peace and liberation from all afflictions. This method, called the thirty-seven branches of enlightenment, shows us that we must free our mind from all negative thoughts and develop virtuous and wholesome thoughts and actions. This will help purify the gross negative thoughts of anger, hatred, pride, jealousy, attachment, and so forth that obscure the subtle nature of the mind and that inhibit the manifestation of wisdom and compassion.

In the second turning of the wheel, the Buddha teaches us that everything is emptiness, that what we perceive to be substantial reality is more like an illusion, a cloud, a magician's display, or a reflection of the moon. Phenomena manifest and dissipate like a mirage. Emptiness means that phenomena—*all* phenomena, including ourselves—arise in dependence on other phenomena, causes, and conditions. When we consider a table, for example, we can see that it cannot exist independently of its constituent parts and the causes that gave rise to its construction. It may seem strange at first to think that things are empty of inherent existence when phenomena appear to us so clearly and substantially. However, sacred texts such as the *Heart Sutra* and the rest of the perfection of wisdom literature provide contemplations and practices that facilitate our complete realization of emptiness.

In the third turning of the wheel, the Buddha taught the inconceivable nature of the mind both in the relative and absolute states, the nonduality of appearances and emptiness, and the unity of relative and absolute truth. In relation to this, the Buddha explained how every sentient being has buddha nature, the personal potential to become a buddha, as well as the infinite qualities of a buddha's enlightened mind. These subjects are detailed in texts such as the *Mahaparinirvana Sutra,* the *Tathagatagarbha Sutra,* the *Avatamsaka Sutra,* and the *Samdhinirmochana Sutra.* In particular the

Uttaratantra Shastra is relied on for an extensive description of the qualities of a buddha.

It is said that there are 84,000 negative mental states, and that the Buddha taught 84,000 teachings as their antidote. Desire, aversion, and ignorance are each associated with 21,000 teachings in the vinaya, sutras, and abhidharma, with an additional 21,000 directed toward the most subtle obscurations that are addressed through tantric methodology. There, the four empowerments—vase, secret, wisdom or transcendent knowledge, and fourth or precious word—provide the means for total transformation.

The Buddha taught continuously for more than forty-five years. The depth and breadth of his imparted wisdom are immeasurable. We ordinary, unenlightened people who have gross obscurations cannot comprehend this; it is like trying to measure an ocean with a small cup. For that reason, we have come to depend on commentaries written by great masters such as Nagarjuna, Asanga, and Naropa. The coming of these great teachers was foretold by the Buddha in many sutras and tantras. Through rigorous training, they acquired vast knowledge and the high realization of enlightenment. In other words, they firmly established themselves in the realization of relative and absolute truth. They wrote unmistaken commentaries from within that state, in an abbreviated form so that we can more easily and productively follow, study, and practice.

All the teachings, whether they are sutras, tantras, or commentaries, were given for the same purpose: to purify our obscurations and enable us to develop enlightened qualities, to uproot samsara, and to lead us to actualize buddhahood. They all come to the same point; there is no internal division or contradiction. The Buddha embodies the Dharma, and all his teachings flowed from that state. Jigten Sumgön also achieved full enlightenment, and in that state saw that there is no contradiction among the sutras, tantras, and commentaries. Che-nga Sherab Jungne said:

> You [Jigten Sumgön] have realized that all phenomena of samsara and nirvana without exception do not exist. But neither do they exist. Nor do these statements contradict each other. Although you display not even the slightest sign of elaboration, your dharmakaya has the quality of action.

Thus, Jigten Sumgön said here that he *realized the unity,* the nondual nature, of the various teachings.

When Jigten Sumgön wrote *I have no need of written texts,* he meant that he no longer had to depend on texts because he had fully experienced the meaning of all the Buddha's teachings. Milarepa also said, "I don't need written texts. I see all this as a text." Whatever we see, hear, smell, or taste is all a Dharma teaching. Everything is an example of the movement of the mind, of illusion, and of the nature of noninherent existence or emptiness. Everything is an expression of emptiness.

> **I, a yogin, realized the unity of this life, the next, and the bardo.**
> **There is no boundary of death.**
> **In non-effort I, the yogin, am happy.**
> **This happy yogin experiences joy.**
> **This experience of joy is the guru's kindness.**

In this verse, Jigten Sumgön writes of his accomplishment regarding the bardo teachings. *Bardo* is a Tibetan word meaning "in between" and implies a transition. He first mentions *this life,* the bardo of living, which encompasses the period from conception until death. We are under the care of our parents as soon as we are born. After that, we go to school and then start our working life; we gradually age and finally die. Throughout, we are entangled in a web of confusion and suffering. We continually swing back and forth to bring some happiness and comfort to our lives.

The bardo of sleep or dreaming occurs within the bardo of living. We go to sleep, and the next day we wake up and start another day. Every day we start a new life again and then again. During this time, studying and practicing Dharma gives us the idea of how to relate to our life, how to work in our best interest, and how to maintain our mind more positively. By dedicating our life to Dharma, we take the task of transforming our negative thoughts more seriously and we build the resources we need to face the obstacles of life. This is how to live life more positively and happily. This is the purpose of life.

If we are without Dharma teachings, we face more difficulties because we lack the pristine wisdom to see causality precisely, and we also lack the skillful means to handle confusion. Without Dharma teachings, there is little to direct the mind in a positive direction. When the mind is insidiously polluted by delusion, some use drugs and other means to provide some relief. But that is no real solution, based as it is in delusion. Even some of those who have encountered Dharma teachings choose drugs and other negative solutions without making a real effort to implement wisdom and compassion or to change their negative patterns. There is no end to the predicaments in their life, and in the end they destroy their health and waste their precious human birth.

Dharma is so precious because it is not just a concept to believe in. Dharma means peace and wisdom, and is an empirical method that shows us how to handle the mind. It gives us an opportunity to live more positively and more harmoniously, by choosing the right over the wrong way. If we put energy into understanding Dharma, and reinforce this by doing practice, the result will be a more peaceful life. We will face adverse circumstances more positively and live with dignity.

When this life ends, we experience three different bardos: the bardo at the time of death; the bardo of dharmata; and the bardo of becoming.

Bardo at the time of death. The bardo at the time of death consists of the dissolution of the four elements, and the three subtle experiences. As death approaches, signs appear to indicate that the four elements are dissolving. First, the earth element dissolves into the water element, and the sign of this is that the dying person feels like they are falling or sinking into the ground. Sometimes they raise their hands as if to be pulled back up. After that, the water element dissolves into the fire element, and the dying person feels as if they are drowning or being swept away by a huge river. Then the fire element dissolves into the wind, or air, element, at which time the heat draws into the center of the body. The limbs, feet, and hands become cold and the color of the body becomes pale. The dying person feels like they are in the midst of a great fire. Next, the wind element dissolves into the consciousness. At this time, the dying person feels like they are being taken by a tornado, and it becomes difficult for them to breathe in and out. When consciousness dissolves into the space element, the breath stops.

One may be declared clinically dead when the breath and heart stop, but one is not yet fully deceased because the consciousness has not yet left the body. The dying person now feels three subtle experiences: the white appearance, the red increase, and the darkness experience of near attainment. In the first, the dying person experiences a light that is white as a full moon on a clear night, and the thirty-three mental factors related to aversion cease. Next, during the red increase, the dying person experiences a light as red as the sky at dawn or dusk, and the forty mental factors related to attachment cease. Then during the dark experience of near attainment, the dying person experiences a darkness like that of a clear, moonless night sky, and the seven mental factors cease to function. After the dying person passes through the experience of darkness, the total, ultimate nature of dharmakaya is experienced. This state is all-pervading, free from all spheres, and luminous; this is called ground luminosity. When that passes, the three subtle experiences are experienced again, but in reverse order. Only then does the consciousness leave the body, completing the dying process. All those who have a body will experience this, whether briefly or for a longer period of time.

Bardo of dharmata. The bardo of dharmata occurs after the dying person experiences buddha nature, dharmakaya, or ground mahamudra. At this point, the consciousness is disembodied and, because of that, the being can travel from place to place as fast as light. An unenlightened being in this unstable condition will have a great variety of pleasant and unpleasant experiences. Since one has only a mental body, this is a restless state. Those who have experience with meditation, especially with Vajrayana deity practice or mahamudra, have a great opportunity to recognize all these experiences as manifestations of dharmata. Those without such experience are just lost and confused. The life span in this bardo is one week. After each week the being dies again and takes rebirth within that state. This bardo can last up to forty-nine days, or about seven weeks.

Bardo of becoming. Midway through the seven weeks, the bardo of becoming starts and the being looks for its next rebirth. The being is attracted to parents, conceived, and reborn in one of the six realms, depending on its particular karma and mental state. Then the next life begins and we start the cycle over again. This is what is called samsara—migrating from life to life in confusion. No matter what kind of skills you may have, there is no method other than Dharma to sever this chain of predicaments. How kind are the buddhas and great teachers who, out of pristine wisdom and unfailing compassion, inspire us to follow the path of Dharma! They open the path so that everyone can have an opportunity to escape this great saga of delusion.

Jigten Sumgön says here that he has *realized the unity of this life, the next, and the bardo.* This means that there is no duality, no demarcation in the realization of mahamudra. Therefore, there are no transitions between this life and the next. An analogy for this is the rising of the sun before the full moon sets, leaving no intervening gap of darkness. His mind remains in the dharmakaya without confusion.

We are very fortunate to have all the teachings of Buddhism, both sutra and Vajrayana, available to us. This complete method lacks nothing and teaches us how to reveal our own buddhahood. By manifesting in the form of the yidam deity and perceiving all others as the deity, we reveal our own buddha nature. We can then perceive the dreamlike nature of all phenomena—interdependent, interconnected, with nothing substantially or independently existing. This allows us to stabilize our mind, experience clarity, and attain buddhahood.

There are two qualities of the mind: clarity and purity. The purity aspect of mind perceives all sentient beings as being of the same nature as the Buddha. The clarity aspect is the stability, calmness, and one-pointed focus of the mind in the mahamudra state. If we die with realization of these two mental qualities, we would experience enlightenment at the time of death, because clarity transcends duality. If we had realization, the clarity of the mind would not be blocked by sleep; we could sleep and awaken without a break in awareness. When one has realization that comprehensive, this life, the next life, and the period in between are of one nature. Thus, we should enjoy our Dharma journey and feel fortunate to have this opportunity.

When there is no obscuration, life and death are of one nature, nondual. Because great yogis and buddhas realize this, they do not experience fear, expectation, or grasping at hope. Death and rebirth are like merely changing the house we live in. Jigten Sumgön attained that great level of realization, so he said *I, a yogin, realized the unity of this life, the next, and the bardo.*

> **Day and night, in all six sessions, through strong devotion,**
> **I am always with the authentic guru.**
> **I, the inseparable yogin, am happy.**
> **This happy yogin experiences joy.**
> **This experience of joy is the guru's kindness.**

Dividing the twenty-four hours of a day into four-hour segments results in the *six sessions.*

When Jigten Sumgön says *I am always with the authentic guru,* he means that his devotion to his lama is so strong that he is never separated from his guru. The great Milarepa said, "In this solitary, lonely place my devotion is always with the lama; there is no separation from him." Milarepa also told his disciple Gampopa, "Sometimes if you miss the lama, you can meditate that he is inseparably present on the crown of your head and in your heart. Keep this in your heart." In the same way, Jigten Sumgön was never separated from his lama, Phagmo Drupa. Moreover, Jigten Sumgön, as was mentioned earlier, realized the inseparability of his mind and the mind of the guru. This does not mean that Phagmo Drupa's mind somehow became mixed with Jigten Sumgön's mind, but rather that in the absolute state there is no higher or lower, more wisdom or less wisdom. His realization of enlightenment is free from such arbitrary divisions, and no different from Phagmo Drupa's.

Che-nga Sherab Jungne said:

> The configuration of your body, speech, mind, activities, . . . realms, and qualities are neither one nor separate, and are beyond conceptual thought. This is the inexhaustible proclamation of the buddhas of the three times.

Since Jigten Sumgön abides in that state, there is nothing to separate him from his guru, so he expresses great joy and happiness. Even though we are not enlightened, we still have all the great lineage masters with us. Because of this, we can practice meditation, study sutra and commentaries, help other sentient beings, and live the Dharma teachings with confidence. Thus Jigten Sumgön wrote *This happy yogin experiences joy. This experience of joy is the guru's kindness.*

> **This "Song of the Six Confidences"**
> **I offer to the ear of glorious Taklung Thangpa.**
> **I don't feel that the time I attended the guru was short.**
> **He accepted me, and taught me fully.**

As mentioned earlier, Taklung Thangpa was one of the very closest disciples of Phagmo Drupa and the founder of Taklung Yarthang Monastery. He had strong devotion for the lama and was himself a great master who gathered many disciples. To this day, there are many Taklung monasteries in different parts of Tibet.

Now we must encourage ourselves to study and practice. There is nothing more precious than the Dharma teachings. We have to spend time with them so that we don't forget and revert to "samsara practice." It is common to become inspired as we read books or attend teachings, but after a few days that inspiration often disappears, and we go right back to samsara. It's not enough for us to say, "I don't want any more suffering." The great masters, those who put all their time and energy into Dharma study and practice, successfully purified the causes of their suffering and became the most victorious people in the world. Regardless of who we are—whether we know what suffering is or not—we all desire to be free of suffering. Dispelling the cause of suffering is the purpose of the Dharma. It is very important to be aware of this.

Those who wander in samsara are unsuccessful beings. No matter how hard we work or how much energy we put into this samsaric existence, we are unsuccessful because we have not succeeded in becoming free from suffering or in achieving a true sense of peace. We may flourish materially and technologically, but this kind of success won't stop us from suffering. It doesn't provide us with true and lasting satisfaction, peace, or harmony. When you read the life stories of the great masters you can see that they may have had very little material wealth, yet they were the happiest people in the world.

9. Supplication to the Seven Taras

In the unborn dharmadhatu
abides the Reverend Mother, the deity Tara.
She bestows happiness on all sentient beings.
I request her to protect me from all fears.

Through not understanding oneself as dharmakaya
one's mind is overpowered by the kleshas.
Our mothers, sentient beings, wander in samsara.
Please protect them, Deity Mother.

If the meaning of Dharma is not born in one's heart,
one just follows the words of conventional meaning.
Some are deceived by dogma.
Please protect them, Perfect Mother.

It is difficult to realize one's mind.
Some realize but do not practice.
Their minds wander to worldly activities.
Please protect them, Deity Mother of Recollection.

Nondual wisdom is the self-born mind.
By the habits of grasping at duality,
some are bound no matter what they do.
Please protect them, Deity of Nondual Wisdom.

Although some abide in the perfect meaning,
they don't realize the interdependence of cause and result.
They are ignorant of the meaning of objects of knowledge.
Please protect them, Omniscient Deity Mother.

The nature of space is free from boundaries.
Nothing is different from that.
Still, practitioners and disciples don't realize this.
Please protect them, Perfect Buddha Mother.

INTRODUCTION

JIGTEN SUMGÖN received the complete lineage teachings from his root guru, Phagmo Drupa, over the course of thirty-two months. After the Lord of Beings, Phagmo Drupa, passed away, Jigten Sumgön went to Wön, where he studied with a teacher named Lobpön Tsilungpa. From him, he received the teachings of Vajrayogini. Then, from Dakpo Gomtsul, Gampopa's nephew, he received the four yogas of mahamudra and became completely engaged in that practice. At that time Lama Yäl invited him to practice at the Echung cave.

Jigten Sumgön stayed in retreat there for seven years, never giving a thought to worldly affairs. He realized that the cause of wandering in samsara is one's inability to direct the winds into the channels, and so he concentrated his efforts on this practice and became fully enlightened. At the time that his impure vision dissolved into emptiness, many lineage gurus and yidam deities appeared to him, including the seven Taras. They appeared holding utpala flowers, and gave him vast and profound teachings. After receiving them, Jigten Sumgön sang this powerful song of supplication. This song is not one that he composed from his intellect, but rather it spontaneously sprang forth from his realization.

This prayer contains profound teachings related to the entire Buddhist path. Even though it has only seven verses, it is a comprehensive teaching. Recite this supplication with strong devotion and an earnest determination to realize its meaning. You can repeat this prayer as many times as you like. If you are interested, it would be beneficial to memorize this song and chant it every day.

COMMENTARY

In the unborn dharmadhatu
abides the Reverend Mother, the deity Tara.
She bestows happiness on all sentient beings.
I request her to protect me from all fears.

Dharmadhatu is the sphere of the dharmakaya, the primordial nature of all buddhas. It cannot be seen with the physical eyes, touched by the body, or heard with the ears; it can only be experienced by an enlightened mind. There *abides the Reverend Mother, the deity Tara*. This line means that Tara's innate nature is the dharmadhatu and that she is inseparable from the dharmakaya of all the buddhas. This state is also the nature of our own mind. In order to achieve buddhahood, we must each personally actualize it.

From there, *she bestows happiness on all sentient beings*. Tara manifests infinite activities to benefit all sentient beings, not only humans. Sometimes a refreshingly cool breeze will come along when we are feeling very hot. At other times, we may shiver with cold, and then the sun will come out and bring some heat, so warm and pleasant. These are the activities of dharmakaya.

In other words, all the good feelings that we experience come from positive karma. If we find some delicious food to eat, or friends to share a good time with, this arises from our positive karma. Good karma arises through the power of all-pervading wisdom, and the suffering we experience comes from delusion, or negative karma. The more we practice, understand, and experience the Dharma, the more delusion is reduced. Confusion's grip is loosened and negative karma loses ground. It is also the activity of the dharmakaya that causes us to see physical and mental suffering as something positive. For example, the experience of suffering purifies the related negative karma. Our own suffering encourages us to develop compassion for others. And for some individuals, suffering creates an opportunity to awaken and to open the wisdom mind. Once we realize our afflictions do not "really" exist, they disappear completely into the dharmata. But as long as we remain deluded, we will continue to create negative karma and helplessly suffer.

In the last line of this verse, Jigten Sumgön supplicates Tara *to protect me from all fears*. He himself was already enlightened, so he wrote this out of great compassion as a representative of the sentient beings who are still in samsara. Samsara is a state of fear. From the strongest leader to the poorest slave, there is no one in the six realms who is without fear. Weapons will not protect us; money cannot buy us respite. We can be free of fear only when we realize the nature of all phenomena, the dharmadhatu or mahamudra. This is what the Dharma is really about. We are so fortunate to be exposed to these teachings that lead to the elimination of all suffering! Now that we have heard them, though, we must make the effort to purify our negative thoughts at every possible opportunity.

How, then, does Tara protect us? We should think of her as a symbol or as an embodiment of the wisdom of all the buddhas. She protects us and leads us out of samsara by instilling in us the ultimate view of dharmadhatu, and by showing us what to take up and what to abandon.

> Through not understanding oneself as dharmakaya,
> one's mind is overpowered by the kleshas.
> Our mothers, sentient beings, wander in samsara.
> Please protect them, Deity Mother.

As mentioned above, our own nature is the dharmakaya, just as it is for all the buddhas. In other words, all beings have buddha nature. This is explained in the first chapter of *The Jewel Ornament of Liberation,* where Lord Gampopa shows, by means of detailed reasoning, how it is that everyone has the same essence and that the suchness of the Buddha and of sentient beings is identical, just as milk is permeated by butter, mustard seed by oil, and silver ore by silver. The difference is that those who are called "buddha" have completely realized this nature, and we have not. This is like diamonds: a buddha is like one that has been cut and polished to perfection, and we are like rough diamonds still encrusted with mud. The polished jewel is not essentially different from the one in the mud, but until the jewel is exposed, it is not very beneficial.

Because we do not perceive ourselves as enlightened beings, we are *overpowered by the kleshas.* "Klesha" is a Sanskrit word that refers to the afflicting emotions of attachment, aversion, pride, jealousy, ignorance, and so forth. We are enslaved by them, are completely under their control, and we suffer in the six realms as a result. Due to the varying levels and degrees of afflicting emotions and karma, the six realms of sentient beings have come about. The feeling of suffering is uncomfortable because it is incompatible with our basic nature, which is happiness. Understanding this is the basis of compassion. We understand that beings do not want suffering and that suffering is actually unnecessary, but that it occurs anyway because of confusion and the afflicting emotions. If suffering were the true nature of beings, there would be no need to develop compassion. But since we know this is not true, compassion can become a very important motivation to dispel confusion and attain enlightenment.

While Jigten Sumgön was in retreat, he became very sick. At first he thought, "This pain is excruciating. I must be the worst, most unfortunate person in the world." But later he realized, "I am very fortunate because I have received all these precious Dharma teachings. If I die now, I can go to a buddhafield. But what about all the other beings in the six realms? They haven't received these teachings, so their endless sufferings are much worse than mine." This inspired powerful compassion in him and allowed him to see himself as an embodiment of compassion. He could then utilize his physical sickness to purify the suffering of all sentient beings without interruption, which alleviated all of his own physical suffering. Within a few days, he was free from all his physical sickness and had achieved enlightenment.

Perceive the immensity of sentient beings' suffering and confusion, and then cultivate compassion from the marrow of your bones. We should treat all sentient beings as if they were *our mothers* or whoever is closest to us. We depend on others for every benefit we receive. For example, shopping at a grocery store would seem to be a simple matter. However, consider that farmers worked hard to produce the food, others processed it, and still others transported it. The store owner has to manage his business successfully, and the government has to maintain a monetary system. We couldn't even survive without the efforts of others! In the same way, businesses depend on customers, and politicians depend on the people who elect them. How could one become famous in a place with no people? Our Dharma practice develops in the same way. Without sentient beings, there would be no way to develop compassion, loving-kindness, or bodhicitta. Can we cultivate patience with a rock? Can we give anything to a desk? We cannot attain buddhahood without the practices of love, compassion, and bodhicitta. We are very much interconnected with all beings, so we must impartially keep each one in our heart.

Our mother sentient beings *wander in samsara* based on each one's unique accumulation of karma. There are six realms in which beings can wander: the hell, hungry spirit, animal, human, demigod, and god realms. Within each realm, beings' experiences depend on their degree of affliction and the quality of their karma. For example, some have a high mental capacity that affords them the opportunity to seek better conditions for this life. Some are born into a difficult life and don't have much capacity to create a better one. Therefore, it is important for each of us to take responsibility for ourselves, to appreciate our opportunities, and support those who need help.

Beings endlessly cycle through these states, and only very rarely does one happen upon these precious Dharma teachings. How does this happen?

First, beings have ignorance. That ignorance obscures the clarity of mind. For that reason, they mistakenly perceive duality, "themselves" and "others." Then perceptions of good and bad, like and dislike arise. Growing stronger, these become attachment and aversion. Pride and jealousy follow soon after. We are not taught to be ignorant; we are not taught to desire or hate. These emotions just pop up because they are deeply rooted habits that have developed over many lifetimes. None are unique to Asia or to the West, or even to humans. We share this sad heritage with all beings. Through these disturbing emotions, variegated karmas are created.

We can see that there are different types of suffering. Even though some pleasant things seem to bring happiness and joy, they don't last very long because they are impermanent. When they deteriorate or when our perception of them changes, suffering results. This is called the suffering of change. Thus, knowing external phenomena to be unreliable, we won't be so attached to them and will be better able to accept our situation. The pervasive condition of suffering will exist as long as the five aggregates are pervaded by afflicting emotions. On the basis of this understanding, we should purify our karma and mental afflictions as much as possible. This wisdom brings more peace into our mind, and our suffering will naturally decrease. Further, we can develop compassion for those who do not have this understanding.

The Buddha taught this from the point of view of omniscience. He precisely knows how every individual functions, how each one exists, and what they need to purify. He did not create samsara, but he understands every part of it without exception. So we, too, must study samsara and realize how it is made up from our delusion and negative thoughts. Understanding that phenomena are transitory and untrustworthy will lead us to develop renunciation for samsara and a wholehearted yearning for enlightenment.

> If the meaning of Dharma is not born in one's heart,
> one just follows the words of conventional meaning.
> Some are deceived by dogma.
> Please protect them, Perfect Mother.

Even though we have begun the path toward enlightenment, if our mind has not truly changed, we will continue to gravitate toward samsara. Intellectually understanding, and even agreeing with, concepts such as impermanence is not enough. The real meaning, the experience of Dharma, must be *born in one's heart* for it to take root. Our mouths say may, "Yes, yes, samsara is a terrible state of suffering." But if our actions show that we still enjoy samsara, we are merely following the *words of conventional meaning* and intellectualizing. The actual meaning of Dharma has not been born in the heart. We don't get much benefit from this, and there is a danger of straying from the path and becoming lost. That would be most unfortunate.

If we do the practices as instructed, and achieve some experience, we can be more like Milarepa. His sister visited him once while he was meditating in a mountain cave. He had absolutely nothing—no food, no clothes. She was a beggar herself, and wailed, "We are the most unfortunate people in the world! I thought you could do better than this. Here I am begging door to door and here you are with nothing. Won't you at least go to a monastery where you can get food and clothing?" Milarepa replied, "When I hear of the eight worldly concerns, I am disgusted. I know the world of samsara very well, so I have no interest in it at all. I received the precious Dharma teachings, so I have no time to waste. Please don't speak to me of such things." You see, he had experienced Dharma deeply, so he had no alternative but to live according to his heart with a feeling of joy. This is how Dharma practice becomes a way of life, a way of peace and freedom.

When Dharma remains intellectual, it is reduced to dogma. Instead of proceeding out of confidence based in experience, we merely become attached to our tenets. Rather than being a path out of samsara, the Dharma can be perverted and become an even stronger tie to confusion. Thus, we can be *deceived by dogma*. Jigten Sumgön saw this very precisely, so he prays for our protection from this fault. We must take Dharma into the heart, so that we may truly follow the path.

> It is difficult to realize one's mind.
> Some realize but do not practice.
> Their minds wander to worldly activities.
> Please protect them, Deity Mother of Recollection.

Five paths comprise the journey to buddhahood: the path of accumulation, the path of preparation, the path of special insight, the path of meditation, and the path of perfection.

It is difficult to realize the nature of *one's mind*. First, on the path of accumulation, we begin to understand the nature of samsara and renounce it. We receive teachings from a spiritual master, study them, meditate, and experience profound shamatha or calm abiding of the mind.

On the path of preparation, our practice has become well established and meditative absorption is stable. We begin to achieve the experiences of joy, clarity, and nonconceptual thought. Our interest in emptiness grows powerful at this stage as our meditation experience becomes stronger.

Then, on the path of special insight, we can see the subtlety of the nature of mind. This is because we will have developed shamatha or meditative concentration to the point that the mind cannot be moved by discursive thoughts, and on that basis, we can cultivate special insight, also called "critical" or "incisive" insight. The combination of these two meditative states allows us to perceive the total nature of emptiness; no place for confusion remains. We must continue meditating in order to become thoroughly familiarized with the mind, but some who reach this stage of realization are so excited by it that they *do not practice* any more. The old habits of samsara reawaken, interest in the eight worldly concerns grows, and they become completely derailed from the path. Special insight is important, of course, as a necessary basis for the path of meditation, but it is not the end of the road. One needs to continue further.

On the path of meditation, we must concentrate totally on meditation, as Milarepa did. He reached the path of insight while staying with his teacher Marpa, and then spent the rest of his life meditating in the mountains. This is the point at which we progress through the bhumis. If we don't practice like this, we will forget our realization, the mind will *wander* back *to worldly activities,* and our ego attachment will again grow strong. We need to keep up our momentum until realization is perfected.

Here, Tara is called *Deity Mother of Recollection.* Recollection has a very profound meaning. At first, we have to cultivate conventional or artificial recollection. In that, we make an effort to remember something, then forget it, and then remember it again. Sometimes when we meditate, we have an important insight or experience that we don't want to lose. But it fades unless we repeatedly refresh it. With repeated recollection, experiences become habit, and then a part of our very being. When recollection is effortless, this is called "wisdom" or "awareness," and one has achieved the fifth path, that of perfection. A mind that abides in complete recollection at all times is Tara's wisdom mind, or buddhahood.

Nondual wisdom is the self-born mind.
By the habits of grasping at duality,
some are bound no matter what they do.
Please protect them, Deity of Nondual Wisdom.

After we actualize the first bhumi on the path of special insight, we practice step by step, up to the eighth bhumi as our meditation becomes extremely powerful. At the eighth bhumi, we realize or experience *nondual wisdom,* the one taste of samsara and nirvana. First, we see how phenomena—all appearances, all thoughts—are a reflection of mind. We practice that and become more stabilized in that realization until we see that there is no separation between the perceiver and the perceived.

For example, are the sun and its light two separate things? They are two, yet they cannot be separated. If they were separable, we could still have sunlight when there was no sun. But that is not the case. They are two, but also not two, so this is called "nonduality." Duality would mean there were two independent things, and singularity would mean there was only one thing. So "nonduality" means simply that there are *not two,* without implying that there *is one.* Mind and appearances exist in the same way. They are two, but do not separately exist—they are nondual.

In samsara, we think of phenomena as being completely external to ourselves, as being "real." Consider a house, for example. It did not arise by itself. It is made by people, so it is a mental creation. A mind first made an architectural drawing on paper. Then the builder looked at the design and figured out how to put the pieces together to make that house. In the same way, whether directly or indirectly, the whole of samsara is a construction of mind. When we have not realized this, we are confused by the appearance of "reality." But when we meditate well, nondual wisdom is the *self-born mind* that we realize is within us. Because he had complete realization of nonduality, Milarepa could walk through cave walls of solid rock. He realized from his own experience that everything is of the nature of mind, free from elaboration, so rock could no longer block him.

For us, duality is a deeply rooted habit that will be very difficult to break. Even though we may be able to prove any point of philosophy with reasoning and analysis, still, our experience is lacking. This is because of habit. Practice is about countering our habit of *grasping at duality.*

But *some are bound,* caught in duality, *no matter what they do.* Until we realize the inseparability of emptiness and all phenomena, we will be like a cooking pot that hasn't been cleaned in a very long time. The bottom has become so thickly encrusted with dirt that it will take a long time to clean, even with special tools.

We use meditation gradually to instill new habits. We can do the same meditation year after year; there is no need to jump from one to another. If we do one practice consistently, we can enrich it with reflections on impermanence, the suffering of samsara, compassion, and wisdom. There is no need to become discouraged; progress may be slow, but it will come to sincere practitioners without fail. Understanding this, we should be inspired to practice every day as much as possible, to apply whatever antidotes we know with joy and a feeling of good fortune.

> Although some abide in the perfect meaning,
> they don't realize the interdependence of cause and result.
> They are ignorant of the meaning of objects of knowledge.
> Please protect them, Omniscient Deity Mother.

The *perfect meaning* refers to shunyata, or emptiness. Some practitioners are able to meditate well in total absorption in the emptiness state. But they don't *realize the interdependence of cause and result,* so they presume that they have achieved the ultimate exhaustion of mind and phenomena. In truth, the more we practice, the more we purify our conduct so that we can experience the deeper meaning. This is what the Buddha did. Like his, our mind and discipline should also become increasingly pure as we progress day after day, year after year, until we reach the final goal of inseparable emptiness and causality.

Emptiness cannot transcend karma, cause and result. The *Heart Sutra* says, "Form is emptiness and emptiness is also form. Form is no other than emptiness and emptiness is also no other than form." They cannot be separated because no emptiness exists outside of phenomena. The very phenomena that we see are themselves emptiness. This is the point that some practitioners don't have the wisdom to see. Milarepa said, "Emptiness is easier to understand. You can investigate and scrutinize it, and gain understanding. But cause and result are much more difficult to comprehend." Only on the eighth bhumi and above does one achieve the incisive wisdom that sees the nature of interdependence, and only the Buddha's wisdom mind can perceive the most subtle aspects of the relationship between cause and result.

So those highly realized meditators who have not understood the full nature of causality within emptiness remain *ignorant of the meaning of objects of knowledge.* This means that they have not understood or directly realized the functioning of cause and result within emptiness. Therefore, we pray for Tara to *protect them* from their ignorance with her omniscience.

The nature of space is free from boundaries.
Nothing is different from that.
Still, practitioners and disciples don't realize this.
Please protect them, Perfect Buddha Mother.

Can space be said to have a center? If it had boundaries, then perhaps its center could be defined. But without boundaries, margins, or edges, where would the center be? This is the meaning of infinity—freedom from all limitations. The pristine mind is *no different from that.* Liberation is infinite, *free from boundaries,* free of elaboration. So the Buddha's wisdom mind and qualities are limitless, totally beyond measurement by our ordinary mind. Our unenlightened mind, bound by concepts, creates limitations. We must purify even the most subtle thoughts of duality, because they obscure this nature. When we have done so, we will have arrived at buddhahood itself: infinite wisdom, infinite compassion, infinite activities. *Practitioners and disciples* who *don't realize this*—we ourselves and all who follow the path of the bodhisattva—should not restrict our realization but must go forward until we reach freedom from all fetters.

Reflect on Tara, who is inseparable from the dharmakaya and who perfectly embodies wisdom and compassion. She gazes at all sentient beings and manifests infinite activities to free them from delusion and suffering. Visualize Tara in front of you or on the crown of your head and supplicate. Call upon her to shield you from delusion as you practice sincerely by reciting her mantras: OM TARE TUT TARE TURE SOHA and OM TARE TUT TARE TURE MAMA AYUR JÑANA PUNYE PUSHTING KURU SWAHA. The details of the visualization and meditation instructions can be found in *Pearl Rosary.* After reciting this prayer with strong devotion, meditate that Tara dissolves into you, or you can also recite Tara's mantra and then dissolve into emptiness. Rest the mind in the natural state. Meditate that all obscurations have been purified and that the nature of mind has been revealed. You can do this anywhere. You just need to be able to maintain your recollection and mindfulness.

I find this prayer very inspiring. In just seven verses, the whole of the Tripitaka, including the tantra teachings, is contained. We are so fortunate to have come in contact with this kind of teaching! Now that we can see how precious the Dharma is, we can look at samsara with different eyes. No matter how impressive modern technologies may be, they are still part of samsara. We went to the moon and didn't find happiness there. Now we are looking to get something from Mars. But here, if you take these teachings to heart, you will find something that is profoundly worthwhile.

Part Three

THE LIFE AND LIBERATION OF LORD JIGTEN SUMGÖN

10. The Life of Jigten Sumgön
by Drigung Kyabgön Padmai Gyältsen

OM SVASTI

The victorious Shakya saw the five sights.
He showed the victorious path,
and, to expand the teachings, took birth again as the victorious
regent Ratna Shri.
I prostrate to him.

THE GLORIOUS Phagmo Drupa had five hundred disciples who possessed the white umbrella, an honorary title; but, as he said again and again, his successor would be an *upasaka* who had attained the tenth level of a bodhisattva. This is the story of that successor, the peerless Great Lord Drigungpa, Jigten Sumgön.

Limitless kalpas ago, Jigten Sumgön was born as the Chakravartin Tsib-kyi Mukhyu (Wheel Rim), who was the father of a thousand princes. But then he renounced the kingdom, attained enlightenment, and was called the Tathagata Nagakulapradipa (Tib. Lurik Drönma). Although he had already attained enlightenment, he appeared later as the bodhisattva Kun-sang Wangkur Gyälpo. At the time of Buddha Kashyapa, he appeared as the potter Gakyong. At the time of Buddha Shakyamuni, he appeared as the Stainless Licchavi, who was inseparable from the Buddha himself. Later, he was born as Acharya Nagarjuna. Through all these births, he benefited the Buddha's teachings and countless sentient beings.

Then, so that the essence of the Buddha's teachings might flourish, Jigten Sumgön was born into a noble family in Tibet in 1143. His father was Naljorpa Dorje, a great practitioner of Yamantaka, and his mother was Rakshisa Tsünma. Many marvelous signs accompanied the birth. Jigten Sumgön learned the teachings of Yamantaka from his father, and by the age of four became expert in reading and writing. From his uncle, the Abbot

Darma, the great Radreng Gomchen, the Reverend Khorwa Lungkhyer, and others, he learned many sutras and tantras. At that time, he was called Tsunpa Kyab and later, Dorje Päl.

Jigten Sumgön's coming was predicted in many sutras, tantras, and termas. For example, in the *Yeshe Yongsu Gyepai Do* (*Completely Expanded Wisdom Sutra*) it is said: "In the northern snow ranges will appear a being called Ratna Shri. He will benefit my teachings and be renowned in the three worlds." In the *Gongdü* (*Quintessential Sublime Vision*) it is said: "At a place called Dri, the Source of the Dharma, Ratna Shri will appear in the year of the Pig. He will gather a hundred thousand fully ordained monks. After that he will go to the Abhirati (Tib. Ngönga) buddhafield. He will be called Stainless White Sugata and have a large retinue." In the *Gyälpo Kaithang* it is said: "Northeast of glorious Samye, at a place called Drigung, the source of the Dharma, the Lord-King Trisong Detsän will be born in the year of the Pig as the sugata Ratna Shri. He will gather a hundred thousand bodhisattvas. He will go to the Abhirati buddhafield and be called Stainless White Sugata. In that buddhafield, he will become the fully perfected king, the perfected Dharma teacher." Thus, his coming was clearly predicted.

When Jigten Sumgön was still young, his father passed away. His family's fortunes declined, so he had to support his family by reading scriptures. Once he was offered a goat. As he led it away, it tried to break loose; he pulled back, but the goat dragged him for a short distance and he left his footprints in the rock. When he was eight, he had a vision of Yamantaka. On another occasion, while meditating at Tsib Lungmoche, he saw all the phenomena of samsara and nirvana as insubstantial, like a reflection in a mirror. Even when he was in Kham he was renowned as a yogin.

Jigten Sumgön realized the practices of mahamudra and luminosity, and in his sleep he visited the Arakta Padma buddhafield. As mentioned earlier, from the great Radreng Gomchen he learned all the teachings of the Kadam tradition. From Lama Lhopa Dorje Nyingpo he received the teachings of Guhyasamaja and others. Once when there was a drought in Kham, he took the food offered to him as a fee for his reading and distributed it to those who were starving. Thus, he saved many lives.

Many important people began to approach Jigten Sumgön for teachings. One, Gönda Pandita, who came from Central Tibet, told him about Phagmo Drupa. Just by hearing the name of that being, Jigten Sumgön's mind quivered like the leaves of a kengshu tree blown by the wind. Enduring great hardship, he traveled from Kham to Central Tibet. A rainbow stretched the length of his journey, and the protector Dorje Lekpa took the forms of a rabbit and a child and attended him, looking after his needs. When he came to the dangerous, rocky path of Kyere, a natural formation of the six-syllable mantra transformed itself into a vision of the face of Phagmo Drupa.

Jigten Sumgön traveled day and night. On the way, he met a woman and man who said, "We have come from Phagmo Dru." Seeing them as the guru's emanations, he prostrated to them. He arrived at the Phagdru Monastery at midnight, and a Khampa invited him inside. When he met Phagmo Drupa, the guru said, "Now, all of my disciples are present." Jigten Sumgön then offered his teacher a bolt of silk, a bolt of plain cloth, and his horse. Phagmo Drupa refused the horse, explaining that he did not accept offerings of animals. Jigten Sumgön also offered a bag of food, which Phagmo Drupa used to perform a feast offering to Chakrasamvara. Then Phagmo Drupa gave Jigten Sumgön the twofold bodhisattva vow and the name Bodhisattva Ratna Shri. As one vessel fills another, Phagmo Drupa gave Jigten Sumgön all the teachings of sutra and tantra.

At that time, there lived a woman who was an emanation of Vajrayogini. Phagmo Drupa suggested to Taklung Thangpa that he stay with her; but Taklung Thangpa, not wishing to give up his monk's vows, refused, and shortly afterward the emanation passed away. Lingje Repa then fashioned a cup from the woman's skull. This made him late for an assembly, and the food offerings had already been distributed by the time he arrived. Taking the skull cup, he circulated among the monks, receiving offerings of food from each. The monks gave only small portions, but Phagmo Drupa gave a large amount, filling the skull cup completely. Jigten Sumgön gave even more, forming a mound of food which covered the skull cup like an umbrella. Lingje Repa then walked again through the assembly, and as he walked he spontaneously composed and sang a song of praise in twenty verses. Finally, he stopped in front of Jigten Sumgön, offering the food and the song to him.

One day, Phagmo Drupa wanted to see if any special signs would arise concerning his three closest disciples, so he gave each of them a foot of red cloth with which to make a meditation hat. Taklung Thangpa used only what he had. Lingje Repa added a piece of cotton cloth to the front of his hat, and Jigten Sumgön added a second foot of cloth to his, making it much larger. This was considered very auspicious. On another occasion, Phagmo Drupa called Jigten Sumgön and Taklung Thangpa and said, "I think that the Tsangpo River is overflowing today. Please go and see." Both disciples saw the river following its normal course, and returned; but Jigten Sumgön, thinking there was some purpose in the guru's question, told him, "The river has overflowed, and Central Tibet and Kham are now both under water." This foretold the flourishing of Jigten Sumgön's activities, and he became known as a master of interdependent origination.

At this time, in accordance with the prediction made by Phagmo Drupa, Jigten Sumgön still held only the vows of an upasaka. One day, Phagmo Drupa asked him to remain behind after the assembly and instructed him to sit in the seven-point posture of Vairochana. Touching him on his head, throat, and heart centers, he said OM, AH, HUNG three times and told him, "You will be a great meditator, and I will rejoice."

Jigten Sumgön attended Phagmo Drupa for two years and six months. During that time, he received all of his guru's teachings and was told that he would be his successor. At the time of Phagmo Drupa's parinirvana, a radiant five-pronged golden vajra emanated from his heart center and dissolved into the heart center of Jigten Sumgön; this was seen by the other disciples. Jigten Sumgön then gave all his belongings to benefit the monastery and to help build the memorial stupa for his guru.

After this, he met many other teachers. From Dakpo Gomtsul he received the four yogas of mahamudra. A patroness then promised him provisions for three years, and Jigten Sumgön, earnestly wishing to practice the teachings he had received, retired to Echung Cave to meditate. In those three years, he gained a rough understanding of the outer, inner, and secret aspects of interdependent origination. He then realized that the cause of wandering in samsara is the difficulty wind has in entering the channels, and so he practiced moving the wind, saw many buddhas and bodhisattvas face to face, and had visions of his mind purifying the six realms. Then he went on a pilgrimage to Phagdru and other holy places.

On his return to Echung Cave, he practiced with one-pointed mind. In the same way that Mara arose as obstacles to Lord Buddha at the time of his enlightenment, and the Five Sisters and others tried to hinder Milarepa, the final fruition of Jigten Sumgön's karma then arose, and he contracted leprosy. Becoming intensely depressed, he thought, "Now I should die in this solitary place and transfer my consciousness." He prostrated to an image of Avalokiteshvara that had been blessed many times by Phagmo Drupa. At the first prostration, he thought, "Among sentient beings, I am the worst." At the second, he thought, "I have all the teachings of my guru, including the instructions of bardo and the transference of consciousness, and need have no fear of death." Then, remembering that other beings didn't have these teachings, he sat down and generated profoundly compassionate thoughts toward others. His sickness left him, like clouds blown away from the sun, and at that moment he attained buddhahood. He had practiced at the Echung cave for seven years.

Shortly after this, he had a vision of the seven Taras. Because he had a full understanding of interdependent origination, and had realized the unity of discipline and mahamudra, he took the vows of a fully ordained monk. From this time on, Jigten Sumgön did not eat meat. As he had already been named Phagmo Drupa's successor, the chief monks of his guru's monastery invited him to return.

After taking the abbot's seat at the monastery, Jigten Sumgön insisted on a strict observance of monastic discipline. One day, some monks said, "We are the 'nephews' of Milarepa and should be allowed to drink *chang*." Saying this, they drank. When Jigten Sumgön admonished them, they replied, "You yourself should keep the discipline of not harming others." Phagmo Drupa then appeared in a vision to Jigten Sumgön and said to him, "Leave this old, silken seat and go to the north. There you will benefit many sentient beings."

Jigten Sumgön went north and, on the way, at Nyenchen Thanglha, he was greeted by the protector of that place. At Namra, a spirit king and his retinue took the upasaka vow from him, and Jigten Sumgön left one of his footprints behind as an object of devotion for them. He gave meditation instructions to vultures flying overhead, and they practiced according to those teachings. Once, at a word from Jigten Sumgön, a horse that was running away returned to him. He also sent an emanation of himself to Bodh Gaya to pacify a war begun by Duruka tribesmen.

On another occasion, at Dam, he gave teachings to a large gathering and received many offerings. At the end of a day which had seemed very long, he told the crowd, "Now go immediately to your homes," and suddenly it was just before dawn of the next day. To finish his talk, Jigten Sumgön had stopped the sun. When he was at Namra Mountain, Brahma, the king of the gods, requested the vast and profound teachings. On the way to Drigung, the great god Barlha received him. The children of Dzänthang built a throne for Jigten Sumgön, and he sat there and instructed the people of that town. Even the water, which has no mind, listened to his teachings and made the sound "Nagarjuna."

Then he came to Drigung Thil. In his thirty-seventh year, he established Drigung Jangchub Ling and appointed Pön Gompa Dorje Senge as supervisor for the construction of the monastery. Many monks gathered there and enjoyed the rainfall of profound Dharma.

In Tibet, there are nine great protectors of the Dharma. Among them, Barlha, Sogra, Chuphen Luwang, Terdrom Menmo, and Namgyäl Karpo bowed down at Jigten Sumgön's feet, took the upasaka vow, and promised to protect the teachings and practitioners of the Drigung lineage.

At one time, water was very scarce in Drigung. Jigten Sumgön gave 108 pieces of turquoise to his attendant, Rinchen Drak, with instructions to hide them in various places. Rinchen Drak hid all but one, which he kept for himself and put in his robe. The pieces he hid became sources of water, and the one he kept turned into a frog. Startled, he threw it away, and in falling it became blind in one eye. Where the frog landed, a stream called "Blind Spring" arose. Most of the streams were dried up by fire when Drigung Thil was destroyed around the end of the thirteenth century, but some still remain.

Twice a month, on the new and full moons, Jigten Sumgön and his monks observed a purification ceremony called *sojong*. Once some monks arrived late, and Jigten Sumgön decided to discontinue the practice, but Brahma requested him to maintain that tradition, and he agreed.

Jigten Sumgön continued to look after his old monastery at Phagdru, Dänsa Thil. Once when he was at Daklha Gampo, Gampopa's seat, dakinis brought an assembly of 2,800 yidams on a net of horsehair and presented them to him. To memorialize Phagmo Drupa, he built an auspicious stupa of many doors, and placed images of those yidams inside compartments, with a door for each of them. The tradition of building stupas of this type originated from this. While he was visiting Daklha Gampo, light rays streamed forth from Gampopa's image, merging inseparably with Jigten Sumgön, and he attained both the ordinary and extraordinary siddhis of the treasure of space. In a vision, he met with Ananda and discussed the teachings.

Once Lama Shang said, "This year, the dakinis of Oddiyana will come to invite me and the Great Drigungpa to join them. He is a master of interdependent origination and won't have to go there, but I should go." Soon after this, the dakinis came for him and he passed away; but when they came to invite Jigten Sumgön, he refused to go, and the dakinis changed their prayer of invitation to a supplication for the guru's longevity. Then all the dakas and dakinis made offerings to him and promised to guide his disciples.

Jigten Sumgön had many important students. Among them, the leaders of the philosophers were the two Che-ngas, the great abbot Gurawa, Nyö Gyälwa Lhanangpa, Gar Chöding, Pälchen Chöye, Drupthob Nyakse, and the two Tsang-tsangs. The foremost vinaya holders were Thakma Düldzin and Dakpo Düldzin. The Kadampa geshe was Kyo Dorje Nyingpo. Among the translators were Nup, Phakpa, and others. The leaders of the tantrikas were Tre and Ngok. The leaders of the yogins were Düdsi, Bälpu, and others. When Jigten Sumgön taught, rainbows appeared and gods rained flowers from the sky. Machen Pomra and other protectors listened to his teachings, and the kings of Tibet, India, and China were greatly devoted to him. At this time, Jigten Sumgön had 55,525 followers. To feed this ocean of disciples, Matrö, the king of the nagas and the source of all the wealth of Jambudvipa, acted as patron for the monastery.

Near Drigung Thil there was a rock called Lion Shoulder, which Jigten Sumgön saw as the mandala of Chakrasamvara. He established a monastery there and, to spread the teachings and benefit sentient beings, built another auspicious stupa of many doors using a special method. He also repaired Samye Monastery.

Jigten Sumgön's main yidam practice was the Chakrasamvara of Five Deities, and he sometimes manifested in that form in order to work with those who were difficult to train. When a war began in Minyak in Eastern Tibet, he protected the people there through his miracle power. The number of his disciples increased to 70,000. Many of the brightest of these attained enlightenment in one lifetime, while those of lesser intelligence attained various bhumis, and everyone else realized at least the nature of his or her own mind.

In one of the predictions about Jigten Sumgön it was said, "A hundred thousand incarnate great beings, tulku, will gather." Here, "tulku" meant that they would be monks and have perfect discipline, and "great beings" meant that they would all be bodhisattvas. In other life stories, it is said that in an instant Jigten Sumgön visited all the buddhafields, saw buddhas such as Amitabha and Akshobhya, and listened to their teachings. Jigten Sumgön himself said that whoever so much as heard his name and had the chance to go to Layel in Drigung would be freed from birth in the lower realms, and that whoever supplicated him—whether from near or far away—would be blessed, and his or her meditation would grow more firm. He also said that all sentient beings living in the mountains of Drigung, even the ants, would not be born again in lower realms.

From the essence of the instructions of sutra and tantra, Jigten Sumgön gave teachings which were compiled by his disciple Che-nga Sherab Jungne into a text called *Gong Chig,* which has 150 vajra statements and 40 additional verses in an appendix.

A naga king named Meltro Zichen once went to Drigung for teachings. Jigten Sumgön sent a message to his disciples to remain in seclusion so that those with miracle power would not harm the naga, and those without such power would not be harmed themselves. The message was given to everyone but the Mahasiddha Gar Dampa, who was in meditation in the depths of a long cave. When the naga arrived, he made a loud noise which was heard even by Gar Dampa. He came out to see what was happening and saw a frightening, dark blue snake whose length circled the monastery three times and whose head looked in at the window of Jigten Sumgön's palace. Without examining the situation, he thought that the naga was there to harm his guru, so he manifested as a giant garuda which chased the naga away. At Rölpa Trang, there is a smooth and clear print left by the naga, and at Dermo Mik there is a very clear claw mark left by the garuda when it landed on a rock. Near the river of Khyung-ngar Gel there are marks left by both the garuda and the naga.

A Sri Lankan arhat, a follower of the Buddha, once heard that Mahapandita Shakya Shri Bhadra was going to Tibet, and he gave that teacher's brother a white lotus, asking that he give it to the Mahapandita to give to Nagarjuna in Tibet. When Shakya Shri Bhadra arrived in Tibet, he ordained many monks, but didn't know where to find Nagarjuna. When giving ordination, he would usually distribute robes, but once, when an ordinary disciple of Jigten Sumgön approached him for ordination and asked for a robe, none were left. Nonetheless, he insisted strongly. One of Shakya Shri Bhadra's attendants pushed him away and he fell, causing blood to come from his nose.

Before this, Shakya Shri Bhadra had been accustomed to seeing Tara in the morning when he recited the seven-branch prayer, but for six days after this incident she didn't show herself. Then, on the seventh day, she appeared with her back turned to him. "What have I done wrong?" he asked her. "Your attendant beat a disciple of Nagarjuna," she replied, "and brought blood from his nose." When he asked how he could purify this misdeed, Tara told him, "Make as many Dharma robes as you have years, and offer them to fully ordained monks who have no robes." Shakya Shri Bhadra then searched for the monk who had been turned away. When he found him, and learned the name of his teacher, he realized that Jigten Sumgön was Nagarjuna's incarnation. So he sent one of his attendants to offer the white lotus to Jigten Sumgön. In return, Jigten Sumgön sent many offerings of his own and asked that Shakya Shri Bhadra visit Drigung, but the Mahapandita could not go there, though he sent many verses of praise. Because Nagarjuna had knowingly taken birth as Jigten Sumgön in order to dispel wrong views and was teaching at Drigung, Shakya Shri Bhadra saw that there was no need for him to go there.

At this time, many lesser panditas were visiting Tibet. One of them, Vibhuti Chandra, said, "Let us talk with the Kadampas; the followers of mahamudra tell lies." Shakya Shri Bhadra replied, "Because Jigten Sumgön is a great teacher, you should now apologize for having said these things." Vibhuti Chandra then went to Drigung, made a full apology, and constructed an image of Chakrasamvara at Sinpori Mountain. He also translated into Sanskrit one of Jigten Sumgön's writings about the fivefold path of mahamudra, named *Tsin-dha Mani*.

One day, a great scholar named Dru Kyamo came to Drigung from Sakya to debate with Jigten Sumgön. When he saw the guru's face he saw him as the Buddha himself, and his two chief disciples—Che-nga Sherab Jungne and Che-nga Drakpa Jungne—as Shariputra and Maudgalyayana. There was no way he could debate with Jigten Sumgön after this. His devotion blossomed fully, and he became one of Jigten Sumgön's principal disciples. Later, he was called Ngorje Repa and wrote a text called *Thegchen Tenpai Nyingpo* as a commentary on Jigten Sumgön's teachings.

The number of Jigten Sumgön's disciples continued to increase. At one rainy season retreat, 100,000 morality sticks were distributed to count the monks attending. Not long after that, 2,700 monks were sent to Lapchi, and equal numbers were sent to Tsari and Mount Kailash, but by the next year 130,000 monks had again gathered at Drigung.

Karmapa Düsum Khyenpa once came to Drigung after visiting Dak-lha Gampo. At Bam Thang, Jigten Sumgön and his disciples received him warmly. At that time, the Karmapa saw Jigten Sumgön as the Buddha and his two chief disciples as Shariputra and Maudgalyayana, surrounded by arhats. When they returned to the main assembly hall, the Serkhang, the Karmapa again saw Jigten Sumgön as the Buddha, with his two disciples appearing as Maitreya and Manjushri, surrounded by bodhisattvas. Thus, Düsum Khyenpa showed great devotion and received many teachings. He also saw the entire area of Drigung as the mandala of Chakrasamvara.

The question arose of who would hold the lineage after Jigten Sumgön's passing. Jigten Sumgön had confidence in many of his disciples, but had thought for a long time that the succession should pass to one of his family clan, the Drugyäl Kyura. Since he had been born in Kham, he sent one of his disciples, Pälchen Shri Phukpa, there to teach his family members. Displaying miracle power and proclaiming his guru's reputation, Pälchen Shri Phukpa taught Jigten Sumgön's uncle Könchog Rinchen and his uncle's son Anye Atrak and grandsons. Their minds became attracted to the teachings, and they moved to Central Tibet. Their stories are told in the *Golden Rosary of the Drigung Kagyu.*

One day Jigten Sumgön told his disciple Gar Chöding to go to the Soksam Bridge and offer a torma to the nagas living in the water. "You will receive special wealth," he told him. A naga king named Sokma Me offered Gar Chöding a tooth of the Buddha and three special gems. Generally, it is said that this tooth had been taken by the naga king Dradrok as an object of devotion. This was the same naga who usually lived in the area of Magadha but had access to Soksam by way of an underwater gate. Gar Chöding offered the tooth and gems to Jigten Sumgön, who said, "It is good to return wealth to its owner," indicating that the tooth had once been his own. "As you are wealthy," he continued, "you should make an image of me and put the tooth in its heart." A skilled Chinese artisan was then invited to build the statue, and the tooth was enshrined there as a relic. Jigten Sumgön consecrated this statue hundreds of times. It was kept in the Serkhang and called Serkhang Chöje (Dharma Lord of Serkhang). Its power of blessing was regarded as being equal to that of Jigten Sumgön himself. It spoke to many shrine keepers, and to a lama named Dawa it taught the Six Dharmas of Naropa. Later, when Drigung was destroyed by fire, it was buried in the sand for protection. When the Drigung Kyabgön returned to rebuild the monastery, a search was made for the statue, which came out of the sand by itself, saying, "Here I am!" Thus, this image possessed great power. Gar Chöding made many other images of Jigten Sumgön at this time.

Jigten Sumgön had by then grown old and could not often travel to Dänsa Thil. He sent Che-nga Drakpa Jungne there as his Vajra Regent, and that disciple's activities were very successful. Under the leadership of Panchen Guhya Gangpa, Jigten Sumgön sent 55,525 disciples to stay at Mount Kailash. Under Geshe Yakru Päldrak, 55,525 were sent to Lapchi. Under Dordzin Gowoche, 55,525 were sent to Tsari. Even at the time of Chungpo

Dorje Drakpa, the fourth successor to Jigten Sumgön, there were 180,000 disciples at Drigung.

Once, Jigten Sumgön went to the Dorje Lhokar Cave at Tsa-uk. "This cave is too small," he said, and stretched, causing the cave to expand and leaving the imprint of his clothes on the rock. Because the cave was dark, he pushed a stick through the rock, making a window. He then made shelves in the rock to hold his belongings. All of these can be seen very clearly. Jigten Sumgön also left many footprints in the four directions around the area of Drigung.

One day, Jigten Sumgön fell ill. Phagmo Drupa appeared to him in a vision and explained a yogic technique by means of which he became well again. Jigten Sumgön taught according to the needs of his disciples. To some, according to their disposition, he gave instructions in the practice of the Eight Herukas of the Nyingma tradition.

Toward the end of his life, he predicted a period of decline for the Drigung lineage. Taking a small stick that he used to clean his teeth, he planted it in the ground and said, "When this stick has reached a certain height, I will return." This foretold the coming of Gyälwa Kunga Rinchen. Jigten Sumgön asked Che-nga Sherab Jungne to be his successor, but the latter declined out of modesty. Then he asked the great abbot Gurawa Tsültrim Dorje, who agreed.

In order to encourage the lazy to apply themselves to the Dharma, Jigten Sumgön entered parinirvana at the age of seventy-five, in the year of the Fire Ox (1217). His body was cremated on the thirteenth day of the month of Vaishaka. Gods created clouds of offerings, and flowers rained down from the sky to the level of one's knees. His skull was untouched by the fire, and his brain appeared as the mandala of the sixty-two deities of Chakrasamvara more clearly than if a skilled artist had painted it. His heart also was not touched by the fire and was found to have turned a golden color. Likewise, countless relics appeared.

After Jigten Sumgön's passing, most of the funerary responsibilities were taken on by Che-nga Sherab Jungne, even though he had earlier declined the succession. He went to Lion Shoulder (Tib. Senge Phungpa) Mountain to view the mandala of Chakrasamvara, saw Jigten Sumgön there, and thought that he should build a memorial in that place. Jigten Sumgön then again appeared in a vision on the mountain of the Samadhi Cave and said to him, "Son, do as you wish, but also follow my intention." Then he disappeared. Doing as he wished, Che-nga Sherab Jungne built an auspicious stupa of many doors called "Sage, Overpowerer of the Three Worlds." In that stupa, he put Jigten Sumgön's heart and many other relics. Following his guru's intention, he built the stupa "Body-essence, Ornament of the World," which was made of clay mixed with jewel dust, saffron, and various kinds of incense. In that stupa, he put Jigten Sumgön's skull and brain, along with many other relics, including vinaya texts brought from India by Atisha, and the *Hundred-Thousand-Stanza Prajñaparamita*.

Jigten Sumgön now abides in the Eastern Great All-Pervading Buddhafield, surrounded by limitless numbers of disciples from this earth who died with strong devotion to him. When such people die, they are immediately born there. Jigten Sumgön places his hand on their heads, blessing them, and welcoming them there.

11. THE PRECIOUS JEWEL ORNAMENT

BY NGORJE REPA

OM SVASTI

There was one who for countless previous kalpas
Possessed the power of the gathering of accumulations and excellent
    training,
Whose activities were unequaled in the three worlds.
I pay homage to the lord of beings, the Drigungpa.
His body is inseparable from the buddhas of the three times.
He is the emanation of glorious Vajradhara.
He perfected the ocean of limitless good qualities.
His life is beyond thought and expression.
His enlightened activities are inconceivable.
Even the aryas, who possess the perfectly pure wisdom eye,
could not describe them, even if they were to try for kalpas.
Here, I will write a little, according to my own understanding.

HE IS THE precious lama, the protector of the three worlds, the essence of all the buddhas of the three times. He was born in Drongkhyer Tsungu in the snow land of Tibet, in the left-hand valley of upper Tsar in a land in Do-Kham enriched by the holy Dharma. This is the land of the red-faced rakshasa, on the heights of the snow mountains of the yakshas, a place of many gods and rishis, the fifth of ninety-nine border lands.

In particular, the clan of his birth was the Drugyäl Kyura, which is like the Shing-sa-la of the Brahmin caste. His mother was the hidden yogini Tsünma. When he was conceived in his mother's womb, he entered in the form of a white text called *Thunderbolt Vajra*. His mother experienced the glory of joy and peace in the daytime and in dreams. A special samadhi was also born in her mind.

At the time of his birth, that region was pervaded by auspiciousness and excellent goodness in all directions. After that, though still young, that Dharma lord abided in the stainless state. He became expert in all worldly and transcendent knowledge. Many others followed his example. Many disciples whose mind streams were ripened by the Dharma appeared. At that time, he received from revered lamas the cycle of the three kinds of Vajrakilaya and other teachings. He received instructions on mahamudra from the great reverend called Khorwa Lungkhyer. Under others, including Lobpön Kyebupa and Radreng Gomchen, he studied and trained in the stages of the Buddha's teachings.

When he was twenty-five, he thought of going to Central Tibet. At that time, just by hearing the story of Phagmo Drupa from Gönda Pandita, his mind quivered like the leaves of a kengshu tree blown by the wind. He then set out for Central Tibet. On the road, many auspicious signs appeared in the daytime and in dreams. When he met Phagmo Drupa, their body, speech, mind, and activities were united in one nature. He pleased the holy lama with the offering of practice.

When the precious lord Phagmo Drupa attained parinirvana, a golden vajra emerged from that lama's heart and dissolved into his own. This was seen by all. To show how the buddhas of the three times attained buddhahood through the practice of austerities, he stayed seven years at a place called Echung and gave up all comforts of body and life. At that time, he subdued all demons who create obstacles to the samadhi of emptiness and compassion. The ushnisha appeared as a sign of his perfection of the two kinds of bodhicitta. Then, at the age of thirty-five, he received the bhikshu ordination from Khenpo Shangsum Thokpa, Lobpön Denma Tsilungpa, and Sangtewa Nyälwa Dülwa Dzinpa. He directly perceived the inseparable nature of that which is forbidden by vow and that which is naturally proscribed, and of the mode of abiding of virtue and nonvirtue. He realized all outer and inner dependent arisings without exception. Because of this, he possesses inconceivable compassion, power of blessings, wisdom, samadhi, and the gateways to samadhi, clairvoyance, and so forth. Because of these inconceivable qualities, he possesses limitless confidence to benefit others.

Now I will also explain these things in verse:

Countless kalpas in the past,
he perfected the two accumulations for the benefit of beings.
Even though he had already achieved supreme unsurpassable
    enlightenment,

he took an inconceivable birth through the power of compassion.
In the supreme valley of Dri, enriched by Dharma, in the east,
he emanated as a powerful thunderbolt vajra
and was born in the Kyura clan
for the liberation of beings.
He became learned in all classes of knowledge.
Others followed his example.
He remained in the unafflicted state.
He arose as the glory of the joy and happiness of all beings.
Guided by the reverend called Khorwa Lungkhyer,
by Kyebupa, and by Radreng,
he developed his mind and studied the commentaries
to the tantras, mahamudra, and the stages of the path.
Driven by the wind of the blessings of glorious Phagmo Drupa,
who dwelled at the tree of virtue at the border of India and Tibet,
and by the blessings of the Compassionate One,
he set out for Central Tibet to ripen the fruit.
On hearing his lama's precious name from the spiritual friend,
his mind moved like kengshu leaves quivering in the wind.
As in the stories of Norsang and Taktugnu,
he endured heat, cold, and countless hardships on his journey to the
    Dharma king.
Along the mountain range from Kham to Central Tibet he saw
    continuous rainbows and lights.
On a cliff road at the mouth of the valley of Phenyul, the source of
    knowledge, at the palace of the six syllables,
he saw the Lord of Beings, Phagmo Drupa,
in the form of a stainless white bhikshu.
In the forest of Tha-tsa, graced by spontaneously established blessings,
at the vajra throne, the seat of the glorious lama, just by his meeting
    that unequaled lama,
his body, speech, mind, and activities
merged inseparably with the lama's.
He pleased the lama by offering his life, wealth, and practice,
and the lama's blessing established him
in the nature of the buddhas of the three times.
From the subtlest conceptual thought
to the primordial-awareness wisdom of the buddhas,

he opened the door to the profound and vast Dharma.
He actualized the meaning of stainless speech.
With the roar of a lion, the lama prophesied in the assembly:
"You will become an unsurpassed, noble, great meditator."
He attained the fame of a lineage holder dwelling on the tenth bhumi.
The lama's vajra mind dissolved into his in nondual primordial
    awareness.
Like the buddha at the river Nairanjana,
He also—in an isolated place—performed austerities
with no concern for his life.
Like a moon without clouds and free from eclipse, that sage's mind was
    fully freed.
He became completely victorious over all faults,
the enemies, the four maras.
Because of this, he perfected bodhicitta,
and the ushnisha appeared on the crown of his head.
Even though he was enlightened from beginningless time
and was victorious over all faults and obscurations,
he took on full ordination for the benefit of beings
in accordance with the example of the buddhas of the three times.
He studied the vinaya, the root of the Buddha's teachings.
He fully realized the meaning of the inseparability
of that which is forbidden by vow and that which is naturally
    proscribed,
as well as the meaning of virtue and nonvirtue.
In an instant, he understood the interdependence of "this cause" and
    "that result,"
of all vessels and their contents of samsara and nirvana without
    exception,
and of "this cause" and "that outcome" of all outer and inner things,
and of different states of mind.
In brief, he understands the births of beings,
including the dragon in the sky and the conch in the sea,
and the way that faults and qualities arise
through the interdependence of prana and the secret body and mind.
Through the power of truth of his speech,
he pacifies others' sufferings of sickness and harm
and all dangers arising from fire, water, rock, and so forth.

He spontaneously accomplishes all wishes without exception.
With his wisdom, he perceives all dharmas without obstruction.
He is famous for teaching meditation to birds in the sky.

Thereafter, the Dharma lord, the precious protector of beings, went to the forest of glorious Drigung in the northern region of U-ru. After he arrived there, his fame and renown spread in all directions. Because of this, in the same way that a great shade tree attracts many flocks of birds, he unceasingly gathered from all directions noble beings who had not fallen away from the Mahayana: scholars and practitioners who aspired to the qualities of the holy lama, who had gathered great accumulations of merit and wisdom during limitless kalpas in the past, who had attended previous buddhas, who had gathered such skillful means, who were not afraid to receive the profound teachings of dependent arising, and who had the great courage to enact the vast conduct of skillful means.

The stainless speech of the Prajñaparamita, the precious sutras, all profound classes of the tantras of secret mantra, and supports of body, speech, and mind—profound and full of marvelous blessings—arose like a mountain of treasure. Enjoyments and necessities excelling those of Vaishravana or a universal monarch, marvelous wealth, precious jewels, and so forth—all wish-granting things without exception—gathered like rain clouds in a summer sky.

He overpowered, with the strength of his loving-kindness, those who were arrogant with pride or anger and who, motivated by jealousy and harmful thoughts, contended with others. He conquered, with his great compassion, all demons and obstructing forces. Beings in that land had no power to harm each other, and their joy exceeded that of the god realm Shen-trul Wang-je. Even birds and wild animals lived in peace. Thus, he spontaneously accomplished the benefit of others.

Now, I will express all this in verse:

In the sky of the naturally pure dharmadhatu,
the sun-rays of his great compassion
are fully freed from the clouds of faults and obscurations.
Because of this, his fame and renown pervade all worlds.
Those who aspire to that lord's qualities
are amazed by receiving them
through seeing, hearing, and recollection,

as in the pure land of Lord Amitabha.
Hundreds of thousands of disciples
and countless spiritual masters sat at his feet,
developed the power of wisdom through his limitless teachings,
and trained their minds in the meaning of the Tripitaka.
All proud and accomplished ones of Central Tibet
without exception—Kharak Nyö, Mänlung Lotsawa,
Yarlung Khu, Dritsam Shang, and others—
took the dust of his feet on the crowns of their heads.
All kings without exception,
the virtuous ones in all directions such as north and south,
together with their noble families in the world,
bowed down respectfully at that lord's feet.
Those who had not fallen away from the Mahayana,
who gathered the accumulations from beginningless kalpas,
and who had the fortune to attend the holy lama
assembled unceasingly from all directions.
The marvelous supports of body, speech, and mind—the shrines
    worshipped
by the three worlds, together with the gods,
the treasury of joy and happiness of all beings—
he gathered in his hands like a limitless treasure.
The supports of speech—the sutras and tantras with their
    commentaries,
and the stainless Prajñaparamita,
the mother of all buddhas and disciples of the three times—
fell into his hands like a summer rain.
Gold, silver, brocades, horses, and fine clothing—
whatever marvelous things existed in the world—
he spontaneously obtained
like opening a treasure that grants all wishes.
Like the abundant wealth of a universal monarch,
the joy and happiness of the gods of Shen-trul Wang-je,
or the enlightenment at Magadha,
he spontaneously accomplished the benefit of himself and others.
Those who resented that lord
because of hatred, pride, or arrogance arising from jealousy and
    harmful thoughts,

he subdued with the power of loving-kindness and compassion.
He defeated all maras with his mind of compassion.
As in the country of King Maitribala,
all enmity ceased among the people, birds,
animals, and so forth where he lived,
and they dwelt in harmony and peace.
There, those who were intent on full liberation
gathered at one time in the hundreds of thousands, like those
    gathered before Lord Maitreya in Tushita.
Because of his perfected accumulations, he is unchallenged in the
    world,
like Indra in the realm of the gods.
He provided whatever was desired:
enjoyments of food and drink, shelter, clothing, conveyances,
    precious jewels, grains, and so forth,
along with pleasant words, the example of his practice, and his living
    according to the meaning of the teachings.
In this way, he possessed the four ways of gathering disciples.
He possessed blessings and virtue equal to the limits of space.
The three realms and all worlds without exception came under his
    power,
and the treasury of all supreme and ordinary siddhis
arose like a mountain of glory and auspiciousness.

When that lord of beings thought to give teachings to those assembled hundreds of thousands who were intent on the fruit of full liberation, many great omens never seen before appeared in all the buddhafields of the ten directions. Using their inconceivable miracle power, all the bodhisattvas of those realms appeared in the sky with clouds of offerings in order to see that holy lama's display and to hear his teachings. From those buddhafields also appeared shravaka arhats possessing limitless miracle power. Brahma and Indra, the lords of the gods, together with the four protectors of the world and so forth, appeared in space with a rainfall of offerings. Gods, nagas, yakshas, gandharvas, mahoragas, asuras, garudas, kinnaras, and so forth, with their own clouds of offerings, also appeared to hear the holy lama's teachings and to offer their protection. Also, the Glorious Protector Mahakala and others—all protectors of the teachings—along with the eight assemblies of gods and spirits, gathered to protect the Buddha's teachings and to fulfill the intention of the holy lama. This cannot be comprehended by ordinary beings. Instead, it is a matter for the pure primordial awareness of all buddhas and bodhisattvas.

Now I will describe these things in verse:

Then this unequaled lord of beings
thought to give teachings to those of varying capacity
concerning dependent arising, which is free from the eight extremes.
In all the buddhafields, these kinds of signs appeared:
Flowers rained from the sky, the earth shook six times,
the smell of incense arose by itself, and rainbows appeared.
Powerful bodhisattvas asked the buddhas the reason for this,
and the buddhas proclaimed:
"This is a sign that the precious, unequaled, victorious teacher of
    Dharma
is alive and giving teachings in this long-suffering world,
at this time of the degeneration
of Shakyamuni's teachings."
Those bodhisattvas were amazed,
and, in order to enact conscientiousness,
to see the display of the unequaled lama, and to hear the Dharma,
appeared in the sky with clouds of offerings.
From those buddhafields, assemblies of shravakas
appeared in that place with displays of miracles,
emitting blazing fire from their upper bodies and water from their
    lower halves,
and manifesting many bodies from one and dissolving them back
    again.
Brahma, Indra, and the four protectors of the world,
together with their families,
appeared in order to hear the Dharma,
and made offerings of divine substances, filling space.
Gods, nagas, yakshas, gandharvas, garudas,
kinnaras, and mahoragas also appeared there in person
with their own clouds of offerings
in order to hear the Dharma and to offer their protection.
All protectors of the teachings, mahakalas and mahakalis,
assembled like clouds in the sky

in order to fulfill the intention of the glorious lama
and to spread the Buddha's teachings.

Thereafter the Dharma lord, the precious lord of beings, directly actualized
the dharmakaya, which is like space. He then manifested as the glorious
sambhogakaya, adorned with the major and minor marks, in order to tame
the bodhisattvas in the buddhafields. In the same way, through the three
kinds of nirmanakaya, he accomplished the benefit and training of bodhisattvas, arya shravakas, pratyekabuddhas, accomplished siddhas and yogins,
scholars learned in the five classes of knowledge, universal monarchs of
humans and gods, rishis of non-Buddhist schools, Brahma, Indra, Ishvara,
and even animals and so forth—taming each in their own way.

In the marvelous speech of the tathagatas, he gave—from within the
inexhaustible dharmadhatu—limitless, pacifying teachings of the 84,000
doors in the languages of the six realms and of the gods and nagas and so
forth. To tame through the five kinds of wisdom mind of the tathagatas,
such as the vajra-like samadhi and so forth, he emanates according to the
needs of individual beings through the limitless doors of the four kinds of
inconceivable activity.

Thus, the unceasing jewel-wheel of the body, speech, and mind of that
precious Dharma lord, that lord of the three secrets, is as vast as space and
as deep as the ocean. Even though it cannot be measured, I will still partially
relate these things in more detail in verse:

That lord abandoned all obscurations
and directly actualized the three kayas, the fruit of nonabiding.
He possesses the two kinds of purity, the stainless dharmakaya,
the unified one taste of inseparable wisdom and space.
His one body pervades all buddhafields of all buddhas of the ten
    directions without exception,
and all buddhafields without exception appear within his body.
His emanations for the benefit of beings do not conflict.
His supreme emanation performs the twelve deeds of a buddha.
His birth emanations appear even in animal forms.
Through these various births of family and form,
he manifests in the god realm as the king of the gods
and in the human realm as a universal monarch.
He emanates as superior, unequaled masters,

as a captain for those who set out to sea,
and as a warrior to turn back the tide of war.
Because of his compassion, he awakens the potential
for the enlightenment of all beings
through his emanation of various kinds of birth:
hell-being, preta, animal, and asura.
Moreover, he fully manifests as earth, water, fire, wind, forests,
    medicine, doctors,
nurses, bathing pools, various jewels, clothing, and conveyances,
mansions, food, drink, seats, a wish-granting tree,
a wish-granting cow, and attractive gatherings of parents and relatives.
He fully manifests as whatever is desired by any being
and fulfills the benefit of others.
As the sun, the moon, and clouds of rain,
he grants fearlessness and protection to those who suffer.
To the shravakas, who have entered the path to peace
and who possess inconceivable birth and death,
he fully displays his love and compassion
and establishes them in the supreme state of vastness and profundity.
For the pratyekabuddhas, he gradually opens all doors
of the Dharma of interdependence
and establishes them in the liberation that does not abide in samsara or
    nirvana
and that is free from grasping and fixation.
To bodhisattvas who have attained the ten bhumis,
he appears as the sambhogakaya, which is adorned with the major and
    minor marks,
teaches the Mahayana,
and brings them to the primordial wisdom of the Buddha.
He emanated, greater than others, for the benefit of beings
in that forest of Drigung,
in the northern region of the Land of Snow in Jambudvipa,
in this world of the Buddha's teachings.
That guide is an object of offerings for gods and humans.
His merit is like a mountain of gold.
For all who encounter him, there is no disagreement.
He is an ocean of good qualities, meaningful to behold.
At Namra mountain, Brahma supplicated him.

At Thanglha, he was received with offerings by assemblies of gods.
He received blessings directly from lamas,
from assemblies of yidams and dakinis, and from buddhas.
He bound by oath all the eight classes of worldly gods and rakshasas
    without exception.
When he turned back the Duruka army at Bodh Gaya in India,
he appeared as a white bhikshu with a staff and bowl
and pacified the harmful forces of the enemy through the power of his
    loving-kindness.
In order to fully accomplish the intention of all lamas, to spread the
    teachings of the buddha,
and to increase the two accumulations of beings,
he built a glorious Auspicious Stupa of Many Doors
at the glorious center of enlightenment, Drigung.
Through the power of the blessings of that peerless compassionate one,
countless artisans—emanations of awakened beings—
arrived from all directions.
He blessed various precious materials.
From within the lotus bed of that stupa,
made of precious things and unsurpassed in the world,
arose the shapes of many buddhas, together with their complete body
    forms, postures, and attributes.
The more one sees of these, the more one is amazed!
On each of eighty pillars made from precious materials
were carved four bodhisattvas, two facing out and two facing in.
Eighty and sixty offering goddesses held up that palace of the gods,
which was adorned by many hangings, canopies, and pediments.
Through the activities of various skillful means
of building this unsurpassed, precious shrine imbued with sacred
    power—
this vast mansion of the outer, inner, and secret—
he satisfied all beings according to their wish.
Through his activities of speech, empowered by compassion,
he gave 84,000 kinds of teachings in the languages of gods, nagas,
    yakshas, gandharvas, kinnaras, and mahoragas.
He clearly proclaimed the sixty branches of profound, melodious
    speech
which possesses the four powers of unmistaken meaning: soothing,

gentle, endlessly fascinating, and clearly proclaimed to all worlds,
including the gods'.
For those of superior, middling, and ordinary capacities,
he opened the door of the inconceivable Dharma
through grammar, syntax, and various sounds,
names, words, and letters.
In the middle of many assemblies of hundreds of thousands of
bodhisattvas,
he proclaimed—free from hesitation or self-consciousness—
the lion's roar without distinguishing
among "close" or "distant," "greater" or "lesser."
Though some possess the four kinds of discerning awareness and
training
in limitless hearing, contemplation, and meditation,
they lack experience of the realization
of the pinnacle of the view.
They don't understand the noncontradictory nature
of the various tenets of the Buddha's teachings.
Their intelligence is scattered, and they don't understand
the interdependence of those things to be abandoned and their
antidotes.
For all of them, he extended the power of his compassion
and established the intention of the buddhas of the three times by
means of the four kinds of proof:
the words of the Buddha, his own experience, the instructions of the
lineage, and general accounts.
He showed the appearance of all phenomena of samsara and nirvana
to be merely mental formation,
and all objects of knowledge to be equal in one taste,
primordially unborn like the sky.
He taught that ground, path, and fruition are empty in one taste
and that emptiness and compassion are inseparable in one taste.
He blessed those of superior power
with the meditation of uncontrived spontaneity.
The undefiled three trainings—which are the meaning of the Tripitaka,
the holy teachings of the Sage—
are the foundation of the three vows,

all the antidotes for the objects to be abandoned.
He taught that these can be held together in the mind, at one time,
    without contradiction.
The unmistaken method of glorious Naropa,
which is the essence of all the classes of tantra of secret mantra,
is the technique of the path—the mode of abiding of body and
    mind.
Through this profound instruction, he ripened all who were proper
    vessels.
He cut their doubts regarding the Dharma of perfect meaning.
He gave instructions inspiring the certainty of experience.
Through his primordial, unobstructed, omniscient wisdom
he expanded their understanding to all objects of knowledge without
    exception.
Like Mentok Dazey in the All-Good Forest at the time of Buddha
    Padmai Lama's teachings,
he gave instructions in the sublime samadhi of emptiness.
He established many beings on the path of nonreturning.
His awakened activities are the embodiment of the five kinds of
    primordial wisdom, fully free from the elaborations of striving
    and effort.
He perceives all objects of knowledge without obstruction.
His dharmakaya is free from sickness, aging, birth, and death.
He abides beyond the qualities of purity, self, bliss, and permanence.
May he hold us with the hook of his compassion!

Thus, for thirty-seven years from the time of his enlightenment until he attained parinirvana, that peerless, precious lama sustained his sangha. As described above, wealth was gathered and distributed. Spiritual friends assembled there. Accomplished sanghas came and went. He displayed inconceivable manifestations of body. He pointed out inconceivable doors to the Dharma. It is impossible to comprehend or describe even one day of these activities. What need to mention them all?

The meaning of this will now be described further in verse:

Thus, the holy lama, the Dharma lord, turned the wheel of Dharma
    for forty years in the All-Good Forest of glorious Drigung.

By means of the four ways of gathering, he perfected the benefit of
  beings.
In this way, this great earth was filled with those who realized
  awakened qualities
by hearing the Dharma from that victorious one.
Countless disciples gained critical insight into the truth of dharmata;
actualized the Dharma of outer, inner, and secret interdependence;
  and accomplished equanimity.
They could display miraculous powers of body and transform all
  elements without exception.
They accomplished the qualities of the methods of the path.
He possessed the activities of taming all those to be trained without
  exception
by subduing them, accepting them, leaving them as they were, and so
  forth.
He possessed direct insight to bless the mind streams of others.
The fame of that lord of all pervades the whole world.
Inconceivable gatherings of spiritual friends,
retreatants intent on full liberation,
came and went in their hundreds of thousands
without increasing or diminishing the assembly.
At Oddiyana, Dzalendara, Kailash, Gangha, Serkyi Ja Khyib, Jakang,
  Asura, Bodh Gaya, Tsari, Lapchi, and Chuwar—well-known as
  holy places—
and in Nepal, Minyak, Jang, Hor, and so forth—less well-known as
  holy—
in caves, under trees, and in monasteries:
in all these places, his disciples surpassed the number of stars in the sky.
Thus, at this time of the flourishing of the activities of that peerless
  Dharma Lord, I also arrived.
For twelve years, my karmic connections to practice were awakened.
I received recognition as a rebirth of Naropa in the midst of the
  assembly.
He held me in his heart with unmatched kindness.
He sustained me like a son with food, clothing, wealth, and teachings.
He possesses the riches of a universal king.
He is a mountain of samadhi, enriched by the forest of awakened
  qualities,

and fully ornamented by the Dharma of knowledge and realization.
In order to repay the kindness of the glorious lama,
the peerless Kharak of Nyö, together with spiritual friends possessing
  knowledge and realization
and monks possessing the three trainings,
offered many tens of sutras written in gold
and the most desirable things among the treasures of man:
gold, turquoise, horses and saddles, specially dyed woolen robes, pearls,
  coral, tigers, leopards, medicines, and so forth:
limitless special and marvelous things, each in limitless hundreds of
  numbers.
Parasols, conch shells, pavilions, and so forth—
these great seventeen were offered on the Drigung plain.
At one time, a hundred thousand bodhisattvas received summer retreat
  sticks
and made offerings of desirable things—
the wealth of the four directions of India and China—
in the presence of that victorious one.
By turning the vast, great, and universal Dharma wheel,
he caused all to give birth to supreme bodhicitta
and established all beings in the supreme Mahayana.
E MA! How marvelous and inconceivable!

Thus, the holy lama fully completed all his deeds and activities without
exception. When he was seventy-five years old, he taught the limitless ultimate meaning in the middle of the assembly according to the Buddha's third
turning of the wheel. He also displayed many emanations of his body. To
the great meditators, he pointed out limitless doors to samadhi, along with
limitless signs and symbols. For those who had arrived from different directions, he fully perfected the accumulations of merit and wisdom.

Thus, from space, many rainbows appeared, along with a rain of flowers,
and so forth. Marvelous, amazing, and inconceivable miraculous displays
unfolded themselves. On the twenty-seventh day of the third month of the
Fire Ox year, he entered into parinirvana.

Now these things will be described in verse:

Thus, the Dharma lord, this lama of all beings, fully completed his
  deeds and activities.

When all who could be trained by that body had been trained, so that
    his teachings would not decline,
he passed the activities of his teaching to the Khenpo who held the
    disciplines of the Sage;
to Che-ngawa, the chief of his disciples; and to the precious Chökyi
    Gyältsen, who held the family lineage.
In order to inspire lazy ones to diligence,
and to sadden those who believe in permanence,
he entered into the peace of parinirvana
like a fire whose fuel is spent.
At that time there were inconceivable, marvelous signs.
So that the continuity of the Three Jewels would not decline,
he gave blessings from within the sphere of great luminosity.
His wisdom body became an object of recollection.
According to the vision of ordinary persons,
his form body passed into a buddhafield.
The minds of the sangha gathered there
mixed with unmoving samadhi, the mind of the Dharma lord.
The four kinds of sangha without exception
also made offerings of body and wealth
and supplicated him with one-pointed yearning.
I, too, lamented: "Now we have no protector or lord!"
I collapsed on the ground with the suffering of grief.
Helplessly, I shed tears like blood.
I offered vast clouds of real and imagined offerings.
In the Fire Ox year, on the twenty-seventh day of the month of
    enlightenment,
the Dharma lord displayed the entry into parinirvana.
A month later, on the third day, a fragrance pervaded all directions
when his body was touched by the wisdom fire.
In the sky, many gods received him,
offering numerous parasols, victory banners, and canopies,
together with the sounds of cymbals and other kinds of celestial
    music,
the varied fragrances of the best incense, a rain of flowers, and clouds
    of offerings.
From space, gatherings of gandharvas gazed down
with displays of limitless celestial music,

melodious songs,

and many varieties of inner and outer offerings.

On the earth, many beings lamented, wailed, and cried aloud.

The sorrow of their grief was unbearable,

as though they were bewildered without refuge

in the darkness of a desolate plain.

That lord has inconceivable manifestations.

As objects of offering for future generations,

his body emanated limitless deity forms and relics

that filled the center of enlightenment, Drigung.

On the thirteenth day of that month, the close disciples, the chiefs
    of the assembly who were highly accomplished,

made the great promise not to go to Kham but to stay in Central
    Tibet and go into retreat.

At that time, rainbows filled the sky,

and a rain of relics of the Sugata filled every part of Jambudvipa.

Those who were fortunate met the right path.

Those burdened by desire had their wishes fulfilled.

Those oppressed by fear, together found refuge from fear.

All were established on the noble path of enlightenment.

Concerning the vajra body, speech, mind, qualities, and activities
    of the Drigungpa,

the holder of the treasury of the three secrets of all the buddhas of the
    three times without exception:

the more one looks, they are unending.

What a great wonder!

An unsurpassed guide like this never came in the past

and will not come again in the future.

Therefore, I pray to this precious one, excellent in the three times:

"Please hold me and all beings with your compassion."

Your excellent virtues are immeasurable.

Your inexhaustible qualities, like the limits of space, could never be
    described,

even by buddhas as innumerable as the sands of the Ganges,

even if they proclaimed them for many hundreds of thousands of
    kalpas.

I take refuge in your innumerable marvelous disciples, both direct
    and indirect,

who perceive the meaning of objects of knowledge from within the
    state of equipoise,
who actualize samadhi,
and who accomplish direct insight.
Vajradhara, lord of beings in this degenerate time,
you fully awaken my lazy mind.

COLOPHON

I clearly perceived the image of the lama's life and liberation and, inspired by
devotion, wrote down what I perceived. A frog in a well cannot comprehend
the ocean's depth. A fly cannot measure the limits of space. How can my
small mind measure the vastness and profundity of your life and liberation?
However, for my own inspiration, I have briefly set down a little in order to
recall it. By this virtue, may the teachings of the glorious lama spread like
the light of the sun.

I have adorned the pure gold of the lama's life and liberation with many
precious gems of poetry. This ornamentation with stainless jewels was done
by me. By this virtue, may all beings quickly attain buddhahood.

Furthermore, according to the Phakpa Yeshe Yongsu Gyepai Do: "In the
future age of degeneration, in the northern ranges of snow, will appear a
victorious Dharma lord, a guide of humanity known as Ratna Shri. That
supreme being will be renowned throughout the world. He will perform
deeds in accordance with my doctrine. That sugata's supreme disciples,
who will be free from the afflictions of anger and arrogance, will gather as
a sangha of eighty million. They will attain buddhahood for the benefit of
beings." This is what the Buddha foretold.

This story of the life and liberation of the glorious Drigungpa, called *The
Jewel Ornament*, was written by Shedang Dorje, who brings joy to the heart.

12. Jigten Sumgön: The Second Nagarjuna
by H. H. the Drigung Kyabgön Chetsang Rinpoche

Prophecies of the Precious Lord's Coming

THE COMING of the Second Nagarjuna, the Victorious Lord, the Dri-gungpa, the Protector, Jigten Sumgön, was prophesied very clearly in the sutras and tantras of the Perfect Teacher, Lord Buddha, and in the hidden treasures of Padmasambhava. The *All-Victorious Wisdom Sutra** says,

> He, a supreme being, will spontaneously appear. Known as Rin-chen Päl, his fame will spread to the whole world. The virtuous sangha accompanying this exalted being will be eighty million shravakas. When the spiritual sons of the Supreme Tathagata have freed themselves from emotions, anger, and pride, there will be eight million bodhisattvas accompanying this exalted being.

The *Maha Guhyasamaja Yoga Tantra*† relates that

> The lord of the secret path
> will appear as a glorious Vajradhara teacher,
> the very quintessence of the three kayas,
> to accomplish the benefit of beings.
> He will manifest in the forest home of mighty beasts
> as the glorious King of Munis,
> a Shakya bhikshu

---

*From the *All-Victorious Wisdom Sutra,* vol. GA of the Derge edition of the Kagyur, f. 136.
†From the *Maha Guhyasamaja Yoga Tantra,* vol. TSHA of the tantra section of the Kagyur, f. 101.

endowed with supreme intelligence
which will blossom both gradually and all at once.

Another sutra says,

> The sole lord, King Trisong Detsän, will manifest to the north-
> east of Samye at the place famed as *Dri,* Source of the Dharma,
> as the great being born in the Pig year known as Rinchen Päl, sur-
> rounded by hundreds of thousands of emanated bodhisattvas. In
> the future in the buddhafield of True Joy, he will become the fully
> enlightened sovereign known as the Tathagata Stainless White.

And from the hidden treasures of Padmasambhava:

> In Tso-ngu,
> near the lake of Upper Dän,
> Ratna Shri will appear
> as a son of the great yogin Dorje.

A Brief Account of the Dharma Lord's Life

There are many brief and detailed biographies of Jigten Sumgön. Most of
the following stories are taken from *The Blazing Vajra,* written by Che-nga
Drigung Lingpa (also known as Che-nga Sherab Jungne), who attended
Jigten Sumgön for many years and was a master of the ten aspects of knowledge. Jigten Sumgön passed away in the fourth month of the Female Fire
Ox year. In the fifth month, this biography was composed by some principal
disciples, headed by Che-nga Drigung Lingpa. They wrote this life story,
and that evening they read it to the assembly of monks and all were very
pleased. Che-nga Drigung Lingpa wrote:

> The disciples of the Lord of Beings asked me to write the life
> story of the Precious Lord. This cannot be done by anyone, even
> by gods; therefore it is beyond my own inferior ability. But I will
> set forth a little, according to his own words.

In Kham, there is a village called Chökyi Tsuklakhang that lies between
Upper Dän, which is like a golden stupa, and Lower Dän, which is like a

turquoise mandala. Near that village, in a valley called Tsar Töyön Lung, is a village called Tsung-ngu. It is here that Jigten Sumgön was born.

Jigten Sumgön's father was Naljorpa Dorje, an emanation of Bhagavan Bhera and a descendent of the Drugyäl Kyura clan, who understood well the abhidharma, the paramitas, and the tantra of the secret mantra, and who was a yogin of Vajrabhairava. His mother's name was Rakshisa Tsünma. She was a hidden yogini. When Jigten Sumgön was conceived, he entered his mother's womb in the form of a white text that had the nature of Vajrapani. He remained in the womb for nine months and fourteen days, and was born in the Water Pig year (1143). His uncle gave him the name Welwa Thar. This beautiful child, established in limitless virtues, far surpassed ordinary beings. He was accomplished in reading at the age of four, and his style of reading, called "thel-lok," in which all the syllables are pronounced, was later brought by him to Drigung.

Once he read the *Manjushri Namasangiti* and that evening his father asked him to recite it. To the great surprise of his family, he repeated almost all of it from memory. He studied all the teachings held by his father, and at the age of nine began to instruct others. His uncle, Darma, taught him the *Three Aspects of Vajrakilaya*. From Lhopa Dorje Nyingpo and his disciples, he learned about Guhyasamaja, and he also received teachings on this yidam according to the tradition of Gö Lotsawa. Under Jetsün Khorwa Lungkhyer, he studied mahamudra, practiced, and became accomplished in the samadhi of illusion. He saw the Arakta Padma buddhafield. From Lobpön Kyebupa and Radreng Gomchen he learned the stages of the teaching and the stages of the path, and received many instructions of the Kadam tradition. He was overwhelmed by great compassion. A woman who had lost her limbs to leprosy was once carried to town by Jigten Sumgön so that she could beg for food. He placed a lump of sugar in the mouth of a blind beggar. He regarded all sentient beings as his mother.

When he was fifteen, there was a famine in the land, and his father passed away. His mother and teachers died the next year. Then he moved south and supported himself and his host by reading scriptures. Once, he was offered a goat. Because he was young, the goat dragged him and he left his footprints in the rock. These footprints are called the "goat-dragged footprints" and can still be seen in a rock close by a river near Lhadra in Upper Ga in Kham. From Lobpön Sangye Yeshe, he received the empowerment of Vajrayogini. Then, at the invitation of the patron Akhar, he went into retreat at Tsib

Lungmoche. There, he saw samsara and nirvana as though reflected in a mirror.

Gönda Pandita arrived in Central Tibet. Jigten Sumgön met him and asked about the wonderful teachers who were then in that region. Gönda Pandita replied that the great scholars in philosophy were Cha, Yor, Nya, Tsang-nak, Nyenbak, and many others; that the great meditators were the Kadampas. There were also many yogins, but the most wonderful of all was Phagmo Drupa. Just by hearing Phagmo Drupa's name, Jigten Sumgön's mind was moved like a steed encouraged by a whip. That evening, he left his retreat cave and went to the house of Pön Chöye, who discouraged him from going to Central Tibet. But Mokchen A-Me Gese helped him get permission to go. Many wonderful omens occurred on the road; he saw all of them as the emanations of Phagmo Drupa and continued on his way as in the stories of Taktugnu, Norsang, and other bodhisattvas.

Finally, in the Glorious Samantabhadra Forest, he met the Lord of Beings, Phagmo Drupa. The guru declined Jigten Sumgön's gifts of a horse and silk, but accepted a brick of tea, which was then boiled and served to eighty disciples. Phagmo Drupa's face became brighter as he drank the tea, and Jigten Sumgön felt uplifted on seeing this. Phagmo Drupa noticed this and said, "I have great hopes for you. All this is my blessing. For you, I underwent many trials."[*]

On that day, Phagmo Drupa said, "Today my retinue of disciples is complete," and he gave a teaching on the aspiration of bodhicitta. Step by step, he gave Jigten Sumgön the bodhisattva vow and teachings on mahamudra, the Six Dharmas of Naropa, and other topics. Jigten Sumgön was satisfied with them. Three times Phagmo Drupa gave him the teachings on the true nature of mind. The third time, he actualized those instructions. He was fully satisfied with his realization of mahamudra and thought, "There is no need for anything more than this." He went to the Lord of Beings and said, "All apparent phenomena are included in the dharmakaya of mahamudra, so there is no need for other teachings. One should have devotion and confidence in the guru because of his kindness." The Lord of Beings said, "What are you saying? Until you achieve enlightenment, you will need the five dharmas. You should not abandon the Five Profound Paths of Mahamudra.[†] You may be satisfied with your realization, but there is much farther to go on the path." After that, Jigten Sumgön put all his energy into the practice of these five profound paths. He gained certainty in these teachings and sang this song:

> I bow at the feet of glorious Phagmo Drupa!
>
> If the steed of love and compassion
> does not run for the benefit of others,
> it will not be rewarded in the assembly of gods and men.
> Attend, therefore, to the preliminaries.
>
> If one's body, the king of deities,
> is not stabilized on this unchanging ground,
> the retinue of dakinis will not assemble.
> Be sure, therefore, of your body as the yidam.
>
> If, on the guru, snow mountain of the four kayas,
> the sun of devotion fails to shine,
> the stream of blessings will not arise.
> Attend, therefore, to this mind of devotion.
>
> If, from the sky-like expanse of mind's nature,
> the clouds of conceptual thought are not blown away,
> the planets and stars of the two wisdoms will not shine.
> Attend, therefore, to this mind without conception.
>
> If the wish-fulfilling gem of the two accumulations
> is not polished by aspiration,
> the results we have hoped for will not arise.
> Attend, therefore, to this final dedication.

Once, Jigten Sumgön went to visit the Lord of Beings and found him in the company of Khenpo Shang, Geshe Dän, and many other great teachers. The Lord of Beings said, "All of you, please go. I want to give a special teaching to Jigten Sumgön." They all left. Phagmo Drupa told Jigten Sumgön to

---

meditation on the yidam, meditation on the teacher, meditation on mahamudra, and dedication.

sit in the center of the room. He then approached him, placed his walking stick on Jigten Sumgön's heart, and loudly spoke the three syllables OM, AH, and HUNG. "You will be a great meditator," he told him, "and I will rejoice."* This made Jigten Sumgön confident and dispelled his hesitations. After that, he didn't care for food, clothes, or fame. He spent most of his time secluded in meditation, and became known as Silent Kyura.

On another occasion, food offerings of hard brown sugar were distributed to the assembly. Drupthob Lingje was late and missed his portion, but he brought a cup made from the skull of a dakini and received small amounts of food from everyone there. Phagmo Drupa gave him a large amount, which filled the skull-cup to the brim and beyond. Drupthob Lingje walked up and down in the assembly, singing:

> Principal heart-son of the Precious Dharma Lord,
> who brings together all his teachings,
> Dharma Regent who comes from magnificent blessings,
> who has the power of confidence and devotion,
> I prostrate to you!

In this way, he sang this and other verses, and when he came to the end of the line, he gave the skull-cup to Jigten Sumgön. His song has twenty verses and is called "Twenty Verses of Praise." Around this time, Jigten Sumgön took the bodhisattva vow with his friend Tonpa Sherab Lama and was given the name Rinchen Päl.

Jigten Sumgön spent thirty-two months at the feet of the Lord of Beings, and received all his teachings. When the Lord of Beings passed away, a five-pronged, golden vajra emanated from his heart and dissolved into the heart of Jigten Sumgön, and this was seen by everyone present.[†]

After the Lord of Beings passed away, Jigten Sumgön went to Wön, where he lived with a teacher named Lobpön Tsilungpa. From him, he received the teachings of Vajrayogini. From Dakpo Gomtsul, he received the four yogas of mahamudra. He became completely engaged in practice. At that time Lama Yäl invited him to practice at Echung Cave, and he went into retreat there for seven years. He realized that the cause of wandering in samsara is one's inability to direct winds into the channels, and so he concentrated his

---

*Collected Works of Kunga Rinchen, vol. KA, f. 36a1.
†Chos 'byung mkhas pa'i dga' ston of dPa' bo gtsug lag 'phreng ba, vol. NA.

efforts on this practice. Then the seven Taras appeared holding utpala flowers, and gave him very vast and profound teachings. Jigten Sumgön sang a song of powerful blessings, supplicating the seven Taras:

> In the unborn dharmadhatu
> abides the Reverend Mother, the deity Tara.
> She bestows happiness on all sentient beings.
> I request her to protect me from all fears.
>
> Through not understanding oneself as dharmakaya,
> one's mind is overpowered by the kleshas.
> Our mothers, sentient beings, wander in samsara.
> Please protect them, Deity Mother.
>
> If the meaning of Dharma is not born in one's heart,
> one just follows the words of conventional meaning.
> Some are deceived by dogma.
> Please protect them, Perfect Mother.
>
> It is difficult to realize one's mind.
> Some realize but do not practice.
> Their minds wander to worldly activities.
> Please protect them, Deity Mother of Recollection.
>
> Nondual wisdom is the self-born mind.
> By the habits of grasping at duality,
> some are bound no matter what they do.
> Please protect them, Deity of Nondual Wisdom.
>
> Although some abide in the perfect meaning,
> they don't understand the interdependence of cause and effect.
> They are ignorant of the meaning of objects of knowledge.
> Please protect them, Omniscient Deity Mother.
>
> The nature of space is free from boundaries.
> Nothing is different from that.
> Still, practitioners and disciples don't realize this.
> Please protect them, Perfect Buddha Mother.

At Echung Cave, when he was near enlightenment, he contracted leprosy as a sign of the exhaustion of his negative karma. He became depressed by this illness and immeasurable compassion was born in his mind through his reflections on the suffering of all beings. The power of his compassion forced the evil nagas and their retinues to leave his body, and he saw them go. At that moment, he was completely free from sickness, and he sang this song:

> I, your son, on the path of the secret Vajrayana, searched for an
> authentic guru.
> I saw you as the Buddha himself.
> From the body-mandala of the Jetsün
> I took many full empowerments and was magnificently blessed
> by your body, speech, and wisdom mind.
> I realized the meaning of nonduality.
> Lord of Beings, you passed away before I could attend you for very
> long.
> Remembering the kindness of the Lord of the World,
> my mind is completely moved by affection and devotion.
> By staying alone in a solitary place,
> one throws the eight worldly concerns far away.
> Cutting attachment to food and clothing,
> I meditate in the continuity of the nonduality of mind.
> The kindness of the authentic guru
> and the continuity of joyful effort
> ripened the obscurations of negative karma
> that had accumulated from beginningless time.
> I contracted leprosy, a disease difficult to cure, and thought,
> "Maybe it would be better to die."
> This mendicant remained in a solitary place,
> with no texts around me, with no one asking, "Are you sick?"
> with no one administering medicine or saying mantras.
> At that time, I experienced uncontrived devotion to the peerless
> guru,
> and realized the samadhi that understands sickness as the mind.
> I maintained this awareness without interruption.
> In three nights and four days,
> my karma and obscurations were purified.
> I realized the cause and effect of interdependent origination.

The treasure of the profound tantra revealed itself.
In the oneness of the great luminosity,
the two fixations of meditation and activity were purified.
I recognize that I am now a lord of yogins.
Because of the leprosy born from negative karma,
I realized the teachings of emptiness and compassion.
These are famous for driving away leprosy.
This is the blessing of the precious guru.
I became motivated to study the teachings of previous gurus.
I learned the stories of the liberation of their own body, speech,
    and mind.
Making feast offerings without random actions or concern for
    meat and beer,
I haven't disgraced the Lord of Beings.
Now I will have no regrets, even if I die.
I will not lack confidence, even if I grow old.
I haven't been partial, even as the leader of disciples.
In samsara, I have had no thought of accepting or rejecting.
I haven't given teachings in exchange for wealth.
Whatever I have done has been in the service of the gurus of the past.
Even if I spoke a lot, I led disciples as did the gurus of the past.
I haven't disgraced the teachings of the Protector, the Lion of the
    Shakyas.
Now I will have no regrets, even if I die.

Thus he sang this song called "Driving Away Leprosy." He accomplished the major and minor marks of a buddha. The ushnisha appeared on the top of his head, and he attained the state of Vajradhara.

Jigten Sumgön often said, "I practiced meditation for seven years. For five years, I didn't know how to practice, and for two years I practiced with full understanding, achieving this much realization. So, if you practice for some years, through the power of taming your mind you can go either to a pure buddhafield or to a higher realm. I realized that all things depend on cause and effect. Ultimately, all causes and effects appear from emptiness. This is my special understanding."*

Jigten Sumgön then left his cave. When Lama Yäl invited him to lead a

---

*The Blazing Vajra Jewel, a biography of Kyobpa Jigten Sumgön by Che-nga Drigung Lingpa (sPyan lnga bri gung gling pa), f. 56b7.

ceremony, Namkha Gyän (the daughter of Thöpa Drupse) ran and danced naked through the assembly. Jigten Sumgön thought, "This is because I am not a monk." Following this, he put on robes and went to Wön. When he was thirty-five, for the benefit of beings, he received the vows of a bhikshu from Khenpo Shang, Lälop Lobpön Tsilungpa, and Sangtewa Nyälwa Düldzin. Because he was not satisfied with his own study, analysis, and meditation, at Chungpo Phuk he studied the root text of the vinaya, along with many other teachings, from Nyälpa Duldzin. He reached the limits of scholastic knowledge. Although he had realized the interdependence of cause and effect, he didn't teach without reference to the scriptural authority of the Buddha and lineage gurus, and he said that even if he were to remain in a buddhafield, he would not be separated from the Buddha's teachings even for an instant.

In the Fire Bird year of the second cycle, Jigten Sumgön was enthroned at the Phagdru monastery. He stayed there for three years. However, because of the poor discipline in that place, he felt that he shouldn't stay any longer and supplicated the Lord of Beings, who appeared in the clear light. As instructed, Jigten Sumgön went to Drigung. There, Tokden Minyak Gomrim offered him a place for a monastery. At Drigung Thil, Jigten Sumgön built a residence, an assembly hall, and a temple for the protectors with images of silver, along with many other buildings. In the Earth Pig year of the third cycle, because of his fame, he founded the seat of the Drigung Kagyu order. In that year alone, more than a hundred monks gathered there.

Soon after, Jigten Sumgön was invited to Damzhung in the north, where he was received by the great Dharma Protector, Nyen Thanglha Chenpo. While giving teachings there, he arrested the course of the sun. The kings Thangde and Wöde requested him to come to Namra in the north. He stayed there from late winter through the summer, and gave meditation instruction even to animals such as deer, horses, and vultures. On his return, he sang this song called "Lakma Trakar":

> I bow down at the feet of all gurus!
> At the monastery of Lakma Trakar,
> I am unhappy and my mind wanders.
> These thoughts occur to me:
> The son of the nephew of King Tsede,
> and Kundrak De, the lord-king,
> born in Upper Tibet,

descendants of the three families* and, as humans, descended from
    a god,
are the lords who wonderfully established
the teachings of the Lion of the Shakyas
and caused them to flourish.

To the north of Thanglha Mountain,
these kings, the lords of the powerful gandharvas,
offered many hundreds of texts, including *Sangne Tö*.
They bowed their crowns at my feet.
Although I have no desire for worldly things,
and though they requested me to practice there,
like a bird freed from its bonds,
I am leaving sadly for the south.

From the three regions of Upper Tibet to Minyak,
all are devoted to me.
The elder and younger brothers of the spirit Namra
and all wrathful gods and demons
bow down and attend me.
Even though I became the lord of beings there,
I left that evil place without attachment.
Like a bird freed from its bonds,
I am leaving sadly for the south.

In the country of those Dharma kings,
many thousands of disciples
cultivated the mind of supreme enlightenment,
establishing their own and others' benefit
through the practice of the six paramitas,
giving up the defilements of nonvirtuous actions,
and obeying whatever I commanded.
Many disciples who are proper vessels
are overpowered and tightly bound
by the demon of mental afflictions.
Each year, I freed hundreds from such childishness.

*Three families of wisdom, compassion, and power.

I leave behind many disciples who are proper vessels,
who became monks through confidence
in the teachings of the Lion of the Shakyas.
Like a bird freed from its bonds,
I am leaving sadly for the south.

For the benefit of others, I went north
to no particular place.
The Dharma king Lhawö and I received each other.
Even though, to benefit the Dharma king,
I satisfied his mind
with the vast and profound teachings,
he wasn't ripened and freed
by the teachings of the glorious Mahapandita Naropa,
through which one can attain supreme siddhi
in one lifetime.
Like a bird freed from its bonds,
I am leaving a little sadly for the south.

From Chang Lhanyen Sangsang to Khem Naklha Jampo,
all beings think of me.
Impartially, I establish many in peace and happiness.
Many others, without refuge,
deceived by wrong view and nonvirtuous friends,
take birth in lower realms.
Without having established them in enlightenment,
like a bird freed from its bonds,
I am leaving a little sadly for the south.

By not staying in a hermitage in snow mountains
solitary, complete with qualities
praised by the buddhas of the three times,
a place where yogins of the past stayed,
or on an island in the middle of a lake
with no one else around,
I do not fulfill the wishes of the Protector,
the Lord of the Three Worlds, glorious Phagmo Drupa.
Like a bird freed from its bonds,
I am leaving sadly for the south.

Innate self-awareness is the supreme seat
of the buddhas of the three times,
a completely solitary place
held by yogins of the past,
and especially by the precious guru.
Without having established the qualities
of the three bodies,
like a bird freed from its bonds,
I am leaving sadly for the south.

Nyenchen Thanglha Yarlha Mountain
is like a giant lion leaping into the sky.
This is the monastery for the master yogin
who cuts attachment to this life.
Without having continued, in this place,
in the experience and realization
of the practice of nonduality,
like a bird freed from its bonds,
I am leaving sadly for the south.

Namtso Chukmo Lake in the north
is like a beautiful turquoise mandala.
It is difficult to measure its breadth and depth.
This is the monastery of Pema Gyälpo
and other yogins of the past.
Without having settled my mind,
like a bird freed from its bonds,
I am leaving sadly for the south.

The monastery of the elder and younger brothers of Namra
is a gathering place for evil gods and demons.
Without having subdued through immeasurable compassion
these gods, and without having benefited
other sentient beings,
like a bird freed from its bonds,
I am leaving sadly for the south.

The peak of Tsälchen Lhago Mountain
is like a spear held in the sky.

This is a place where Lord Marpa and Pälchen Galo
cut the elaborations of mind.
Like a bird freed from its bonds,
I am leaving sadly for the south.

To the north of snow mountains,
whose nature is effortless accomplishment,
are four marvelous monasteries.
Without having accomplished all benefits
of myself and others,
like a bird freed from its bonds,
I am leaving sadly for the south.

The lord of the land with his retinue—
although I dare not separate from them,
I find that I have to leave.
In general, the samaya of the secret tantra is very strict.
In particular, in the lineage of glorious Naropa,
the guru is the profound path.
I have no choice but to go to Ngamshö.

The two spiritual friends, the Khenpo and the Lobpön,
are like parents.
They grow old and are close to death.
Through their compassion, they sent messengers.
Thinking that I might not come, they invoked my samaya.
For this reason also, I have no choice but to go.
They sent an image of the Dharma Lord and a letter.
Because they invoked my samaya,
I have no choice but to go.

The vajra Dharma friends who entered the path
like passengers boarding a ship
gather around me with affection.
With compassion, they request teachings.
The lord of the land acts as their patron.
Lord of the Land, don't scold me.
You patrons in all directions, don't be disappointed.

I must go this once.
I will return again.

In general, I, a bhikshu of the Shakyas,
no matter where I stay,
think of the lords of the land and their retinues
as my patrons, without doubt.
All power and strength that I have,
according to the Dharma,
I will use again to benefit the king.
All virtues accumulated in the three times
I offer to you and all sentient beings.
I am not selling my affectionate respect.
I have no choice but to go.
I must leave this once,
but I will see you again soon.

Thus he sang.

He traveled through Drigung.* The children of Dzänthang built a Dharma throne on which he sat and gave teachings. In the summer, the river there is turbulent; but where Jigten Sumgön taught, the river made no sound. This is so even today.

Then he arrived at his seat. Khenpo Kolti had been giving monks' vows without encouraging the development of bodhicitta. This made it difficult to observe the ceremony of sojong,† and Jigten Sumgön thought to discontinue the practice, but Brahma and Indra requested him to maintain it. The naga king Matrö bowed at his feet and asked for teachings. He had been asked to come to Ngamshö, but went first to Phagdru. He could not bear to see the decline of his guru's seat, so he restored that place to its former strength. At that time, a large golden parasol was brought from Nepal and placed atop the Tashi Wöbar stupa, which contained the relics of Phagmo Drupa.

All the texts at Phagdru were brought to Daklha Gampo to pacify local

*Drigung is located about ninety miles northeast of Lhasa, near the upper waters of the Kyichu River. The name of this place comes from the name of one of the four chief ministers of Songtsen Gampo, Driseru Gungthun, who lived there. Phagmo Drupa manifested as a *dri* (female yak) and pointed out that place as the location for a monastery.
†A ceremony to purify monks' vows that is observed at the full and new moons.

quarreling, and this caused Phagdru to flourish a hundred times more than before. Jigten Sumgön assigned Che-nga Drakpa Jungne to act as his regent there. In the autumn, he returned to Drigung.

As time passed, it became increasingly clear that Jigten Sumgön was indeed the incarnation of Nagarjuna. One time Karmapa Düsum Khyenpa came from Daklha Gampo to establish his seat at Tsurphu and do other things. On the way, he visited Drigung to see Jigten Sumgön. Jigten Sumgön and his disciples received him at Bam Thang. At that time, Karmapa Düsum Khyenpa saw Jigten Sumgön as the Buddha, and the two Che-ngas* as the Buddha's two chief disciples Shariputra and Maudgalyayana, surrounded by many arhats. Karmapa Düsum Khyenpa bowed down to him. They returned to the Serkhang assembly hall, and again, Karmapa Düsum Khyenpa saw Jigten Sumgön as the Buddha, with the two Che-ngas appearing this time as Maitreya and Manjushri, surrounded by the eight bodhisattvas and other great beings. Karmapa Düsum Khyenpa saw this and said, "You are the Acharya Nagarjuna." Strong devotion arose in him. He asked for teachings, and regarded Jigten Sumgön as one of his gurus.

In this regard, the history written by Pawo Tsuklak Trengwa says,[†]

> Again, in the autumn, Jigten Sumgön came to Drigung. Düsum Khyenpa went to Drigung and was received at Bam Thang. Düsum Khyenpa said, "Precious Lord, you are the Acharya Nagarjuna," and asked for teachings. He made a large offering of brown sugar and other things.

From Situ's *Rosary of Moon Water Crystal, the Successors of the Karma [Kagyu]*:[‡]

> Düsum Khyenpa went through Drigung Thil. Jigten Gönpo received him at Bam Thang and gave him teachings. Their minds merged inseparably. The Precious Guru said, "You are the Lord of Beings, Nagarjuna."

---

*Che-nga Sherab Jungne (also known as Che-nga Drigung Lingpa) and Che-nga Drakpa Jungne.

[†]*Chos 'byung mkhas pa'i dga' ston* of dPa' bo gtsug lag 'phreng ba, vol. NA, f. 50a12.

[‡]*A Moonlight Crystal*, a religious history of the seat-holders of the Karmapa lineage, f. 12a7.

From *The Blue Annals:**

> Düsum Khyenpa came to Drigung and said, "You are the Arya Nagarjuna."

Another story tells of an arhat in Ceylon (Sri Lanka) offering a flower to Jigten Sumgön. *The Blue Annals* relates:

> When Jigten Sumgön was sixty, an arhat from Ceylon sealed up a fourth lotus and gave it to the younger brother of Khache Panchen, asking him to give it to Khache Panchen to take to Tibet. The arhat blessed the flower so that it would not fade, and said that it should be given to the bodhisattva Rinchen Päl, the incarnation of Nagarjuna, at a place called Dri(gung).

From the religious history by Kunkhyen Pema Karpo:†

> An arhat from Ceylon gave three golden flowers to Khache Panchen and asked him to take them to Tibet. He said that one should be given to the incarnation of Arya Nagarjuna, but Khache Panchen didn't know where to find him. When Khache Panchen was staying at Lemoche, he announced that whoever came to him for bhikshu ordination would receive a Dharma robe. A Khampa monk from Drigung received ordination and asked for a robe, but none were left. He insisted, and tugged at the robe of Khache Panchen. Khache Panchen's attendants beat him, and blood flowed from his mouth and nose.
>
> Ordinarily, White Tara would appear in Khache Panchen's meditation, but for seven days after that incident she didn't show herself. Khache Panchen did purification practices and supplicated her. After seven days had passed, Tara appeared with her back turned to him. "Arya Tara," he asked, "what have I done wrong?" She replied, "You defiled your karma by beating Nagarjuna's disciple." "I don't remember that," he said, and Tara answered, "You beat him until he bled." Khache Panchen asked

---

The Blue Annals, by 'Gos lo-tsa-ba gzhon-nu-dpal, NYA section, f. 86b2.
†*The Religious History of Pema Karpo* (*Chos 'byung pad ma nyin byed*), f. 279a5.

how he could purify that misdeed, and Tara replied, "You should give Dharma robes equal in number to your years to those monks who have none." He promised to do that, and then searched for the monk who had been beaten. He found him, learned the name of his teacher, and realized that Jigten Sumgön was Nagarjuna. He offered the flower to him.

From *The Smiling Face of the Wondrous Lotus,* a collection of the life stories of Indian panditas:[*]

When Jigten Sumgön and Sangye Öntön of Gyama were arranging the invitation of Khache Panchen, Vibhuti[†] said: "Drigung has a lot of wealth, and these followers of mahamudra tell lies." Khache Panchen replied, "Vibhuti, that can't be!" and continued, "A disciple of the Drigungpa from Kham asked for a robe. Even though I offered him cloth for a robe he pulled at mine. My disciple, Jo-se Nyima, beat him and wounded him, bringing blood. For seven days after that, Tara didn't appear during my Seven-branch Prayer. I strongly supplicated her, and she finally showed me her back, but not her face. When I asked her why, she said, "You committed a great bad deed by abusing Nagarjuna's disciple. To purify that, you should distribute a hundred Dharma robes to those monks who have none.' So I did that. You, Pandita, should purify your own bad karma of speech, and build a temple of whatever kind you like."

Vibhuti then went to Drigung and composed verses of praise [to Jigten Sumgön]. Later, at Sinpori Mountain[‡] he built a Chakrasamvara temple with an image of the same height as Khache Panchen. That image is called "Staying in Space" and has great power of blessings. Vibhuti remained in Tibet for many years.

---

[*]*The Smiling Face of the Wondrous Lotus,* f. 868.
[†]Vibhuti Chandra (1129–1225) was an erudite Indian scholar, famous for his knowledge of Sanskrit and abhidharma, who accompanied Kashmiri Pandita Shakya Shri to Tibet with eight others. He received the lineage of Six Yogas from Päl Shawari and transmitted the lineage to Chäl Amogha. Thus, this lineage came to be known as the Six Yogas of the Jonang tradition.
[‡]Sinpori Mountain is known for an image of Chakrasamvara situated amidst a forest to the other side of Tshe chu sgrub sde on the bank of the Chagsam River.

On seeing the text *Fully Clarifying the Three Vows,* he understood the sequence of these vows and wrote a text of his own,* saying, "Nowadays, following the Buddha's teaching regarding the different explanations of the three vows, . . ." which established them as victorious in all directions. He translated many books from Sanskrit into Tibetan.

Similarly, there are many other stories, well-known in Tibet and India, referring to Nagarjuna's reincarnation as Jigten Sumgön.

Around this time, the naga king Sokma Me offered the fourth tooth of the Buddha to Jigten Sumgön. Lord Buddha said to Ananda in the *Karuna Pundarika Sutra:*

> After my passing, a place called Shingkün Kyewa will appear in the northern hemisphere. There, to honor my tooth, they will offer flowers, garlands, incense, ointments, music, parasols, banners, draperies, a victory throne and other things, cloth, silver, gold, and many precious jewels. They will attend my tooth and regard it as a guru. Ananda, my stupa will be adorned with gold. Ananda, many hundreds of monks with pure morality will appear at that place. At that time there will also appear many lay practitioners with pure morality, learned, sincere, and strongly devoted to my teachings. Those lay people will respect, attend, and regard as gurus those who become monks within my path.

As had been clearly prophesied, Jigten Sumgön said to Drupthob Gar Chöding, "Go to the Soksam Bridge, make camp, and offer a torma to the nagas. You will receive special wealth." Gar Chöding went there and offered a torma to the nagas, whereupon the naga king Sokma Me offered him the fourth tooth of the Buddha and three special gems. Gar Chöding brought them to Drigung and offered them to Jigten Sumgön, who said, "It is good to return wealth to its owner. As you are wealthy, build my image and put these inside." Drupthob Gar invited artisans from China. They built a workshop below the monastery and constructed an image of Jigten Sumgön out of many precious metals. They placed the Buddha's tooth inside. Jigten Sumgön consecrated this image hundreds of times. It was called the

---

Rosary of the Light of the Three Vows.

"Dharma Lord of Serkhang" and regarded as Jigten Sumgön himself. This image spoke to many of Jigten Sumgön's successors, and to many shrine keepers. Later, when Drigung was destroyed, the image was buried in a large hill of sand, and when a search was made for it at the time of the monastery's restoration, it raised its hand out of the sand, saying, "Here I am." Similarly, there are many other marvelous stories about this image.

The Buddha made many prophecies concerning the holy place Tsari Tra, which is called Devi Kota, the Palace of Shri Chakrasamvara. Once, the dakinis of Tsari Tra brought an assembly of the 2,800 enlightened deities of that place on a net of horsehair and presented them to Jigten Sumgön. He perceived each deity directly. To commemorate the glorious Phagmo Drupa, he built an auspicious stupa of seven different precious materials with many doors. At that time, four thousand bhikshus were gathered at Drigung. When Jigten Sumgön was thirty-nine, Drigung had seven thousand bhikshus divided into thirteen groups. By the time he was forty-nine, the victory banner of practice was planted firmly on the pinnacle of samsara in Tibet.

From the relative point of view, because so many disciples had gathered around him that he had begun to feel crowded, and from the absolute point of view, in order to open a secret place and further establish the victory banner of practice, Jigten Sumgön went to Tsa-uk at the upper end of the valley, opened the meditation caves of Dorje Lokar, Samadhi Cave and others, and practiced there.

From the *Guidebook to Lapchi:**

> One night, to maintain the continuity of Buddha Shakyamuni's teachings, Jigten Sumgön brought about the subjugation of others and entered samadhi for a moment. Immediately the deity king of Mount Kailash, the Protector of Lapchi, the Protector of Tsari, and many other protectors from Tibet gathered before him, bowed at his feet, and requested him to come to their places as an object of refuge. At that moment, through his miracle power, he sent many emanations of himself to each of their places, and subdued and gave teachings to all the local deities and spirits. In each place, those nonhuman beings asked him

---

*La phyi gnas yig, by Drigungpa Tenzin Chökyi Lodrö ('Bri gung pa bstan 'dzin chos kyi blo gros), f. 15b3.

to send lamas to be their guides. He agreed to send great hermit
practitioners.

Jigten Sumgön's disciples went looking for him, found him at Tsa-uk,
and asked him to return to his seat. Jigten Sumgön said, "Phagmo Drupa
ordered me to practice in retreat," and sang this grand song:

> I bow at the feet of glorious Phagmo Drupa.
> By the great kindness of glorious Phagmo Drupa,
> certainty was born in my mind.
> I obtained the confidence of bodhicitta.
> I, a yogin, remain in solitude.
>
> My experience and realization come out as mere words.
> Even for you disciples who are proper vessels,
> experience and realization are difficult.
> I, a yogin, remain in solitude.
> My qualities have become a source of wealth
> that provokes attachment and aggression.
> Consuming the food of Mara is a cause of many faults.
> I, a yogin, remain in solitude.
>
> My attendants are distracted.
> It is not helpful to keep bad company.
> There is no end to the actions of attachment and aggression.
> I, a yogin, remain in solitude.
> My monks are insincere.
> Many don't think about the needs of this life and the next.
> Feeding a retinue of cattle is a cause of many faults.
> I, a yogin, remain in solitude.
>
> My actions have been [only] for this life.
> I [only] aspire to worldly dharmas.
> This deceives faithful disciples.
> I, a yogin, remain in solitude.
>
> A phantom crosses a mirage river.
> Dream bees sip a sky lotus.

The son of a barren woman plays and sings the music of gandharvas.
Those who are childish and have no experience or realization
say that one can realize the absolute truth through worldly activities.

[But] one's pure and stainless mind
abides with the precious teachings
on the mountain of nonduality.
The forest of great bliss grows dense.

The wild animals of recollection and mindfulness roam about.
They consume the grass and water of bliss, clarity, and
    nonconceptual thought.
If you desire solitude, practice this way.
I, a yogin, remain in solitude.

Then he said, "Either you all go into the mountains and I stay in the monastery, or I go into the mountains and you stay in the monastery." His disciples agreed to go into retreat.*

On three occasions, the chief disciples who had finished the preliminary practices and realized the nature of their mind were sent to the three holy places. The first time, under Geshe Ngayphuwa, eighty were sent to Mount Kailash, eighty to Tsari, and eighty to Lapchi. There were 240 altogether. Jigten Sumgön said, "All you disciples, my sons, don't wander or be attached to leisure. Persevere in your practice in retreat. Don't return here until you have achieved special realization. With patience, bring suffering and unfavorable conditions into your practice. All phenomena depend upon causes and effects, so be careful of your karma. If doubts or unhappiness arise, supplicate the guru." In this way, he sent the first group.

In the area of Ngamshö, people were unhappy. Jigten Sumgön went there with three hundred disciples and stayed at the three snow mountains of Chewa, at the plain of Lochu, at Thilma, and at other places. Through his motivation and prayers, local quarrels were pacified for eighteen years. He provided the wealth to repair Samye Monastery, which had fallen into decline. He was then invited to Daklha Gampo. Dakpo Düldzin and other great teachers there received teachings from him and asked to be placed under his authority. From *The Blue Annals:*†

---

*A Guide to Lapchi, f. 16b1.
†The Blue Annals, NYA section.

Although he didn't accept the seat, he made a great offering to Dakpo Düldzin and said, "Only you can hold this seat, so you must govern the monastery." The Lord Drigungpa gave much wealth to build Tapho Chamar Lungshak and other temples.

At that time, there was a great famine in Dakpo. A gold coin could buy only seven measures (*dre*) of barley, and many people ate the flesh of the dead.

If Jigten Sumgön had only a piece of fruit to eat, it would become larger through the Buddha's blessing. Because of this, he became famous. He was invited to Lower Dakpo, where people respectfully gathered around him and made inconceivable offerings. He was then invited back to Daklha Gampo by Dakpo Düldzin, and was again offered the seat. Dakpo Düldzin also offered him a rosary of a hundred gold coins. Jigten Sumgön went into retreat there for three months and supplicated an image of Lord Gampopa from which light streamed forth, illuminating the entire region of Dakpo. For seven days, people could not distinguish day from night. Many yakshas and Dharma protectors made offerings of wealth, filling the area of Gampo. To relieve the drought, people made offerings of the first part of their tsampa to Jigten Sumgön, and asked him to provide rain. He brought that food to the image of Gampopa and said, "Don't let me be embarrassed." Immediately, there was a great rainfall, and that year the country of Dakpo had its best harvest of barley. In this way, through Jigten Sumgön's unsurpassable great kindness, the people there were saved from famine.

Once Lama Shang Tsälpa said, "The Lama Drigungpa, the Lama Tsurphupa, and I will be invited by the dakinis of Oddiyana. The Drigungpa, who is a master of interdependent origination, won't go, but we two will have to." Jigten Sumgön heard what Lama Shang Tsälpa had said. That year, Lama Shang Tsälpa and Düsum Khyenpa passed away. One morning, when Jigten Sumgön was in his room at glorious Phagdru, the dakinis formed a reception line that stretched from Phagdru to Oddiyana. Immediately, he performed a special meditation. His body transformed itself clearly into Shri Heruka, the lord of those dakinis, and he made the mudra of subjugation. In this way, he subjugated them. The dakinis built a lion throne and prayed for Jigten Sumgön's longevity. Thus, all happened as Lama Shang Tsälpa had said.

At Drigung Thil, the number of monks was steadily increasing. Nyö Gyälwa Lhanangpa made an offering of brown sugar to them, and made 1,700 offerings of different kinds of wealth to Jigten Sumgön. At that time,

Che-nga Sherab Jungne counted those who had assembled, and found that 55,525 monks were present.

There was once a severe drought in that area. Jigten Sumgön said to Düdsi Shikpo, "Go to the spring behind the upper part of the monastery and sing this song. Rain will fall." Jigten Sumgön sang this song, called "Supplication for the Mist of Great Blessings":

Namo Guru!

In the vast sky of the glorious dharmadhatu,
you pervade all dharmas without limitation of boundary or center.
Remembering again and again great Vajradhara, the dharmakaya,
I supplicate you with one-pointed mind filled with yearning.
Guru! Grant your blessings that I may be realized like you.

Clouds gather in the east over the land of Sahor.
Billowing mists of blessings arise.
Remembering again and again Tilo Prajñabhadra,
I supplicate you with one-pointed mind filled with yearning.
Guru! Grant your blessings that I may be realized like you.

Red lightning flashes over Pushpahari in the north.
You underwent twelve trials for the sake of the Dharma.
Remembering again and again the learned mahapandita Naropa,
I supplicate you with one-pointed mind filled with yearning.
Guru! Grant your blessings that I may be realized like you.

The turquoise dragon thunders over the valley of Drowo Lung
    in the south.
You translated the teachings of the Hearing Lineage into Tibetan.
Remembering again and again the great translator Marpa Lotsawa,
I supplicate you with one-pointed mind filled with yearning.
Guru! Grant your blessings that I may be realized like you.

A gentle rain is falling in the highlands of the Lapchi snow range.
The instructions of the Hearing Lineage flow together into a lake.
Remembering again and again glorious Shepa Dorje,
I supplicate you with one-pointed mind filled with yearning.
Guru! Grant your blessings that I may be realized like you.

The earth is soaked in the Daklha Gampo hills in the east
by the continuous stream of the waters of clear light.
Remembering again and again the Lord, the King of Physicians,
I supplicate you with one-pointed mind filled with yearning.
Guru! Grant your blessings that I may be realized like you.

Shoots sprout in the land of Phagmo Dru.
You opened the treasure of the profound secret tantra.
Remembering again and again the Lord, the Self-born Buddha,
I supplicate you with one-pointed mind filled with yearning.
Guru! Grant your blessings that I may be realized like you.

The six grains ripen in the region of Drigung in the north.
The six grains pervade all the six realms.
Remembering again and again the kind Lords of Dharma, the uncles
    and nephews,
I supplicate you with one-pointed mind filled with yearning.
Guru! Grant your blessings that I may be realized like you.

Upon the crown of my head, on a sun and moon disk seat,
sits my kind root lama, inseparable from the glorious Vajradhara.
Remembering you again and again,
I supplicate you with one-pointed mind filled with yearning.
Guru! Grant your blessings that I may be realized like you.

Rain fell, and there was a great harvest. Lhamo Metok Jorma and others said in the *Precious Collection: The Mantra's Top,* "There was a great harvest, and a large measure of the goddesses' barley grain was offered. Because of the great quantity of barley there, the people of Kyishö came to get some."

The number of disciples at Drigung continued to grow, and Jigten Sumgön sent a second group. Under Geshe Nyö and Garpa Changdor, 900 went to Mount Kailash, 900 went to Lapchi, and 900 went to Tsari. There were 2,700 altogether, most of them highly realized. By the following year, the number of disciples had increased even further. From the life story *The Flower of Mahamudra:** "Last year at this time, 2,700 yogins went to the mountains. This year, 13,000 disciples have gathered." After a few

*The *Prayer Text of Drigung Kagyu,* vol. 1, f. 8a4.

years, the community had grown even larger. From the *Explanation to the Assembly:** "One hundred eighty thousand disciples gathered in the plain of Layel at Drigung."

In the Fire Mouse year (1216), when he was seventy-four years old, Jigten Sumgön sent the third group of hermits. Under Panchen Guhya Gangpa, 55,525 went to Mount Kailash; under Geshe Yakru Päldrak, 55,525 went to Lapchi; and under Dordzin Gowoche, 55,525 went to Tsari. Those who had been sent to Mount Kailash stayed at Sheldra, Nyänti, Tarlung, Lhalung, Tsegye, Lemi, Bum, Guge, and other mountains. There, they built meditation caves.† Those who had been sent to Lapchi arrived at Latö and stayed at Gyälgyi Shri, Rongshir, Drinlha Mar, Upper and Lower Lapchi, Nyanang, the three parts (upper, lower, and middle) of Mangyül, Tsum, Kuthang, and other mountains. There, they also built meditation caves.‡

Thus, in Tibet, the essence of the Buddha's teachings raised the victory banner of practice to the summit. Until recently, it was a tradition in Drigung to send vajra-holders and hermits to the three sacred mountains. In those days, the life style of the hermits was like that of Jetsün Milarepa. They followed the example of the early Kagyu lamas and lived as simply as birds. They were supported by the kings of the three parts of Western Tibet, Tö Ngari Korsum,§ the king of Yatse,¶ and other kings, along with the people, who were faithful patrons.

At one time, the king of Ladakh was Lhachen Ngödrub Gön, the king of Guge was Tri Tashi Detsän, and the king of Purang was Lhachen Taktsha Tribar. These kings and their princes also became patrons.** Later, Che-nga Drigung Lingpa came to the area of Mount Kailash. The king of Purang, who was then Jowo Atikmen, Nadak Drakde, and the king of Mön Yatse

---

*The *Prayer Text of Drigung Kagyu*, vol. 1, f. 11a5.
†*A Guide to Mount Kailash* by Drigungpa Chökyi Lodrö, f. 26b2.
‡*A Guide to Lapchi*, f. 17a2.
§*Ngari* means subjects of a king. In 894 C.E. the forty-second king Ngadag Pakor Tsan was killed during a civil war, and his two sons escaped to the western region of Tibet. The younger son, Tashi Tsegpa, settled in upper western Tibet, whereas the elder, Kyide Nyima Gön, escaped to the Ngari region. The latter had three sons; the elder, Pälgyu Gön, ruled over Ladakh; the middle, Tashi Gön, ruled Purang; and the youngest, De-Tsug Gön, ruled Zhang Zhung (Kinnaur, Lahaul, and Spiti). Thus, these districts were known as the three parts of Ngari.
¶Yatse kings descended originally from the eleventh king of Purang. The capital of Yatse is known as Jumla, presently identified with the district of Karnali to the west of Nepal.
**A Guide to Mount Kailash*, f. 27a5.

Dzublang, became his patrons. The details of this can be read in the guide-books to Mount Kailash, Lapchi, and Tsari. *The Jewel Tree of the Expressions of Realization* gives a full account of the lineage of retreat masters of the Drigung Kagyu; therefore, I haven't gone into more detail here.

Jigten Sumgön could, in a moment, benefit many sentient beings with many manifestations. Once, through his miracle power, he stopped a war begun by Duruka tribesmen in Bodh Gaya. He also went to Kasha, the Land of Dakinis (Lahaul), and explained the qualities of the holy mountain Drilbu Ri. From the *Guidebook to Drilbu Ri and Gandhola*:

> The Drigungpa, Jigten Sumgön, said, "The Land of the Dakinis is located west of here and to the north of Dzalendara. In that supreme, peerless place, the upper end of the valley points to the east, and the lower end points to the west. That valley has two upper points and one lower point. In the center is the Unified Great Middle Mountain. There abides the assembly of deities who are Dharma protectors. Behind that is the path to circum-ambulate the secret dakinis. On the way, you will see the hand and body symbols of gods and goddesses. There also is the water of method and wisdom, the stream of siddhi. Farther on are the water of immortality and the water of eight qualities. On the mountain can be seen many spontaneously self-arisen syllables of *ali* and *kali*. Fortunate sons should go to that holy place."

The meditator Sherab Wö once asked Jigten Sumgön to write some stories about his life, such as the story of his reception by Thanglha, but the lama declined. The head monastery of the Drigung order near Nepal was in Kyirong and was called Rishong. There can be seen Jigten Sumgön's residence and footprints. There are other stories like these that were never written down.

When he was seventy-five, Jigten Sumgön began to think that he should dissolve the manifestation of his vajra body. He said, "Now there are no beings I have not helped; there are no teachings I have not given; and there are no activities I have not accomplished. Therefore, I am happy. My respon-sibilities are over. You all should work hard." To the four khenpos and lob-pöns and the meditation instructor Dorje Senge, he gave the precious seat, along with limitless teachings of absolute meaning. The sky was filled with rainbows and with many signs of his miracle power. According to his wish, he passed away into the ultimate state of peace and accomplishment at dusk on the twenty-fifth day of the fourth month, the month of enlightenment, in the Female Fire Ox year (1217).

In later years, people celebrated Jigten Sumgön's parinirvana on different days. In Drigung, the parinirvana is celebrated on the twenty-fifth day of the third month. In Eastern Tibet, in Kham, some monasteries celebrate the parinirvana on the twenty-fifth day of the second month. In Western Tibet, in Lemi (Nepal), and in other places, the parinirvana is celebrated on the twenty-fifth day of the fourth month. These dates are different because, in ancient times, even though Jigten Sumgön's teachings flourished, it was difficult to travel from one place to another, and his followers gradually lost touch with each other. Due to a lack of interest in the stories of his life, even among later lineage holders, these discrepancies arose. This is a reminder of impermanence, the nature of all phenomena. But the great offering of the twenty-fifth day of the fourth month for Jigten Sumgön should be observed without error because of his own concern for that date, and so that the Drigung Kagyu teachings may flourish. Because this is important, I will now clarify the matter of the month in which this ceremony should be observed.

At Drigung Thil, the observance of the parinirvana ceremony of Jigten Sumgön declined after some time. Later, at the time of the thirty-third throneholder of the Drigung Kagyu, His Holiness Tenzin Chökyi Lodrö, Changchen Khenpo Pema Lhündrub and his attendant Könchog Tsöndru (who had the confidence to restore the teachings of the second Nagarjuna) reintroduced the ceremony. The chant leader of Drigung Thil, Döndrup Karpo, and the great scholar Könchog Norsang took on the responsibility to make an embroidered silk thangka of Jigten Sumgön that was eighteen feet high. Another name of the great scholar Könchog Norsang is Jampäl Gyepäl Dorje. He composed a very poetic seven-branch offering to the guru called *Essence of the Ocean of the Two Accumulations,* which is the actual realization of the Ser Khangma. In that excellent text, he mentions without bias the names of many buddhas, bodhisattvas, and great teachers of India and Tibet. But that ceremony was observed on the twenty-fifth day of the third month, a date that was given in the *Golden Rosary of the Drigung Kagyu.* From the *Golden Rosary:*

> On the twenty-fifth day of the third month in the Female Fire Ox year, when he was seventy-five, the mandala of his manifestation dissolved into the expanse of Dharma.

This may have been an error on the part of the author's secretary, who may have mistaken the name of the month. This history was written by Tenzin Padmai Gyältsen, the twenty-ninth throneholder, in the Water Pig year of the thirteenth cycle (1803). That was 584 years after the passing away of Jigten Sumgön.

In Eastern Tibet, at Lungkar Monastery, Thubten Shedrub Ling, the ceremony was observed on the twenty-fifth day of the second month. This date seems to be derived from a religious history called *Entering the Ocean of the Teachings,* which was written by Könchog Lhündrub, the ninth Khenpo of the Ngorpa Sakya.* That text says,

> When the protector was seventy-five, he passed away on the twenty-fifth day of the second month of the Female Fire Ox year. One of his two chief disciples asked him to return to the assembly, and he came back from the clear light. For two days, he gave teachings, and passed away again on the twenty-seventh day. His students then asked him on what day they should perform the ceremony, and he said that it should be observed on the twenty-fifth.

Regarding the third date, Che-nga Drigung Lingpa spent seven years in the area of Mount Kailash. King Yatse of Nepal and the king of Dzublang became his patrons, and the Drigung Kagyu teachings were widely spread in western Nepal. Monasteries remain there even now, such as Waltse Rinchen Ling in Limi in Upper Lo. They performed the ceremony from the time that Che-nga was there. From then until now, Jigten Sumgön's parinirvana has been observed without fail on the twenty-fifth day of the fourth month. That is the correct date. This is so because a month after Jigten Sumgön had passed away, in the mornings his disciples, led by Che-nga Drigung Lingpa, brought his life stories together into a collection called *The Blazing Vajra,* and in the evening read it to the assembly of monks. That text says,

> In the Female Fire Ox year, in the month of enlightenment (fourth month), at dusk on the twenty-fifth day, his thought and speech passed away into the ultimate state of peace and accomplishment.

---

* *The Gateway to the Ocean of Doctrine,* a religious history of the Ngor throneholders of the Sakya tradition, by Könchog Lhündrup, the tenth abbot, f. 45a7.

Che-nga also composed *The Praise of Absolute Meaning to Jigten Sumgön*,* which says,

> In the king of times, the Female Fire Ox year, on the tenth day of the waning moon, the first month of summer (the fourth month of the year), in the All-Good Forest at glorious Drigung, the mandala of the body of the wisdom emanation demonstrated the passing away into the full liberation of the expanse of Dharma.

Likewise, Pälden Bälpu Gongpa, one of Jigten Sumgön's chief disciples, wrote a biography of the lama called *The Precious Jewel Ornament*, which says,

> At that time, in the Female Fire Ox year, on the twelfth day of the waning moon in the month of enlightenment, the Dharma Lord demonstrated the passing away.

And, from the religious history by Pawo Tsuklak Trengwa:†

> He passed away on the fifth day of the month of enlightenment. His attendant disciples supplicated him, and he returned for two days. He showed his face to the assembly and gave teachings. They asked him to stay, and he said, "I have finished taming my disciples." Then they asked, "On what day should we perform the ceremony?" And he answered, "Since you are making offerings to the guru, you should do it on the twenty-fifth day." Then he passed away. Marvelous signs appeared without limit.

For these reasons, the Great Ceremony of the Parinirvana of Jigten Sumgön, the Second Nagarjuna, should be performed on the twenty-fifth day of the fourth month, since this is without mistake and is according to his own intention.

Jigten Sumgön's fame pervades India, China, and the whole world. From *The Complete Liberation of the Fortunate*:

---

*Included in the Collected Works of Che-nga Sherab Jungne.
†*The Wondrous Ocean*, f. 44b.

His supreme mind, not stained by obscurations, has become a
radiant field of merit for offerings by gods and men. The activities
of his learned and realized lineage holders illuminate the whole
world like the sun and the moon.

As is said, the king of Varanasi in India, Ghocha Deva, the Indian pandita Vibhuti Chandra, a Ceylonese monk, and others bowed down at his
feet. Khache Panchen, Karmapa Düsum Khyenpa, the translator Trophu
Lotsawa, Kharak Gyälwa Kyö, the translator Mänlung Lotsawa, and many
other scholars and realized practitioners regarded him as their guru. The
proud kings of Li,* Khodän, Yatse, Purang, Upper and Lower Hor, Khache,
Maryül, Garlok, Guge, Jingikhang, Minyak, Jän, and other places received
teachings from Jigten Sumgön and became his devoted patrons. Countless
disciples appeared. Among them were great disciples and successors to the
throne, thirty-seven in all, whose life stories will appear at a later time.

THE PRECIOUS LORD'S LEGACY

Generally, the activities of the thirteen chief disciples were equal to those
of the lama. Even though they caused the teachings to flourish even further
and built monasteries, we have no record of their lives because of the pas-
sage of time. But the life story of Jamyang Khyentse Wangpo† says: "The
Protector's thirteen chief disciples were his equal. The great siddha, glorious
Jangchub Lingpa, was the first to establish Pälpung Monastery." We have
no record of this, but my great teacher, His Holiness Dilgo Khyentse Rinpoche, said, "Above the present monastery of Pälpung are the vast ruins of
an earlier monastery. When glorious Jangchub Lingpa was there, the monastery was so large that it had doors in each of the four directions, and over

---

*Lochawa Shambhala said, "At present, myself and Rendawa are the only two persons who
can locate Shambhala." This is probably true. The identification of Nepal and Liyul as being
different has also been proved by Drolungpa, who said, "To the east of India are Li and
Nepal." Also, Chomden Rigrel has said, "Liyul captured by Sanu is not Nepal at the border
of India and Tibet." Therefore, Liyul is located to the extreme north of Tibet and to the
extreme south of Russia. In the language of India, this place is called Kamadesa, and in other
countries it is known as Turkestan and Xinjiang by the Chinese. See *The White Annals*, Zhol
edition, f. 9a2.
†*A Biography of Jamyang Khyentse Wangpo*, vol. BA, p. 366.

them were gongs that were beaten at the same time to call monks to the assembly." These kinds of stories are told.

Likewise, near Dölma Dratsa in Dän-tö, in the area of Do-tö (Kham), are the ruins of great walls. In ancient times, tens of thousands and hundreds of thousands of monks appeared there. Because of that, this place is known even now as the Valley of Ten Thousands and the Valley of Hundred Thousands. This monastery was built by the glorious Ngayphuwa. Kyo Dorje Nyingpo also built monasteries. In Nangchen, in Gapa, there is a monastery called Kham Kyo Gön.

Lama Rinchen Sangpo was one of Jigten Sumgön's chief disciples, and Jigten Sumgön prophesied that he would practice in retreat at Mänri Nakshö in Do-me (Kham) and at Drak Senge. In the Earth Mouse year, Lama Rinchen Sangpo and his disciples went to Do-me. First, he stayed at Drakmar Serkhang. The upasaka of Tshoshi, Yülkyong Pälsang, Dorsang of Tsongkha, and others became his disciples. Lama Rinchen Sangpo left a footprint near Tsorung. The upasaka of Tshoshi rode a drum to the top of a mountain. Yülkyong Pälsang rode a deer as if it were a horse. The deer's antlers struck the ground, and even today the place is known as Antler Imprint. Dorsang of Tsongkha threw a vajra into space, and it stayed there by itself. These miracles and others were the signs of their realization.

As Jigten Sumgön prophesied, they went to search for the place that he had described. Three ravens flew ahead of them, showing the way, and landed near Drak Senge. Then they disappeared. The lama and his disciples quickly went to where the ravens had landed, and found a Mahakala thangka that had been an inner object of the Mahakala shrine at Drigung Thil. They were overjoyed, built a retreat hut on that site, and practiced there. Nowadays that thangka is kept at Rongpo Tshoshi. Lama Rinchen Sangpo gave the upasaka of Tshoshi a nine-pointed vajra made of iron, along with various texts and the Mahakala thangka, and appointed him the guardian of Drak Senge in Taklung Pälri. Yülkyong Pälsang and Dorsang of Tsongkha were given many texts and appointed the guardians of Drakmar Serkhang and Ri Langchen Nyäldra.

Lama Rinchen Sangpo subjugated nagas, demons, and spirit kings in that area and hid many treasures. Inconceivable numbers of lineage holders and siddhas appeared there. This is described in detail in the religious history of Do-me, *The Ocean of Annals*.*

---

*mDo smad chos 'byung (Lanzhou: Kansu'u mi rigs dpe skrun khang, 1982), 342.

In Ü-Tsang, Gar Dampa Chöding established the Chöding Monastery in Lungshö Sur Ri. That monastery flourished greatly, and Gar Chöding began to feel that it was the equal of Drigung Thil. He took five hundred disciples and went to Kyem in Kongpo. There he built a monastery called Phulung Rinchen Ling. He also built monasteries in Makham and in the area of Nangchen. Gyän Thangpa built a monastery called Gyän Thang Gompa at Ye, a place where torma plates were put out for the raven emanations of Mahakala. Jigten Sumgön's commentary called *The Elephant's Burden** is kept in that monastery. Drupthob Tsangshik built the Ngangkyäl Monastery in Nyal.

In the area of Ngari, Che-nga Sherab Jungne built monasteries at Mount Kailash and Yuru.† Nyö Gyälwa Lhanangpa built a monastery that was like Drigung Thil near Thanglha Mountain. He also built monasteries and fortresses in Bhutan. Panchen Guhya Gangpa built the Gyangdrak Monastery at Mount Kailash. Geshe Yakru Päldrak built the great Düdül Phuk at Lapchi, and others. Dordzin Gowoche built a monastery at Tsari. Many Drigung Kagyu monasteries were also built when Jigten Sumgön was alive.

Both Ga-Ngön Tashi Chödzong Monastery in Ladakh and Rishong Monastery in Kyirong have great annals that describe in the same way how

> at first, headed by the three holy places, 3,535 monasteries were prophesied by Jigten Sumgön; later he sent hermit practitioners to establish them. Finally, many disciples and patrons offered the places for the monasteries and built them. This is described in detail in the six annals that are kept in Drigung Thil Jangchub Ling Serkhang. Also, the great books written by Che-nga Drigung Lingpa, Che-nga Drakpa Jungne, and the Dharma Lord Dharmaradza are kept in Drigung, at the seat of Rinpung, and in the Nedong Palace. In particular, the story of the three phases of the monasteries of Mount Kailash, Ga-Ngön, Yungdrung, and others are in the manuscripts kept at Lapchi and Mount Kailash.

Some of these books may still exist in Tibet. In any case, they are not available now.

---

*Chos 'byung mkhas pa'i dga' ston, f. 43.
†A Golden Garland of the Throneholders, a religious history by Tenzin Padmai Gyältsen.

Disciples of Jigten Sumgön appeared in inconceivable numbers. The religious history *The Precious Rosary,* written by Gyälwang Könchog Rinchen says, in brief:

> The eight Che-ngas, including Wön and Drakjung;
> the eight spiritual sons, including Nyö and Gar;
> the eight great, glorious disciples, including Chöye and Guhya;
> the eight repas, including Ngorje and Tishri;
> the three ascetics, including Uyang Guge and others;
> the eight translators, including glorious Trophu Jampa;
> the ten vinaya holders, including Thakma, Dakpo, and others;
> the eight Kadampa meditation masters, including Kyotrom and
> others;
> the five dispellers of confusion, including Nyima Senge and others;
> countless assemblies of disciples gathered in their inconceivable
> millions.
> The three great seats* flourished greatly.
> Gampo and the seat of Drigung are related like the sun and moon.
> The Drigung Kagyu are the lords of the three great holy places:
> Mapham Lake and Mount Kailash, the residence of Lion Face, the
> body [of Chakrasamvara],
> Lapchi and Chuwar, the residence of Tiger Face, the speech [of
> Chakrasamvara],
> and Tsari Sarbhadra, the residence of Sow Face, the wisdom mind [of
> Chakrasamvara].
> The kings of the four directions are his subjects:
> in India, they call him Mahabodhi;
> in China, they call him Manjushri;
> in Hor and Gyishang, these two, they call him Avalokiteshvara;
> in Tibet and Tasik, they call him Vajradhara.
> The thirteen great kingdoms are under his authority:
> In Upper Tibet, the two kingdoms of Li and Odän;
> Khache, Drili, Maryül, Guge, Yatse, Purang, and Upper and Lower
> Hor;
> In Lower Tibet, Jingikhang, Minyak, and Ga.
> These also are under his authority.

---

*Drigung Thil, Yangrigar, and Tsa.

The eighteen great myriarchies and others also became his subjects:
Do, Rong, Tre, Nyak, Sumdän, Tsa, Me, Tsangpo,
Purang, Nyang, Pheng, Kyi, Yor, Lhopa, Shuk, Tsam, Kongpo, and
　　Charpa.
These eighteen myriarchies became his subjects.
The Drigung lineage became unequaled, and its activities are very
　　well known.

Thus it is said.

CONCLUSION

In brief, in the Land of Snows, it was said that no other tradition flourished
as did the Drigung Kagyu. Kunkhyen Pema Karpo wrote, "Thus, when
the Drigung Kagyu were flourishing, everything came under their authority." Jamgön Kongtrul Yöntän Gyatso wrote,* "It was common to say, 'The
mountains are filled with Drigung hermits. The plains are filled with Drigung patrons.'"

　　Thus, Jigten Sumgön, the Second Nagarjuna, performed limitless activities that filled the whole of space, and the assembly of his disciples gathered
like the disciples of Buddha Maitreya. In this way, he spread the precious
teachings of the Buddha in all directions like the light of a hundred thousand suns.

　　　　The activities of the Second Nagarjuna
　　　　fill the whole of space, like the light of a hundred thousand suns.
　　　　I, who have a childish mind,
　　　　like a frog in a well—
　　　　How can I measure their limit?

*rGya chen bka' mdzod, vol. TA, f. 87a.

Glossary of Enumerations

Two
two accumulations: merit and wisdom
two classes of Buddhist teachings: sutra and tantra
two deity yoga meditation practices: arising or generation and completion
two form bodies: sambhogakaya and nirmanakaya
two wisdoms: knowing reality as it is, and understanding each and every object of knowledge

Three
three collections of Dharma (pitaka):
  1. vinaya
  2. sutra
  3. abhidharma
three kayas or forms (of a buddha):
  1. nirmanakaya, the emanation body
  2. sambhogakaya, the complete enjoyment body
  3. dharmakaya, the perfect wisdom body
three lower realms:
  1. animal realm
  2. hungry ghost realm
  3. hell realms
three qualities of deity yoga:
  1. clarity
  2. purity
  3. divine pride
three trainings:
  1. moral ethics, or *shila*
  2. meditative concentration, or *samadhi*
  3. incisive wisdom, or *prajña*

three types of laziness:
1. discouragement
2. attachment to the pleasures of this life
3. busyness for this life's benefit

three types of suffering:
1. suffering of suffering
2. suffering of change
3. all-pervasive suffering

three vows:
1. pratimoksha vows
2. bodhisattva vow
3. tantric vows

three worlds:
1. desire
2. form
3. formless

FOUR

four causes of samsara:
1. not gathering the accumulations of merit and wisdom
2. gathering the nonvirtues
3. creating obstacles to others' creation of virtue
4. not dedicating virtue

four classes of tantra:
1. action (kriya)
2. conduct (charya)
3. yoga
4. unexcelled tantra (uttaratantra)

four elements:
1. earth
2. fire
3. water
4. air

four foundations, also called "the four thoughts that turn the mind":
1. precious human life
2. impermanence
3. the suffering of samsara
4. karma or causality

four kayas or forms (of a buddha):
1. nirmanakaya (emanation form), the physical form that a buddha manifests whenever needed in any of the six realms
2. sambhogakaya (pure enjoyment form), a subtle form that a buddha manifests for highly accomplished bodhisattvas
3. dharmakaya (truth or wisdom form), the complete buddhahood that can be comprehended by a buddha alone
4. svabhavikakaya (nature form), not a physical form but rather the unified and inseparable nature of all buddhas' forms

Four Noble Truths:
1. truth of suffering
2. truth of the cause of suffering
3. truth of the cessation of suffering
4. truth of the path

four yogas of mahamudra:
1. one-pointed state of mind
2. free from elaboration
3. one taste
4. nonmeditation

FIVE

five aggregates. See *five skandhas.*

fivefold path of mahamudra:
1. bodhicitta
2. yidam deity practice
3. guru yoga
4. mahamudra
5. dedication

five paths:
1. path of accumulation
2. path of application
3. path of special insight
4. path of meditation
5. path of perfection

five precepts (for laypersons):
1. not to kill
2. not to steal
3. not to lie

4. not to engage in sexual misconduct

5. not to take intoxicants

five skandhas (aggregates):

1. form

2. feeling

3. perception

4. formation

5. consciousness

five wisdoms:

1. dharmadhatu, or wisdom of the all-pervading elements of Dharma

2. mirror-like wisdom

3. equanimity wisdom

4. discriminating wisdom

5. all-accomplishing activity wisdom

Six

Six Dharmas of Naropa: the practices of

1. tummo

2. illusory body

3. dream yoga

4. clear light

5. phowa

6. bardo

six grains:

1. barley

2. corn

3. rice

4. wheat

5. pea

6. mustard

six perfections:

1. generosity

2. moral ethics

3. patience

4. perseverance

5. meditative concentration

6. wisdom awareness

six realms:
1. hell realms
2. hungry spirit realms
3. animal realms
4. human realms
5. demigod realms
6. god realms

SEVEN

seven mental factors
1. eye consciousness
2. ear consciousness
3. nose consciousness
4. tongue consciousness
5. body consciousness
6. mental consciousness
7. mental faculty

EIGHT

eight bardos:
1. bardo of view
2. bardo of meditation
3. bardo of conduct
4. bardo of dreams
5. bardo of generation and completion stages of the path (also called bardo of the path)
6. bardo of the essential point
7. bardo of the three kayas
8. bardo of result

eight worldly concerns:
1. gain
2. loss
3. praise
4. blame
5. pleasure
6. pain
7. fame
8. disgrace

TEN

ten bhumis:

1. Great Joy
2. Stainless
3. Radiant
4. Luminous
5. Very Difficult to Train
6. Obviously Transcendent
7. Gone Afar
8. Immovable
9. Good Discriminating Wisdom
10. Cloud of Dharma

ten nonvirtues:

1. killing
2. stealing
3. sexual misconduct
4. lying, especially about spiritual achievements
5. divisive speech
6. harsh words
7. idle talk
8. covetousness
9. malice
10. holding wrong view, especially about causality

ten virtues:

1. refraining from killing, and preserving life
2. refraining from stealing, and practicing generosity
3. refraining from sexual misconduct, and practicing moral ethics
4. refraining from lying, and speaking truthfully
5. refraining from divisive speech, and speaking harmoniously
6. refraining from harsh words, and speaking peacefully and politely
7. refraining from idle talk, and speaking meaningfully
8. refraining from covetousness, and practicing contentment
9. refraining from malice, and practicing loving-kindness and compassion
10. refraining from holding wrong views, and practicing the perfect meaning

TWELVE

twelve deeds of a buddha:
1. descending from Tushita
2. entering the womb and being born
3. training in arts and sciences
4. getting married and enjoying royalty
5. renouncing samsara
6. practicing austerities
7. taking up the seat at Bodh Gaya and gaining enlightenment
8. turning the wheel of Dharma
9. defeating opponents in debate
10. displaying miracle powers
11. passing into parinirvana
12. manifesting relics

twelve links of interdependent origination:
1. ignorance
2. karmic formation
3. consciousness
4. name and form
5. six sense organs
6. contact
7. feeling
8. craving
9. grasping
10. becoming
11. rebirth
12. aging and death

EIGHTEEN

eighteen favorable conditions:
freedom from these eight unfavorable conditions:
1. being born in a hell realm
2. being born a hungry ghost
3. being born an animal
4. being born a barbarian
5. being born a long-lived god
6. holding wrong views

    7. absence of a Buddha

    8. muteness

as well as having these five personal conditions:

    9. being human

    10. being born in a central country

    11. possessing all the senses

    12. having committed none of the heinous actions

    13. having devotion for the Dharma

and having these five external conditions:

    14. a buddha has appeared

    15. a buddha has taught

    16. the Dharma that was taught remains

    17. there are practitioners of the Dharma

    18. there is love and kind support for practice

THIRTY-SEVEN

thirty-seven branches of enlightenment:

four types of essential mindfulness:

    1. sustaining mindfulness of the body

    2. sustaining mindfulness of feelings

    3. sustaining mindfulness of the mind

    4. sustaining mindfulness of phenomena

four types of perfect abandonment or correct trainings:

    5. abandoning nonvirtues which have been created

    6. not allowing new nonvirtues to be produced

    7. producing the antidotes, virtues which have not arisen

    8. allowing those virtues which have arisen to increase

four supports for miraculous ability:

    9. the absorption of strong aspiration

    10. the absorption of perseverance

    11. the absorption of the mind

    12. the absorption of investigation

five powers or faculties:

    13. the power of faith

    14. the power of perseverance

    15. the power of mindfulness

    16. the power of absorption

    17. the power of wisdom awareness

five strengths:

    18. the strength of faith

    19. the strength of perseverance

    20. the strength of mindfulness

    21. the strength of absorption

    22. the strength of wisdom awareness

seven branches of enlightenment:

    23. the perfect mindfulness branch

    24. the perfect discrimination branch

    25. the perfect perseverance branch

    26. the perfect joy branch

    27. the perfect relaxation branch

    28. the perfect absorption branch

    29. the perfect equanimity branch

eightfold path:

    30. perfect view

    31. perfect conception

    32. perfect speech

    33. perfect action

    34. perfect livelihood

    35. perfect effort

    36. perfect mindfulness

    37. perfect absorption

GLOSSARY OF NAMES AND TERMS

abhidharma: Literally, higher teachings. A category of Buddhist scriptures that presents a systematic, abstract description of all worldly phenomena.

afflicting emotions (Skt. *klesha*): In general, any defilement or poison that obscures the clarity of mind.

Asanga (fourth century C.E.): An Indian master who is most remembered for having received five celebrated texts from Arya Maitreya (*Abhisamayalankara, Uttaratantra, Mahayanasutralankara, Madhyantavibhaga,* and *Dharma-Dharmatavibhaga*) and for founding the Vast Action lineage.

bardo: Tibetan word meaning a state between any two things, especially the experiences of the state after an individual's death and before his conception

bhikshu: A fully ordained monk.

bhumi: Literally, "ground" or "foundation." Refers to the progressive levels of a bodhisattva's training, each one of which successively provides the foundation for the next.

bindu: A Sanskrit word meaning essential drop of energy.

bodhicitta: Literally, "mind of enlightenment." The intention to accomplish perfect, complete enlightenment for the benefit of all beings. Buddhahood is the perfection of the practice of bodhicitta.

bodhisattva: Literally, "courageous mind of enlightenment being." One who has generated bodhicitta and who works tirelessly for the benefit of all beings.

buddha: One who has attained unsurpassable, complete, perfect enlightenment; i.e., one who has fully awakened all wisdom and fully purified all obscurations.

buddha nature: The pure essence potential to attain enlightenment that is inherent in every sentient being. It is obscured to varying degrees by afflicting emotions and subtle obscurations, but it can be actualized through the practices of moral ethics, meditation, and wisdom.

Chakrasamvara: One of the principal yidams.

channels (Skt. *avadhuti*): Subtle energy channel within the body, particularly the central channel.

Che-nga Sherab Jungne (twelfth century): One of Jigten Sumgön's closest disciples, known for compiling Jigten Sumgön's teachings into the *One Thought* (*Gong Chig*).

completion stage (of tantric meditation): A meditation performed once one has identified oneself as a yidam deity. There are two types of completion stage practice: with signs and without. Practice with signs consists of reciting mantras, as well as channel and chakra practices. Practice without signs is the practice of mahamudra.

deity yoga: The characteristic type of Vajrayana meditation practice, which is a direct method to reveal and sustain the pure state of the mind and environment. Mundane phenomena are identified with those of a yidam. The term encompasses both the generation or arising stage and the completion stage of meditation.

desire realm: The lowest and largest of the three realms of samsara, it extends from the hell realms to the six classes of desire realm gods. It is so named because beings therein are characterized by gaining pleasure from sensual experience such as seeing objects, hearing sounds, and so forth.

Dharma: The holy teachings of Lord Buddha, categorized in two parts: the Dharma that is studied and the Dharma that has been realized.

dharmadhatu: The uncontrived mode of abiding of all elements of phenomena, both samsara and nirvana.

dharmakaya: One of the three bodies of a Buddha. It denotes the ultimate nature of Buddha's wisdom form, which is nonconceptual and indefinable.

Drigung Kagyu: The branch of the Kagyu tradition founded by Lord Jigten Sumgön.

Drigung Kyabgön Padmai Gyältsen: Fourth Chetsang Rinpoche, known for writing the history of the lineage.

dzogchen: The primordial or natural state of the mind, and a body of teachings and meditation practices aimed at realizing that state.

empowerment: The tantric ritual by which one is empowered to perform a specific meditation practice.

emptiness: The lack of inherent reality of a phenomenon or person.

enlightenment: The ultimate achievement of buddhahood.

formless realm: The highest of the three realms of samsara, experienced exclusively in the highest god realms. It is so named because beings there do not have gross bodies but have a very stable and subtle mental existence.

form realm: The middle of the three realms of samsara, experienced exclusively in the god realms. It is so named because beings there have bodies, but their pleasures come from four stable meditative states with no need for exterior projections.

Gampopa (1074–1153 C.E.): Renowned as one of Tibet's greatest teachers, he is one of the foremost figures in the Kagyu lineage. His writings include *The Jewel Ornament of Liberation* and *The Precious Garland of the Excellent Path*.

guru: See **lama**.

Hearing Lineage: See **Kagyu**.

Hinayana: Of the two major branches of Buddhist philosophy and practice, the Buddhist school that emphasizes individual liberation and practice of the Four Noble Truths.

Jangchub Ling: The principal seat of the Drigung Kagyu, founded by Jigten Sumgön.

Jigten Sumgön (1143–1217): Founder of the Drigung Kagyu tradition. He was the heart-son of Phagmo Drupa and widely recognized as an incarnation of Nagarjuna. His famous teachings include *One Thought* (Tib. *Gong Chig*) and *Heart Essence of Mahayana Teachings* (Tib. *Ten Nying*).

Kadampa: A Tibetan lineage of teachings based on those of the great Indian master Atisha.

Kagyu: Literally, "oral transmission" lineage. One of the four principal traditions within Tibetan Buddhism, it originated with Buddha Vajradhara and was primarily transmitted by Tilopa and Naropa in India, and Marpa, Milarepa, and Gampopa in Tibet. It holds mahamudra and the Six Dharmas of Naropa as its central teachings.

kalpa: Generically, an eon or other nearly limitless length of time. In Buddhist cosmology, it has the specific meaning of a complete cycle of a universe consisting of four stages: emptiness, formation, maintenance, and destruction.

karma: Literally, "action." Physical, verbal or mental acts which imprint habitual tendencies in the mind. Upon meeting with suitable conditions, these habits ripen and become manifest in future events.

kaya: Literally, "body." The various forms in which a buddha manifests.

kleshas: See **afflicting emotions.**

Kukuripa: An Indian mahasiddha.

lama (Skt. *guru*): An authentic teacher authorized to transmit Buddhist teachings to suitable students. Depending on tradition, a lama may or may not be a monk.

Madhyamaka: School of philosophy founded by Nagarjuna that emphasizes the teachings on emptiness.

mahamudra: Literally, the "great seal." The highest, most conclusive view that unites bliss and emptiness, luminosity and emptiness, into one, the primordial effulgent nature of mind, and is the ultimate realization of all phenomena of samsara and nirvana as they actually are. Its practice reveals the practitioner's basic, pure nature and leads to the experience of highest enlightenment.

mahapandita: A Sanskrit title meaning "great scholar."

Mahayana: Literally, the "great vehicle." The Buddhist school that holds the bodhisattva ideal as the highest practice and teaches the aspiration to attainment of enlightenment for the benefit of all sentient beings.

Maitripa (1007–1078?): An Indian mahasiddha and a disciple of Nagarjuna.

mara: Any negative influences that obstruct spiritual development, frequently personified as demon-like beings named Mara.

Marpa Lotsawa (1012–1097 C.E.): A Tibetan layman who is especially renowned for bringing many teachings to Tibet from India and translating them; these include mahamudra texts and the Six Dharmas of Naropa. As Naropa's disciple and Milarepa's primary teacher, he is a major figure in the Kagyu lineage.

meditative concentration (Skt. *samadhi*): A profound mental absorption in which the mind rests in the state free from conceptual thoughts.

Mila or **Milarepa** (1052–1135 C.E.): One of the great masters of the Kagyu lineage, he is often referred to as an example of someone who attained enlightenment in a single lifetime. His vajra songs contain great healing qualities. He was Dharma Lord Gampopa's primary teacher.

morality stick: Sticks used to count the number of monks attending a summer retreat; one stick was assigned to each monk

naga(s): Beings with snakelike bodies who may be benevolent or malicious, often associated with guarding the earth's treasures. They are generally considered to be members of the animal realm.

Nagarjuna (second century C.E.): An Indian master of such critical importance to the propagation of the Mahayana that he is often called the "second Buddha." He founded the Madhyamaka philosophical school which systematized the perfection of wisdom (*prajñaparamita*) teachings, and authored many texts which remain authoritative to the present day.

Ngorje Repa: One of Jigten Sumgön's close disciples, known for having written the *Heart Essence of the Mahayana* (*Ten Nying*), an important summary of Jigten Sumgön's Stages of the Path (Lamrim) teachings that contain an exposition of both sutra and tantra.

nirmanakaya: Literally "emanation body." The physical form of a buddha or other great being, purposefully manifested for the benefit of sentient beings. This is not necessarily a human form; they can appear as whatever is necessary.

nirvana: The unconfused state without suffering; the transcendence of samsara.

parinirvana: The final act of a fully enlightened buddha's life among humans or, in general, the death of any fully enlightened person.

perfections: (Skt. *paramita*): The training to be completed by bodhisattvas, consisting of the perfection of generosity, moral ethics, patience, perseverance, meditative concentration, wisdom awareness, skillful means, aspiration, strength, and primordial wisdom.

Phagmo Drupa: Principal disciple of Gampopa, teacher of Jigten Sumgön, and founder of eight lineages: the Drigung, Taklung, Drukpa, Trophu, Yabsang, Shuksep, Yelpa, and Martsang.

pratyekabuddha: Literally, solitary realizer. Self-liberated buddhas, whose attainment is less than the ultimate buddhahood. While they may receive Dharma teachings during the time of a buddha or now, they do not attain realization until after the buddha's teachings have disappeared. Being without bodhicitta, they do not teach how to reach enlightenment, but they do display miracle powers to inspire devotion.

Ratna Shri: Another name for Jigten Sumgön.

Rinchen Päl: Another name for Jigten Sumgön.

samadhi: See **meditative concentration.**

sambhogakaya: Literally, "enjoyment body." A nonsubstantial yet visible body of a buddha or other great being, manifested to directly benefit bodhisattvas at high stages of realization and to serve as objects of devotion for practitioners.

samsara: The beginningless and endless cycle of rebirths throughout the six realms; the confused state of suffering from which Buddhists seek liberation.

sangha: Generally, the entire community of practitioners. In different contexts, it can refer specifically to the monastic community, to the assembly of highly realized beings (arhats and bodhisattvas at the first bhumi and above), or a group of at least four fully ordained.

sentient beings: All conscious creatures who are reborn within the six realms.

session: A day being divided into six parts, or sessions, a single session is a four-hour period.

Shepa Dorje: Another name for Milarepa.

shravaka: Literally, "hearer." A Hinayana disciple who hears the words of the Buddha and aspires to become an arhat for his/her own benefit.

skandha: Literally, "aggregate" or "heap." The collection of characteristics that constitutes a sentient being. Like a heap of grain, a being appears to be a single entity until, upon closer examination, it is understood to be comprised of many parts.

summer retreat stick: See **morality stick.**

sutra: Literally, a rope or thread that holds things together. Figuratively, it refers to the canonical scriptures that are records of the teachings of Buddha Shakyamuni.

svabhavikakaya: Literally, "nature form." The unified and inseparable nature of all buddhas' forms.

Vajrayana: The diamond path or "vehicle" of Buddhist tantra.

vinaya: The code of discipline for Buddhist practitioners, especially for monks and nuns.

winds (Skt. *prana*): The subtle energy of the body.

yidam: A deity whose form and attributes embody a particular aspect of enlightenment and with whom a practitioner identifies in meditation.

yogin: An accomplished meditator.

SELECTED BIBLIOGRAPHY

CALLING TO THE LAMA FROM AFAR

A collection of prayers and devotions concerning Kyobpa Jigten Sumgön, the founder of the Drigung Kagyu lineage of Tibetan Buddhism. The prayers translated in this text express the depth of genuine devotion in a manner that is characteristic of this genre of Tibetan literature.

Gyaltshen, Khenchen Konchog. *Calling to the Lama from Afar*. Gainesville, Fla.: Vajra Publications, 2002.

A COMPLETE GUIDE TO THE BUDDHIST PATH

Khenchen Rinpoche's insightful and readable commentary on *The Jewel Treasury of Advice*. It contains a complete introduction to the teachings of Buddhism, from the very basic up to the very profound.

Gyaltshen, Khenchen Konchog. *A Complete Guide to the Buddhist Path*. Ithaca, N.Y.: Snow Lion Publications, 2009.

THE GARLAND OF MAHAMUDRA PRACTICES

Translation of a text by Kunga Rinchen (1475–1527). Very helpful for those who already have a little understanding of the Dharma. It contains a description of all the Ngondro practices: the four foundation thoughts (precious human life, awareness of impermanence, karma, and the suffering of samsara); the four extraordinary preliminary practices (refuge, Vajrasattva, mandala offering, and guru yoga); yidam practice; special guru yoga; and a mahamudra session.

Gyaltshen, Khenchen Könchok. *The Garland of Mahamudra Practices: A Translation of Kunga Rinchen's Clarifying the Jewel Rosary of the*

Profound Fivefold Path. Translated and introduced by Khenchen Kön-chok Gyaltshen Rinpoche; co-translated and edited by Katherine Rogers. Ithaca, N.Y.: Snow Lion Publications, 2002.

GARLAND OF THE SUPREME PATH

Gampopa's concise presentation of the essential point of Buddhist training that has been revered and relied upon since it was written in the twelfth century.

Gampopa. *The Precious Garland of the Sublime Path.* Translated by Eric Hein Schmidt. Hong Kong: Rangjung Yeshe Publications, 1995.

Karthar, Khenpo Rinpoche. *The Instructions of Gampopa: A Precious Garland of the Supreme Path.* Translated by Lama Yeshe Gyamtsho. Ithaca, N.Y.: Snow Lion Publications, 1996.

GONG CHIG

A concise presentation of the oral instructions of the Drigung Kagyu lineage that explains the unified, enlightened intention that is a common thread in all the teachings of the Buddha. Usually divided into seven chapters, it consists of vajra statements that were spoken by Jigten Sumgön and recorded by his disciple Che-nga Sherab Jungne.

Jigten Sumgon. *Gongchig: The Single Intent, the Sacred Dharma.* Translated by Markus Viehbeck. Munich: Otter Verlag, 2009.

THE GREAT KAGYU MASTERS

Translation of a thirteenth-century text that gathers the life stories of the founders of the Kagyu lineage together in one volume. It is very helpful to practitioners to have these accounts available for inspiration and guidance.

Gyaltsen, Khenpo Konchog. *The Great Kagyu Masters.* Ithaca, N.Y.: Snow Lion Publications, 1990.

GUIDE TO THE BODHISATTVA'S CONDUCT

A beautiful presentation of the bodhisattva's training in verse form by the Indian master Shantideva. It is one of the most widely read and quoted of all Mahayana texts.

Batchelor, Stephen. *A Guide to the Bodhisattva's Way of Life.* Dharamsala: Library of Tibetan Works and Archives, 1979.

Crosby, Kate, and Andrew Skilton. *The Bodhicaryavatara.* Oxford and New York: Oxford University Press, 1996.

Matics, Marion L. *Entering the Path of Enlightenment.* New York: MacMillan, 1970.

Padmakara Translation Group. *The Way of the Bodhisattva.* Boston: Shambhala Publications, 1997.

Sharma, Parmananda. *Shantideva's Bodhicharyavatara.* New Delhi: Aditya Prakashan, 1990.

Wallace, Vesna, and B. Alan Wallace. *A Guide to the Bodhisattva Way of Life.* Ithaca, N.Y.: Snow Lion Publications, 1997.

IN SEARCH OF THE STAINLESS AMBROSIA

Written by Khenchen Rinpoche as an introduction for beginners and a reminder for more advanced practitioners. It summarizes the fundamental teachings of refuge, love and compassion, and the six paramitas, and also includes short sections on mahamudra and yidam practices, the experience of dying, an explanation of Chöd practice, and Phowa teachings.

Gyaltsen, Khenpo Könchog. *In Search of the Stainless Ambrosia.* Edited by Victoria Huckenpahler. Ithaca, N.Y.: Snow Lion Publications, 1988.

THE JEWEL ORNAMENT OF LIBERATION

Translation of Lord Gampopa's essential philosophy text, which is said to act as Gampopa's regent in these times. This book contains a complete form of Buddhism—right from the starting point, the ground where you enter into the path, until you achieve Buddhahood and manifest activities for the benefit of infinite sentient beings.

Gampopa. *Gems of Dharma, Jewels of Freedom.* Translated by Ken and Katia Holmes. Forres, Scotland: Altea Publishing, 1995.

Gyaltsen, Khenpo Konchog. *The Jewel Ornament of Liberation.* Ithaca, N.Y.: Snow Lion Publications, 1998.

sGam.po.pa. *The Jewel Ornament of Liberation.* Translated and annotated by Herbert V. Guenther. Berkeley: Shambhala Publications, 1971.

THE JEWEL TREASURY OF ADVICE

Translation of a profound teaching in verse, written by Drigung Bhande Dharmaradza ('Bri gung skyabs mgon Don grub chos rgyal, 1704–1754), also known as the second Drigung Kyabgon Chungtsang.

Gyaltshen, Khenchen Konchog. *A Complete Guide to the Buddhist Path.* Ithaca, N.Y.: Snow Lion Publications, 2009.

The Jewel Treasury of Advice: A Hundred Teachings from the Heart. Translated by Khenchen Konchog Gyaltshen Rinpoche. Edited by Rick Finney. Gainesville, Fla.: Vajra Publications, 1997.

PEARL ROSARY

This book describes the methods of tantric visualization and explains how to incorporate their practice into daily life. It was designed for study by individuals or groups without ready access to a qualified spiritual master.

Gyaltshen, Khenchen Konchog. *Pearl Rosary: The Path of Purification.* Gainesville, Fla.: Vajra Publications, 2007.

PRAYER FLAGS

A small book that contains brief life stories of Gampopa, Phagmo Drupa, and Lord Jigten Sumgön, as well as some songs of realization by lineage masters. There are some short teachings on the stages of mahamudra practice, and condensed instructions on how to carry the experiences of sickness and death into one's practice.

Gyaltsen, Khenpo Konchog. *Prayer Flags: The Life and Spiritual Teachings of Jigten Sumgön.* Ithaca, N.Y.: Snow Lion Publications, 1984, 1986.

TRANSFORMATION OF SUFFERING: A HANDBOOK FOR PRACTITIONERS

Contains all the foundations of Buddhism in very accessible terms.

Gyaltshen, Khenpo Konchog. *Transformation of Suffering: A Handbook for Practitioners.* Gainesville, Fla.: Vajra Publications, 1997.

INDEX

abhidharma, 163, 217, 232, 251, 261
Abhisamayalankara, 26, 261
action bodhicitta, 88
action tantra, 75, 252
arising (stage of tantra), 67, 91–92, 251, 262
aspiration bodhicitta, 88
Atisha, 114, 196, 263
Avatamsaka Sutra, 162

bardo(s)
 between lives, 95, 110, 150, 164–67, 189
 eight, 57–70, 255
buddha nature
 counter to laziness, 51
 equality, 35, 42, 156–57, 160
 failure to recognize, 60
 ground, 83, 92, 102–3
 method to realize, 91, 97
 possession of, 13, 15, 159, 162, 174
 realization, 142, 166, 167

Calling to the Lama from Afar, 32, 133
causality
 aspect of four foundations, 84
 emptiness, 125, 180–1
 function, 6, 74
 interdependence, 74–5, 132, 153
 source of all phenomena, 59, 96, 105–6
 study of, 44, 85, 87
 two-types, 45
 wrong view of, 41, 124, 164
 See also karma
Che-nga Sherab Jungne
 author of *Gong Chig,* 192

Jigten Sumgön biographer, 216, 238
Jigten Sumgön disciple, 195–6, 247
 quoted, 163, 168
 vision as Shariputra, 193
 with buddha statue, 32–33
clarity, 48, 106, 132, 146, 178, 236, 261
 aspect of deity yoga, 92, 251
 aspect of mind, 167
 happiness, 48, 74
 increase, 61, 88
 lack, 54, 87, 176
 related to dharmata, 110
 unobstructed, 155
clear light, 4, 25, 224, 239, 243
 aspect of Six Dharmas of Naropa, 254
 description, 26, 70
 realization of, 95
Complete Guide to the Buddhist Path, A, 88, 267
completion (stage of tantra), 57, 59, 65, 91
 aspect of liberating, 76
 practice of, 67–68, 93
 preparation for death, 95

Dagmema, 20
Daklha Gampo, 4, 190, 193, 229, 230, 236, 237, 239
 Gampopa's seat, 29, 30
 prophecy of, 25, 27
Dakpo Gomtsul, 172, 188, 220
death, 28, 150, 167, 206, 209, 228
 fear, 189
 impermanence, 44, 47
 preparation, 95

death (*continued*)
 remorse, 46
 suffering, 85, 112, 115, 120–21
 time of, 32, 39, 110–11, 114, 119, 164–
  65, 167
dedication, 80, 219
 aspect of fivefold path of mahamudra,
  81, 107–9, 253
 prayer, 35, 90, 102
deity yoga, 67, 90, 160
 method, 93–94
 two aspects of, 91
desire world, 59, 103
devotion, 33–35, 126, 157, 172, 181, 222, 230
 and confidence, 12–13
 guru yoga, 79, 96–98
 for Jigten Sumgön, 10, 189, 193–94,
  196, 214
 Jigten Sumgön's, 61, 73, 149–50, 155, 158,
  167–68, 218–20
 Milarepa's, 25, 100
 Naropa's, 16
Dharma center, 53, 115, 140
dharmadhatu, 3, 201, 205, 221, 238
 emptiness, 10–11
 primordial nature, 171–74
dharmakaya, 119, 171, 218
 aspect of buddhahood, 11–13, 68–69,
  98, 106, 173–74
 experience of, 77, 81–82, 166
 and happiness, 44, 155
 manifestations of, 32, 39, 163, 181, 209
 meditation on, 94, 99–100
 realization of, 90, 103, 126, 139, 151–52,
  205
divine pride, 92–93, 251
dream, 57, 61, 132, 197–98, 235
 bardo, 59, 64–65, 164
 metaphor for illusion, 115, 143, 145
 yoga, 70
Drigung Kagyu, 242, 243
 founding, 9, 20, 224
 monasteries, 247–49
 retreat masters, 241
 seat, 263
Drowo Lung, 4, 18, 23–24, 238
duality, 155, 166

as delusion, 70, 121
 grasping at, 64, 76, 179, 181, 221
 as obscuration, 176
 transcending, 42, 59–61, 69, 167, 171
Düdsi Shikpo, 3, 9, 238
dzogchen, 21, 22, 154, 262

Echung Cave, 31, 73, 172, 188–89, 198,
  220, 222
ego, 17, 49, 96, 151, 157, 158
eight unfavorable conditions, 84, 257
eight worldly concerns, 39, 70, 109, 222
 habitual involvement with, 177–78
 quelling, 43–46
 untrustworthy, 114–16, 145
eighteen unmixed qualities, 11, 101
empowerment, 17, 58, 101, 160, 217, 222
 four, 35, 163
 necessity of, 91
 purpose, 93
 qualification of lama, 13
 third, 67–68
 See also initiation
emptiness, 62, 164, 178, 208–9, 223
 and bodhicitta, 119, 122, 159
 and causality, 124–25, 180–81
 and deity yoga, 67–68, 70, 92, 93–95
 genderless, 42
 and luminosity, 81, 99–100
 of all phenomena, 11, 44–5, 75–76, 98,
  122, 154, 162
 realization of, 3, 8–9, 47, 59, 90, 103–4,
  155, 159, 172, 198
 visualization, 33–34, 93–95, 99

first turning, 161
five Kagyu lineages, 30
five skandhas, 57, 65–67, 102
 illusory, 69
 related to suffering, 76
form kayas, 58, 68, 69
form world, 60, 103
formless world, 59–60, 103
four elements, 65, 111, 118
 aspect of dying process, 95, 165
 environment, 74
 relation to space, 102

four fearlessnesses, 11, 97, 99, 101, 159
Four Noble Truths, 161, 253, 263
four thoughts that turn the mind, 84,
    104, 252
fruition, 100, 103–6, 188, 208

Gampopa, 10, 60, 172, 190, 237, 264, 265
    biography, 25–29
    as root lama, 34–35, 97
    student of Milarepa, 40, 59, 125, 167
    teacher of Phagmo Drupa, 82
    teachings of, 55, 107, 126, 143, 174
gender, 42
Great Kagyu Masters, 10, 133
ground (aspect of ground, path, and
    meditation), 90, 100, 208
    mahamudra, 103–5
    perfection, 83, 92
Guhyasamaja, 19, 186, 215, 217
Guide to the Bodhisattva's Conduct, 47, 88
guru yoga, 81, 109
    practice, 96–98, 100
    purpose, 105
Gyangdrak (monastery), 33, 247

Heart Sutra, 162, 180
Hundred Thousand Songs of Milarepa, 113

ignorance, 91, 110, 120, 125, 157, 181
    basis of samsara, 81, 142, 176
    as deluding, 10, 63, 93, 104
    mental factor, 45, 163, 174
    purified, 60, 94
    related to karma, 21, 86–87
    related to wisdom, 26
impermanence, 44–45, 74, 119, 150
    aspect of four foundations, 84–85
    awareness of, 6, 76, 24
    of all phenomena, 49, 242, 153
    reflection on, 47, 51, 180
initiation, 23, 75, 76, 91. See also
    empowerment
interdependent origination, 14, 32, 41,
    73, 222
    Jigten Sumgön's realization of, 74,
        188–90, 237
    twelve links, 16, 257

Jangchub Ling, 3, 9, 135, 190, 247, 236
Jewel Ornament of Liberation, 51, 88, 143,
    174, 263
Jigten Sumgön
    lamas of, 46, 73, 167–68, 197–207, 214,
        244
    realization of, 76, 137–38, 151, 223
    as reincarnation of Nagarjuna, 3, 8–9,
        32, 101, 185, 189, 215, 230–33
    See also under Che-nga Sherab Jungne,
        devotion, interdependent origination,
        mahamudra, Phagmo Drupa, yidam

Kadam tradition, 26, 186, 191, 193, 217,
    218
karma, 21, 85, 133, 153
    emptiness, 180
    negative, 28, 67, 142–43, 173
    positive, 6, 124–25, 173
    purification of, 20–21, 28, 67, 73, 94–95,
        156
    and rebirth, 91, 156, 166, 174–76
    and suffering, 50, 76, 84–86
    visualization, 94–95
    See also causality
Karmapa, 193, 230, 245
Kham, 29, 31, 186–88, 216, 217, 242, 246
Khyunga Rinpoche, 118
klesha, 171, 174, 221, 261, 264
Kukuripa, 19, 264
Kunga Nyingpo, 29

lama, 12
    devotion to, 34, 100–101
    enlightened, 57–59
    married, 50, 138
    qualities of, 13, 96–97
lamaism, 12
Lankavatara Sutra, 9
Lapchi, 4, 20–21, 25–26, 32, 193–94, 234
Lawapa, 14
laziness, 40, 47, 49–52, 150, 252
Lengom Repa, 40, 42
Lobpon Tsilungpa, 172, 220, 224

Madhyamakavatara, 26
Mahamegha Sutra, 9

mahamudra, 79–110, 146
  and bardo, 166–67
  four yogas, 172–73, 188, 253
  and Jigten Sumgön's blessings, 32
  Phagmo Drupa's teaching of, 137, 152,
    218–20
  practice, 35, 44, 46, 64–65, 93
  realization, 68, 117–18, 186
  song, 14, 17, 81–82, 102–6
  study, 49, 217
  view, 59, 62, 154–55
Mahaparinirvana Sutra, 162
Mahayanasutralankara, 26, 261
Maitripa, 19, 264
Manjushri Namasangiti, 217
Manjushrigarbha, 9
mara(s), 110, 131, 203, 235
  four, 200
  as obstacle, 112, 125, 188
  personification of faults, 140–41
Marpa Chökyi Lodrö, 4, 10, 17, 34–35,
    228, 238
  biography, 18–20, 22
  and Milarepa, 15, 43, 59–60, 96, 100,
    157, 178
Meaningful to Behold, 32
meditation instructions
  cultivating bodhicitta, 87–88, 90
  dedication, 109–10
  guru yoga, 98–102
  impermanence, 44–45, 115, 118–19
  love and compassion, 159
  purification practice, 94–96
  receiving lineage blessings, 34–35
  samadhi, 105
  Tara, 181
Mentok Dazey, 27–28, 209
Middle Way School, 9
Milarepa
  author, 113
  biography, 20–25
  example, 156–57, 178–79, 189, 240
  and Gampopa, 28, 126
  as lineage guru, 4, 10, 34–35, 114, 238
  and Marpa, 15, 19–20, 96–97, 100, 157
  and Phagmo Drupa, 30
  quoted, 125, 155, 164, 167, 177, 180

mind training, 26
Mount Kailash, 32, 193, 194, 240,
    243, 247

Nagarjuna, 14, 161, 163
Nalanda University, 15–16
Naropa, 209, 226, 228
  biography, 15–18
  as lineage master, 3, 10, 34–35, 238
  and Marpa, 19, 22
  and Tilopa, 157
nature of mind, 6, 8, 49, 156, 218
  absolute, 27
  innate, 62–63, 81
  pure, 43–45, 83, 181
  realization of, 26, 68, 92, 126, 127, 178,
    179
  recognition in the bardo, 95, 166
  two factors of, 88, 90
Ngok Ton Chödor, 19, 191
Ngorje Repa, 19, 191, 193, 265
nirmanakaya, 69, 94, 126
  guru as, 97, 98
  three types, 11, 205
nirvana, 55, 160, 163, 206, 218
  created by mind, 6, 46, 102, 133, 208
  within dependent arising, 154, 200
  and emptiness, 103–4, 186
  nature of, 44
  ultimate view of, 81
  undifferentiated from samsara, 11, 60,
    67, 103, 124, 155, 179

obscuration(s), 133, 145, 156, 158, 159, 200,
    201, 205, 222, 245
  four, 101
  meditation and, 25, 68, 76, 94–96, 155
  purification of, 15–17, 25–26, 35, 47, 55,
    60, 73, 91, 93, 100, 181
  subtle, 6, 104, 105, 163
  to wisdom, 77, 106
obstacle(s), 112, 125, 126, 134, 188, 198
  countering, 105
  dedication, 108
  gratitude for, 61
  overcoming, 7, 89, 104, 140, 164
Oddiyana, 14, 190, 210, 237

Padmai Gyaltsen, 243, 247, 262
parents, 112, 149, 164, 206, 228
 all sentient beings as, 122–23, 158–60
 in rebirth process, 166
Phagmo Drupa, 111, 131, 136, 185, 226, 235
 biography, 29–30, 82
 guru of Jigten Sumgön, 31, 73, 114, 137,
  152, 168, 186–90, 195, 198–99, 219–20
 guru of Taklung Thangpa, 149, 151
 as lineage master, 10, 34–35, 60, 79, 156
 quoted, 218
 relics, 229, 234
phowa, 128, 254, 269
pratyekabuddha, 62, 109, 133, 205, 206,
 265
Prayer Flags, 133
precepts, 45, 74, 86, 87, 253. *See also* vows
precious human life, 13, 51, 93, 150
 aspect of four foundations, 84–86
 potential, 143–44
 purpose, 135
 rare opportunity, 5, 6
 wasting, 42, 91, 165
primordial wisdom, 17, 26, 60, 106, 206,
 209
proper vessel, 131, 138, 209, 225, 226, 235
 qualities of, 13, 139
purity, 92, 167, 205, 209, 251
Pushpahari, 3, 15, 238

Rechungpa, 25, 40
refuge, 57–58, 97, 100, 213, 226, 234
 comfort, 7
 Dharma as, 55
 method, 86, 90
 protection, 34
renunciation, 24, 85, 87, 127, 154, 176
Rinchen Drak, 111, 113–15, 117, 128, 190
root lama, 4, 33–35, 157–58, 239
rupakaya, 106

Sahor, 3, 13, 238
samadhi, 197, 209–10, 212, 214, 222, 251
 basis of insight, 105
 illusion, 217
 and meaning of *yogin,* 50
 vajra-like, 205

Samadhiraja Sutra, 27, 28
sambhogakaya, 126
 deity yoga, 92
 guru appearing as, 30, 97–98, 205–6
 relation to other kayas, 11, 69
 visualization, 94, 99
Samdhinirmochana Sutra, 162
Saraha, vii
second turning, 161–62
Shakya Shri Bhadra, 192–93
Shantideva, 47, 268
Shariputra, 9, 193, 230
Shepa Dorje. *See* Milarepa
shravaka, 109, 112, 215
 aspect of enlightenment, 133
 assembly of, 203–6, 215
 beliefs, 122–23
 four types, 62
Six Dharmas of Naropa, 27, 194, 218, 254,
 263, 264
skandha, 57, 65–67, 69, 76, 102
solitude, 100, 131–32, 144, 146, 235, 236
 benefits, 140–42, 145
 types, 137–38
spiritual master, 107, 110, 178, 202
 Dharma as, 157
 exemplar, 123
 necessity for, 15, 96, 104
 realization, 98
svabhavikakaya, 11–12, 94, 98, 100, 253,
 266

Taklung Thangpa, 149–51, 168, 187
Tara, 76, 92
 vision of, 32, 192, 221, 231, 232
 visualization, 94, 160
Tathagatagarbha Sutra, 162
ten nonvirtues, 41, 74, 134, 256
ten powers, 11, 159
ten virtues, 41–42, 50, 74, 133–34, 256
third turning, 161–62, 211
three subtle experiences, 95, 165, 166
three types of suffering, 76, 252
Tilopa
 biography, 13–15
 lineage master, 10, 34–35, 60
 with Naropa, 16–17, 157

twelve deeds, 11, 205, 257
twelve trials, 3, 15–17, 238
two accumulations, 79, 107, 207, 219
  perfecting, 104, 105, 198
  wish-fulfilling gem, 108
two wisdoms, 79, 102, 219
  realization, 60, 68, 106

Uttaratantra, 26, 159, 163, 261

Vajradhara, 3, 101, 197, 214, 215, 238
  biography, 11–13
  phowa, 128
  realization, 223
  root lama, 4, 33–35, 239
  teacher of Tilopa, 14
  visualization, 99–100
Vajrayana, 9, 26–28, 67, 167, 222
  essential point, 68
  method, 75, 81, 90–91, 93, 97, 160
  practice, 127, 166
  vinaya, 87
Vimalakirti, 9
vinaya, 28, 248
  as foundation, 87, 200
  sutras, 26, 163, 196, 224

vows
  bodhisattva, 55, 187, 218, 220
  monk's, 187, 189, 224, 229,
  pretense, 45
  three, 208, 233
  upasaka, 188–89, 190
  See also precepts

wealth, 110, 112, 191, 199
  as cause of suffering, 49, 54, 131, 139–41,
  impermanence of, 119–20
  material, 169
  Milarepa, 21
  offering, 108, 194, 201, 209–12, 223, 233,
    235–37

yidam, 76, 79, 149, 207, 219
  aspect of fivefold path, 81, 90–93, 105
  bodhicitta, 109
  Jigten Sumgön, 172, 190–91, 217
  practice, 158–60
  visualization, 67, 99, 167